QUEER LIVES

Queer Lives

❧ *Men's Autobiographies from Nineteenth-Century France*

Translated, edited, and with an introduction
by William A. Peniston and Nancy Erber

University of Nebraska Press ❧ *Lincoln and London*

Acknowledgment for previously
published materials appears on
pp. 249–50, which constitutes an
extension of the copyright page.

LIBRARY OF CONGRESS
Cataloging-in-Publication Data
Queer lives: men's autobiographies from
nineteenth-century France / translated,
edited, and with an introduction by
William A. Peniston and Nancy Erber.
p. cm.
Includes bibliographical references.
ISBN-13: 978-0-8032-6036-8 (pbk: alk. paper)
ISBN-10: 0-8032-6036-9 (pbk: alk. paper)
1. Gay men—France—Biography.
2. Homosexuality, Male—France—
Case studies. 3. Gay men—France—
History—19th century.
I. Peniston, William A., 1959–
II. Erber, Nancy, 1951–
HQ76.2.F8Q44 2007
306.76′62092244—dc22
[B]
2007028544

Set in Monotype Fournier.
Designed by A. Shahan.

For George C. Robb and Leonard O. Green

CONTENTS

ILLUSTRATIONS

ACKNOWLEDGMENTS

We wish to thank the following people for their support: Nicole Albert for conversation and insight; Monte Bohna for assistance with the translation of the Latin passages; David Deiss of Elysium Press for allowing us to scan an image from one of his books; Louis Godbout for sharing his knowledge of nineteenth-century gay literature and images from France; Corinne Keuter for contacting French libraries and archives on our behalf; Jeffrey Moy for technical assistance with the illustrations; Vernon Rosario for help in understanding some of the medical terms; and Daniel Sherman for introducing us to the article on homosexuality and autobiography by Philippe Lejeune. We would also like to thank George Robb and Leonard Green for living with this project as long as we did and for putting up with it and us.

Elizabeth Demers, formerly at the University of Nebraska Press, guided us through the initial stages of this project, and her successor, Heather Lundine, brought it to a successful conclusion. We also want to thank the anonymous reader who reviewed the manuscript for the University of Nebraska Press and who made many detailed, insightful, and useful comments. Ingrid Muller proved to be an excellent copyeditor.

Nancy received financial support from the Professional Staff Congress of the City University of New York Research Foundation, and William received the Bernadotte E. Schmidt Grant for Research in European History from the American Historical Association.

Finally, William wishes to thank Nancy, and Nancy wishes to thank William. Together we somehow managed to complete this project and still remain friends!

In 1770 Jean-Jacques Rousseau finished his remarkable autobiography, *The Confessions*, which was published shortly after his death in 1778. In it he resolved to write his life as an example of the modern individual. He claimed that he was "like no one in the whole world" and that his autobiography had "no precedent" and would have "no imitators." Although he borrowed his title from Saint Augustine's autobiography, his life story was clearly quite different. It was not the story of a sinner's search for God and how that life fit into the overall scheme that God had planned for the world. Instead, it was the story of a man who had accomplished much in his life, but who was still troubled by his personal failings.[1]

Despite his claims to the contrary, Rousseau's autobiography did indeed inspire others in the nineteenth century to follow his example, whether consciously or not. Recently historians have begun to focus on the autobiographies of men and women who did not fill important roles in public life but who nevertheless wrote about their individual personal experiences, uncovering aspects of the human personality and views of historical eras that heretofore remained hidden. Mark Traugott, Alfred Kelly, John Burnett, and Victoria Bonnell have assembled collections of autobiographies of working-class men and women in France, Germany, England, and Russia.[2] Feminist scholars, such as Patricia Meyer Spacks, Estelle Jelinek, Sidonie Smith, and Julia Watson, have analyzed women's life stories by focusing on the genre and its "truth value."[3] In France, Denis Bertholet has written a remarkable study of the entire genre throughout the nineteenth century, situating the passions and ambitions of the great and small in their social, economic, cultural, and political context.[4] He followed the path-breaking work of Philippe Lejeune, who studied the autobiographical writing of commercial agents, industrialists, and financial managers, as well as criminals and teachers. He also identified a number of autobiographical accounts produced by men who were attracted to other men.[5] All of the accounts that he had discovered had been incorporated into case studies and published in medical journals. None of them were unmediated personal expressions, but, despite their disparate origins, these often extremely frank and detailed autobiographies from the nineteenth century expressed the modern conviction that individual lives were worth telling because of their unique sensibilities.

We have translated from French into English eight men's "queer" autobiographies written between 1845 and 1905. They are the ones that Lejeune identified in 1987, and each one addresses the experiences of a man who was sexually attracted to other men. Many of the writers had been charged with a crime, such as public indecency, sexual assault, theft, blackmail, or murder, and while in prison they were asked to write about their lives and the circumstances leading to their arrest. Some of these written confessions served as a means of establishing criminal motives, and the legal experts who elicited them used them to construct prosecutorial arguments.[6] Other life stories in this collection were initiated by medical doctors, who served as experts in the courts or conducted research on convicts in prison or treated patients in private asylums. Forensic scientists used autobiographies as case studies to illustrate their own theories on criminal behavior, while psychiatrists and neurologists used them in their studies of sexual deviance. In some cases the doctors interpreted the men's lives so heavily that their interpretations cannot easily be separated from the men's own words.[7] Nevertheless, some of the narratives that the doctors elicited are indeed extended reflections on the childhoods, adolescences, and adulthoods of these men; others, though truncated and selectively edited by the physicians who first made them public, present tantalizing evidence of long-forgotten men caught up in "the making of a complex machinery for producing true discourses on sex," as Michel Foucault described the process.[8]

In his work *The History of Sexuality*, Foucault argued that historians should focus on how the doctors' implication in "interrogations, consultations, autobiographical narratives, and letters" contributed to "the constitution of a science of the subject."[9] As he put it:

Instead of adding up the errors, naivetes, and moralisms that plagued the nineteenth-century discourse of truth concerning sex, we would do better to locate the procedures by which that will to knowledge regarding sex, which characterizes the modern Occident, caused the rituals of confession to function within the norms of scientific regularity: how did this immense and traditional extortion of the sexual confession come to be constituted in scientific terms?[10]

For the past thirty years many literary and social historians have studied such personal narratives in the context of the evolving legal and medical attitudes toward homosexuality in the nineteenth century. Foucault's cautionary words on the topic distill some of our chief concerns in translating and presenting this collection; he emphasized the importance of considering not only the content of the narratives but also the conditions of their production in a "confessional science . . . which relied on a many-sided extortion."[11] Unlike personal diaries or memoirs, which were written voluntarily for one's own personal use or for future publication, most of the documents in this collection were produced under duress—by men incarcerated in prisons or interned in asylums under the direction of a prosecutor or under the care of a physician. Yet, for the history of science and the study of sexuality, many historians have echoed Foucault's assertion that the nineteenth century was "an important time . . . when the most singular pleasures were called upon to pronounce a discourse of truth concerning themselves, a discourse which had to model itself after that which it spoke, not of sin and salvation, but of bodies and life processes—the discourse of science."[12] As such, we believe that the writing of these men from the nineteenth century deserves a wider audience today at a time when readers are seeking new views on the lives of ordinary men and women from the past, when gay men, lesbians, bisexuals, transsexuals, and transgendered people are looking for the roots of their communities, and when scholars are trying to understand the formation of sexual identities at a crucial moment in the history of modern Europe.

The first autobiography in our collection is by Arthur W——, the pseudonym of Arthur Belorget. Known as "the Countess" in the Paris of the Second Empire, he was the son of a coachman and a dressmaker. As a young man he became the lover of a nobleman who abandoned him after a few years, and thereafter he earned a living as a cross-dressing singer, using a feminine pseudonym and performing in the *cafés-concerts* of Paris. In 1861 he was arrested not for his practice of female impersonation or his liaisons with other men but for desertion and theft. He was tried and condemned to ten years in prison. There he met the man whom he deemed the love of his life—a fellow prisoner named Gustave Engel. In his autobiography Belorget recounts his childhood attachment to his mother, his adolescent experimentations with other boys, and his seduction by the son of a marquis, as well as his career as a performer and his love affairs in prison. His narrative includes a first-person view on aspects of working-class life in Paris, the social atmosphere of the demimonde, the male homosexual sub-culture, and the underground world of men's prisons during the Second Empire.[13] Belorget's autobiography was given to Dr. Henri Legludic in 1874 when Belorget was incarcerated in Angers following his arrest for a public offense against decency. Legludic published it as an appendix to his study, *Notes et observations de médecine légale*, in 1895. In his preface Legludic emphasized the importance of studying "this psycho-sexual disorder . . . that is not rare and has existed throughout history."[14]

The second section of our study includes autobiographies that were presented as medical case studies, along with the commentaries written by the doctors who collected them. As early as the 1850s Dr. Ambroise Tardieu, the leading expert on "pederasty" in France in the middle years of the nineteenth century, had used case studies to great effect in explaining his theories on the relationship between sexual deviance and crime.[15] One case study that he included in the fifth edition of his work was written by the victim of a blackmail scheme, who described his feelings for four young men with whom he had fallen in love. The subject of this study, which we have included in our collection, gave few details about himself, his lovers, or his affairs (unless these details were deleted by the doctor), but his words were used to support Tardieu's contention that pederastic men had exaggerated notions about love, sex, and desire.[16]

In the 1880s and 1890s other medical experts began to publish studies critical of Tardieu's theories. They, too, used autobiographical writings to illustrate their own analyses of sexual deviance. Dr. Jean-Martin Charcot and Dr. Valentin Magnan were two of the most influential theoreticians of this new generation of physicians. They included an autobiography by an effeminate professor in their influential study of "sexual inversion" in 1882. This man explained that he had desired men and boys both emotionally and physically ever since his childhood. In their commentary, Charcot and Magnan concluded that he was suffering from "a neuropathic or psychopathic state of the deepest kind."[17]

Two other case studies included in our collection were elicited by Dr. Paul Garnier, who further developed Charcot and Magnan's theories of sexual deviance in his study on "fetishists," published in 1896. He presented two men's life stories—one by Gustave L——, who described his overwhelming desire and admiration for workers' clothing (and the men who wore them), and the other by Louis X——, who took pleasure in the sight and feel of varnished shoes (and the men who wore them).[18]

The focus of Dr. André Antheaume's and Dr. Léon Parrot's study of sexual inversion is a young man named Antonio, who had attempted to kill himself in 1905. In a letter to his parents he explained his suicidal depression by describing his irresistible attraction to other young men. His parents committed him to an asylum, and there he wrote about his life, thoughts, and desires as part of his treatment. The two doctors who treated him—Antheaume and Parrot—published their patient's suicide note and his reported personal recollections in the prestigious journal *Annales médico-psychologiques*.[19] They destroyed his notebook and sketches.

Charles Double, whose story is the last "case study" in part two, filled a series of notebooks with his autobiographical writings at the request of Dr. Alexandre Lacassagne, the eminent physician and prolific author at the Faculty of Medicine in Lyon. Lacassagne intended to publish them, along with other materials that he had collected from the men whom he had examined in the prisons of Lyon, but he never completed his book. Instead, he preserved the materials among his papers. Double's notebooks provide an especially lengthy example of the kind of autobiographical source materials that doctors like Lacassagne were able to collect in the course of their research. Double was an unsuccessful commercial agent who had killed his mother in 1904 in a fit of rage when she threatened to disinherit him. After he was tried, convicted, and incarcerated, Double agreed to participate in Lacassagne's study. The notebooks show that far from simply recounting his life, Double was able to use this forum to counter the theories of the prosecutor and the doctor who had examined him during the course of his trial. While the notebooks contain a gory, graphic description of his murderous act, they also include Double's rather novel explanations for many of the missteps in his life.[20]

This collection ends with "The Novel of an Invert"—an autobiography that was sent by an Italian man to Émile Zola, the well-known naturalist author. Hoping that his life story would provide material for Zola to use in one of his novels, the anonymous writer had composed his autobiography voluntarily. His first letter focused on his heredity, upbringing, and sexual initiation, presenting the material in a way that resembled the case studies that appeared in the medical literature of the era. His third letter was a character sketch, much like the ones that Zola and other authors are known to have made in the process of writing their novels. In between he described two significant love affairs — one in which he had engaged during his military service, and another one that he had experienced in his youth when he was seduced by one of his father's business associates. Zola did not use these letters in any of his novels; instead, he sent them to a friend, Dr. Georges Saint-Paul, who gave them the ironic title "The Novel of an Invert." Because this man's letters were not written for legal experts or medical practitioners but for one of the greatest novelists of nineteenth-century France, some contemporary scholars have argued that this text is somehow more authentic; others, however, have pointed out that it is not free from the constraints or influences of the legal and medical discourses. After all, it too was first published by Saint-Paul in a medical journal and then reprinted in a medical treatise, where it was used to illustrate the doctor's theory of congenital "inversion." The book caught the attention of the Italian letter writer himself, who then contacted the doctor and provided him with additional details about his life.[21]

We believe that all of these autobiographies give remarkable insights into the lives of ordinary men who were emotionally and sexually involved with other men at a time when criminologists and sexologists were just beginning to develop modern concepts of sexual identities. The men's views of their own lives did not always dovetail neatly with the dominant psychological theories, although the legal experts and medical practitioners clearly thought that they were useful illustrations. Therefore, even though the experts used these autobiographies to strengthen their arguments, the writers themselves used them as a means of self-expression. As Foucault has argued so persuasively, the dominant legal and medical discourses on sexuality in the nineteenth century contained within them the seeds for an alternative understanding, which in many ways was quite subversive.[22] More recently, Harry Oosterhuis has demonstrated that all over Europe men who sought out other men for intimate relationships recognized the medical literature as a place where they could tell their stories to an audience that was, if not always sympathetic, at least open-minded. In fact, in his work on Richard von Krafft-Ebing, Oosterhuis has shown that the upper- and middle-class patients of this famous Viennese psychiatrist influenced him as much as he influenced them.[23]

Our aim in translating these eight autobiographies is to let the words of these men from a different time and place speak for themselves as much as possible on questions about homosexuality and effeminacy, romance and tragedy, fetishism and passion, love and desire, and crime and punishment. Autobiographies have been used as sources in historical investigations, in the social sciences, and in literary analyses. For some who study the genre, the authors' intentions are key, whether the aim is to confess, to justify one's actions, to aestheticize one's experiences, or to trace one's psychological development. For others the dynamics of the texts are preeminent and each narrative of the self is created anew in its interaction with readers, not revealing the truth of an "I" but the uncertainties of a contingent discourse.[24] While we do not make claims for the unmediated "truth value" of these autobiographies, we do believe that their encounter with a new community of readers is imperative, and we urge our readers to enter into what Lejeune has called "the autobiographical pact" —a kind of imaginative collusion with the thoughts, words, and deeds of long-dead individuals.[25] These stories are worth reading not only on their own account but also because they provide documentation of the lives of ordinary men in the nineteenth century—of their family backgrounds, their social and sexual relationships, their problems with their families, the police, the criminal justice system, and the medical profession. These men—and many more who have remained silent far too long—have had a profound, widespread, and lasting influence on the development of modern sexual identities.

QUEER LIVES

The Dramatization of the Self

The Countess

Arthur Belorget was a Parisian, born and raised in the city, the son of a domestic servant and a dressmaker. As an adolescent he became the protégé of a nobleman and as a young man he earned a living as a female impersonator and singer in the theaters and cafés of the Second Empire. Unable to avoid his military service, he served for a short time, deserted, and was eventually caught following a series of petty thefts from the home of one of his mother's former customers. He spent ten years in prison as a result of his crimes. He also wrote an autobiography detailing his unusual life.[1]

His autobiography, "The Secret Confessions of a Parisian: The Countess, 1850–1871," is one of the earliest ones written in French by a man who was sexually involved with other men. It is also the only genuinely narrative work in this collection that conforms to the traditional autobiographical genre of the nineteenth century.[2] It recounts the life of its author from childhood through adolescence and into adulthood, emphasizing the author's psychological development, his sexual awakening, and his romantic love affairs. It seems to have been written for a general audience rather than a prosecutor or doctor. This assumption is suggested by textual evidence, such as the ways in which the author polished his narrative and the attention that he devoted to explaining the family background in which he was raised, the theatrical world to which he belonged, and the prison environment in which he was confined. His direct addresses to the reader refer explicitly to a literary model. In language that seems to echo that of Rousseau in his *Confessions*, Belorget writes: "I am laying myself bare because I have to be honest. What would my confessions be worth if I glossed over things? They would lack clarity as well as truth." He refers to Rousseau by name at the beginning of this section, in which he describes his first sexual encounters with other boys and his only attempt at heterosexual intercourse. That attempt failed, but Belorget justifies his presentation of such humiliating, graphic details by emphasizing their didactic value, as Rousseau might have done: "And if I had held back some of the more revolting details . . . how could I explain my mistakes and the role they forced me to play?"

Belorget's writings about his parents and upbringing emphasize early influences on his tastes and values. He recalls acquiring at a very young age an admiration for the nobility and a fascination with the fashionable demimonde of the Second Empire—two very different, but occasionally intersecting, social realms. His initial sexual experiences were with older youths from his own neighborhood, but when the son of the marquis, who was his father's employer, proposed to educate and support him, he left his parents' home and began an association with the theatrical world of the *cafés-concerts* that was to have a profound effect upon his life.

Cafés-concerts began as a form of working-class entertainment, but by the 1850s and 1860s they were attracting a mixed crowd as the bourgeoisie and the aristocracy began to visit them in their explorations of some of the disreputable attractions of Paris. The ones along the *grands boulevards* were particularly popular and very extravagant. They offered their customers inexpensive alcohol and popular entertainment that was highly satirical and occasionally subversive.[3] Known for an atmosphere that was at the same time "smoky, smelly, badly ventilated, naughty, turbulent, impassioned, noisy, ear-splitting . . . , but rarely violent,"[4] they were notorious sites of prostitution, as female and male prostitutes worked the crowds clandestinely. It was also rumored that many of the stage performers were willing to have sexual relations with customers for the sake of a comfortable living.[5] The Countess knew this world well and described it with sympathy and understanding.

Belorget also knew the male homosexual subculture of nineteenth-century Paris. It was composed of an aggregate of young men in their teens, twenties, or thirties from the provinces and the regions around Paris, working mostly in skilled, unskilled, service, or clerical positions. They were independent from their parents or guardians, struggling to make a living in a difficult urban environment. In their leisure time they sought diversions from their daily lives in the pursuit of sexual pleasures. They often visited areas of the city where they would be most likely to meet other men willing to engage in brief, casual affairs. These affairs took place either immediately in the places of initial contact, like the urinals or the streets, or in more secluded areas, like the parks, squares, or quays of Paris. Male prostitution was very much part of this subculture.[6] The Countess's involvement in this world was indirect, but he knew both male and female prostitutes, and his career in the *cafés-concerts* gave him a great deal of contact with courtesans and their patrons and a number of other sexual nonconformists. His talent for drawing enabled him to illustrate his autobiography with sketches of some of his friends and acquaintances.

In the second half of his autobiography, Belorget turns his attention to an entirely different kind of social world. As a military deserter, who was caught with stolen property, he spent most of the 1860s in prison. There he was exposed to the special argot and protocols of that closed society, and there he had several love affairs with fellow prisoners. His descriptions of relationships with fellow inmates are unlike those featured in Balzac's novels or in the memoirs of police officers and prison wardens—the type of writing that influenced contemporary perceptions of men's relationships in prisons. Rather than entangling Belorget in any kind of criminal conspiracy, as so many prison experts feared, his affairs were sometimes passionate, sometimes friendly, sometimes merely distractions to pass the time, but almost always they were part of a support system upon which he could rely.[7]

Consequently, Belorget's autobiography, structured mainly as a chronological account of the young man's rise as a cherished *mignon*, then as a singer and a successful female impersonator, also addresses his subsequent stumble and fall into casual prostitution, thievery, and imprisonment. As such his story resembles an attenuated *Bildungsroman*. The strategic use of foreshadowing and flashbacks suggests the author's familiarity with the narrative techniques of romantic fiction and morality tales. His first-person narrative maintains an intimate tone and a sharp perspective as Belorget describes his first lessons in female impersonation, his male lovers, and the social rituals of the habitués of certain *cafés-concerts* on the Champs Elysées. Because he enjoyed and had some academic training in drawing, he provides illustrations of himself as the "Countess" throughout his work, along with drawings of close friends and others in Paris's homosexual community. He even includes a few sketches of *tribades* (the contemporary term for lesbians in nineteenth-century France), whom he came to know through his performances. As an insider he offers an opinionated typology of the male homosexual subculture, especially of the *mignons, complaisants, tapettes, garçons,* and *filles,* which he classifies with the assurance and attention to detail of a mid-nineteenth-century social scientist.[8]

Belorget's writing suggests that he might have been familiar with prevailing views of the behavior and mores of men who had sex with other men, such as those published in the memoirs of police officers, courtesans, or criminals,[9] or the theories of medical professionals who specialized in pederasty and sodomy.[10] In fact, he gives his own theories, offering a counterexplanation for the etiology of homosexuality, which he considered an innate condition. He also writes about his feelings of "moral and physical difference," about his pleasure in cross-dressing, and about "fooling Mother Nature," and he repeatedly suggests that his early sexual experiences with older boys and young men, his perception of having undersized genitalia, his close emotional attachment to his mother, and even his love of novel reading has destined him for "the passive role . . . as a *mignon*." In this respect Belorget's self-assessment echoed that of many contemporary experts who implicated both hereditary and environmental influences in an individual's "unnatural" sexual attractions.

Dr. Henri Legludic, who brought Belorget's story to light by publishing it in 1895 as the final chapter of his book, *Notes et observations de médicine légale: Attentats aux moeurs*, presented it with a small measure of sympathy.[11] He claimed to have received it, along with eighteen of Belorget's own drawings, in 1874, when Belorget was one of his patients at the prison in Angers. He included it in his book "for documentary purposes . . . in order to enable readers to understand [the writer's] state of mind and to trace the origin and evolution of his sexual inversion."[12] By doing so, Legludic wanted to dismiss the antiquated view of "pederasty" as "only a vice" that can be detected by anatomical anomalies, which was one of Tardieu's cardinal principles.[13] Instead, he argued that "attraction to members of the same sex" was a "psycho-sexual disturbance . . . which manifests itself in the same way in men and women" and that it was a phenomenon "frequently encountered [by doctors and judges] nowadays and throughout human history." However, Legludic tempered this introduction with an admonitory note: "I realize that these stories have to be treated cautiously and that Arthur W——— is not devoid of this need to pose and show off. After all, it is a temperamental defect."[14]

Despite Legludic's admonitory note, "The Secret Confessions of a Parisian" is an amazing document. It contains a frank admission of a son's admiration for his mother, of his willingness to accept the hospitality of a nobleman, of his struggles to make ends meet, and of his descent into prostitution, thievery, and imprisonment. And with relatively little editorial intervention it brings to life the story of "a lady that all gilded and gallant Paris adored," as the Countess put it so immodestly.

1. "The Countess" putting on her makeup. From a drawing by Arthur W——, 1874. Source: Legludic, *Notes et observations*.

Secret Confessions of a Parisian

By Arthur W——, "The Countess" (1874)

PROLOGUE: HE WHO WAS THE COUNTESS

In the beautiful year of 1860, there lived in Paris a woman whom all gilded and gallant Paris knew. Many gentlemen flattered themselves to have received the favors of this creature, without foreseeing that this boast would later become a certificate of shame and a badge of infamy. Many others boasted of having enjoyed the same rights, but this person, although living in a milieu where she was easily accessible, had a rather difficult manner: she was only a kept woman, not the mistress of everyone.

At that time this woman could have been only twenty-two or twenty-three years old. She was called "Countess Laura." Certain inquisitive persons claimed that she also went by the names "Laura Maxence," "Pauline de Floranges," "Nathalie Pelletier," and "Bertha Lamy," but when they mentioned those names to the *cocottes*,[1] they only made them laugh.

Nobody ever called her anything but the "Countess." "Laura" was used only by a very small number of people, and then they usually added the article "the" — a custom used by pleasure seekers, courtesans, or theater people. The Countess was almost always alone at the park, the races, the theater, or the ball. She was a person of medium height, tall rather than small, with a pleasing figure. At first glance one would consider her pretty, but it was impossible to think that she was beautiful. She was very agreeable in conversation; she pleased by a certain *je-ne-sais-quoi*, which charmed and attracted others spontaneously. Her looks had an appeal that a true beauty did not always possess.

This sinner had a fairly well proportioned oval face; her complexion was pale; her eyes were large, with circles under them; very expressive, tender, and timid at times, they were also as sweet as a child's or as bold, lascivious, and mocking as those of a courtesan. To enhance them, the Countess took care to make them up in the style of Cairo's dancing girls and the beautiful ladies of Constantinople. Her nose was really very ordinary; it was even somewhat common; it didn't have any particular shape; still, the nostrils were pink, pretty, and quivering—a sign of the delicacy of feeling and also of sensuality. Her mouth was small and her lips fleshy, attractive, and of a naturally deep color. Her white teeth were scrupulously straight but a bit large. All in all her whole face was expressive.

The most pleasing thing about the Countess, in addition to her animated and captivating conversation, was a certain melancholic air, a tinge of sadness, which, despite her efforts, changed the expression on her face from laughter to sorrow in an instant. It appeared as suddenly as a lightning bolt in summer in the middle of her gayest hours on the Lake Saint-Fargeau,[2] while she listened to the flirtatious small talk of the dandies who made up her entourage; or it could happen in the Restaurant de Madrid[3] in the middle of the most lively entertainment or at the Maison d'Or[4] in the midst of a banquet while she was sipping *Clicquot*; or it could happen just after she had finished singing one of those obscene ditties that were so well beloved at the dinners of Parisian bachelors and men-about-town.

Her thoughtful head elicited affection; the neck that supported it was rounded, white, and without a single wrinkle or line. The Countess would have been beautiful, except for a terrible deformity that Nature had inflicted on her in one of the most visible parts of her entire body: she had ugly hands. Her hands were small and always marvelously gloved. From far away they could project an illusion of beauty because their owner took care of them religiously, but in vain: neither powder nor cream could elongate those fingers with flat nails and badly-shaped cuticles. No treatment, no doctor, had ever been able to remove the furrows on the palms of her hands, which crisscrossed in all directions. Neither their whiteness nor the brilliant rings that adorned them could change the shape of her hands. Her fingers were too short and the joints that connected them were too bulging. Yet—and this was an exceptional thing—these hands that were so unsightly were charming in their slightest movements, and that grace contributed more than a little to diminishing their ugliness.

As a consolation, and in contrast to the general rule of nature that persons afflicted with bad hands usually have bad feet as well, the Countess had the most beautiful feet in the world.

In addition to the ugliness of her hands, the Countess had one more source of despair related to her beauty; she was extremely thin, and her close friends used to say "as skinny as the Countess."

One day an artist sketched a striking portrait of the Countess, and then he wrote this simple phrase at the bottom of his drawing: "Heartless!" This was in response to her moments of sullen abruptness and based on the testimony of those who accused the Countess of insensitivity.

When the subject saw her portrait, she was silent and motionless for a long time. Her face, already pensive, grew even sadder; burning tears fell from her eyes, and one could hear her repeating, "No, he's wrong, just like all the others. I don't lack a heart. Alas! It's probably because mine is more sensitive than others that I hide it with so much care. With such a heart, how could I have entered this shameful and infamous profession? How miserable I am! I've exchanged all the noble things of nature for the most ignoble and shameful ones. I'm no more than a piece of merchandise sold to the highest bidder, an object that one pays according to the brilliance that it seems to have. Must I keep on besmirching my poor heart with the contact of so much infamy?"

So all was not perfect for this unhappy creature who, at certain times, seemed so foolishly radiant, so playful, so oblivious of all morality and of all self-control. These moments of gaiety, which arose in the midst of the cries of dissolute supper parties through the bluish flames of punch and burning kisses, were for the Countess, as they were for all the rest, a comedy.

You now know the heroine of this book in the physical sense, in her slightest particularities. From the few words of her inner monologue that we reported you've come to understand her morally. We're going to complete this study by sketching the character of this figure with two faces. Laura had literary tastes, she read a lot, she drew passably, and she sang agreeably. Her face lent itself marvelously to makeup, like the faces of all those whose physiognomy is large, full, and marked by strong features. After all, rouge, footlights, and spotlights demand prominent facial features; you should not think that delicate beauty comes off well on the stage. This inspired in one of her friends the idea of launching her in the *cafés-concerts*. The idea was welcomed with joy by one for whom all exhibitionism was charming. Thus it was in 1854 that the Countess made her debut on the stage at a summer pavilion on the Champs-Elysées.

A slave to beauty, luxury, and splendor, the Countess saw her excesses as even more justified when she appeared on the stage of a *café-concert*. She needed a flashy outfit, a new, unprecedented luxury to create an illusion that concealed the imperfections of her fragile beauty. Now her ignoble actions seemed right and in a sense almost indispensable to her; excuses are never lacking in those who want to justify to themselves the shipwrecks of their reprehensible lives. Thanks to this additional income Laura indulged herself in even more prodigious luxuries, if that was possible. But what was real were the amorous customers, the protectors who rushed in. She became even more gay. She laughed often, and this gaiety, which went so well with her youth and finery, made her even more attractive. The dandies of the Boulevard des Italiens feasted their eyes on her every day.

In the public places that she frequented, a young pleasure seeker would often ask an old, handsome man: "Who is that pale woman whom you've just greeted?"

"That! Ah! My dear, that's our beautiful Countess."

"But is it *the* Countess?"

"The Countess, my good man, is the most singular creature that I know, the strangest, most gracious girl that we have among all of our merchants of pleasure. I'm on the best of terms with her!"

Often such boasts came back to the creature who was their object. Then an observer would see a special smile lightly touch the scoffing lips of that sinner, and then sadness would pervade her features just as quickly. But it all happened in a flash. The good girls, her friends, who had despite their frivolity noticed these subtle changes, used to say, "Oh, well! The Countess has her fickle moods!"

She was good, despite her cold air; sensitive, despite her reputation of insensitivity; a little romantic; generous to a fault; alas, the heroine of this truthful tale had already experienced so much deception and ingratitude. These disappointments threw her into the most complete distress and by paralyzing her energy led one day to a frightful fall. It's this *dénouement* that gave me the idea of writing this study.

But before drawing a sketch of those sad episodes, I must narrate the life of the strange being whom I've named the Countess. I have to explain how certain events made this attractive monstrosity develop from a timid child—sweet, studious, and loving—from a young man, in fact—into someone whom everyone on the boulevards knows and who is none other than the author of this book.

Arthur W———[5]

PART ONE: PAULINE DE FLORANGES

Chapter One

My Father and Mother. The House on the Rue Saint-Honoré. The Dressmakers. The *Café-Concert* on the Champs-Elysées.

Our Tastes Are Only Memories. Alfred's Kiss. My Attraction to Luxury. The Evenings at the *Café-Concert*. My Antipathy for Boys' Clothing. Fairy Tales. The Rue de Rumford.

My parents were decent folk in all senses of the word. My father, a former coachman, became a steward thanks to his reputation for absolute honesty and his abilities. My father neither spoke nor acted like a servant; his first master, who greatly appreciated him, had raised him in his household and had given him an education. My father was tall, with a pleasing and friendly face. His character was a bit pretentious, with a streak of egoism. He belonged to the now extinct race of servants who were, in a certain sense, a part of the family for whom they worked. My father adored his masters. For him, being a valet was not a demeaning profession. He'd have readily risked great dangers to help his masters avoid any unpleasantness. Accustomed as he was to the manners and the language of the nobility, he also adopted their likes and dislikes. The result of this, coupled with my father's natural tendencies, was that under their influence he became a spendthrift, generous to the point of recklessness. As a steward he knew full well how to keep accounts and to administer the wealth of others, but he was never able to do the same for himself once he went into business. He always acted as a grand lord, as if he too had the millions that his masters possessed. He was an elegant man, susceptible to praise, even flattery, and attracted to beauty. He dressed like a minor aristocrat and had only one great flaw: a weak character, compounded by excessive vanity. I inherited these two traits almost in their entirety. My father had been one of the most handsome men of his day; the beauty of his face and figure was obvious to me as soon as I was old enough to notice them. He used to say that he had made numerous conquests in his youth, and I could easily believe it.

As for my mother, she was an angel; she had the calm beauty, the purity, the soft caresses, the inexhaustible devotion of an angel. Her face reflected her beautiful soul; her eyes blazed with motherly love. But because she was extremely chaste and calm, she remained ignorant of the stormy passions of earthly beings. For her, her children were everything—the sum total of all of her joys and passions. My God! I feel as if I can still hear her sweet voice, which sounded to my ears like the song of the seraphim. I remember her still, making me kneel, folding my hands together, and teaching me my prayers. Later she taught me to sing lovely songs. When I got older, she was grateful to have such a calm, peaceful child. She was so happy when I would say, "Mother, shall we spend the evening singing and chatting?"

"My dear Arthur, you know how much I'd enjoy that, but you, my sweet child, should not spend so much time indoors. You should play too. You're much too serious. Oh! God is so good to have given me such a son!" And she'd kiss me, the dear woman, as if I were still a baby. Poor mother!

When she was sewing, I'd often read aloud to her from a stack of old novels that were kept locked in an old trunk in the back of a closet. These were the most dangerous books that one could find, but my mother was too ignorant, despite her innate intelligence, to realize the dangers of such readings. For her, every romantic book was lovely and must be good; she thought she was developing the finest feelings in me by awakening a sensibility in me that would later become one of the causes of my downfall. My eyes would often fill with tears, forcing me to stop reading. My dear mother would also cry, and we'd dry our tears with exchanges of kisses. "My dear little boy," she'd say, "you have a good heart."

These emotions, repeatedly stimulated, gave me a distinct taste for solitude. This is quite understandable. The other children my age were so different from me; they played with marbles and pickup sticks; they were noisy in their happiness. Some of them had a vigor that signaled the precocious virility that would make them into men. I looked at them coldly and with surprise. I found no pleasure in chasing a spinning top or aiming marbles at a hole.

Things continued in this manner until I entered a boarding

school. But when adolescence took the place of childhood and when I had become an immoral and degenerate being, I still enjoyed spending evenings with my dear sweet mother, who believed all of my lies with the open heart of a person who doesn't know how to hide anything.

My mother loved singing. She sang with me every day. These golden hours developed a powerful taste for singers and concerts in me. I specifically mean female singers, because my frivolous nature was seduced by the brilliance of their appearance. Thus the first part of my life was one long musical poem. I sang alongside my mother, and I sang as I played the piano with the pretty wife of Monsieur P———. During the tedious hours of my imprisonment these lovely memories of my past often soothed my soul with sweet, consoling dreams and bright, fleeting lights, illuminating the darkness of those ten long years.

When my father met my mother, she was working as a laundress for the Marquise de Y———, but their marriage freed her from that awful position. The newlyweds then moved into their home in a tiny apartment on the rue Saint-Honoré. My mother became a seamstress, and my father returned to the service of the Duchess de Z———. I was born in that house on April 13, 1839.[6]

My mother quickly built up a large clientele for her business. She was skillful, pretty, elegant, and charming. A person didn't need much more than that to become a seamstress for ladies of fashion. Several vaudeville actresses spoke highly of her, which led a great number of women working in the theater to use her services. They treated me very kindly; kept women love children all the more for not having any of their own. All of these ladies gave me presents, which made me, like any child, soon feel confident and at ease with them. They gave me lovely boxes of candy and the painted covers of these boxes attracted me as much as the sweets inside. They gave me books with expensive bindings and beautiful illustrations. Then they'd all hold me on their laps, giving me kisses and praising my good behavior and my clever conversation—the sort of witty and pointed remarks that precocious children usually make.

Those experiences didn't leave me indifferent. The sight of these women, decorated like holy shrines and perfumed like sachets, filled me with all possible joys. I loved to run my fingers over their lace and to play with their jewels. They all seemed like great beauties to me. Their bold and strong-willed natures put me off a little, since I was naturally shy, but their caresses quickly calmed my passing fears. This is what I remember most vividly about my first impressions of the luxury of women's wardrobes.

The rue Saint-Honoré is not far from the Champs-Elysées, and my dear mother loved walking there. We went there frequently during the day, and my mother and I never missed a summer evening stroll, either with my father or with one of the shop assistants who lived with us. My mother also loved the shows at the *cafés-concerts*. As for me, I drank them all in, with my ears and my eyes wide open. These performances strongly attracted me; I'd think about them all day, and each night I'd ask my mother, "Mother, are we going to the *café-concert* tonight?" One day I too would appear on these stages that had charmed me so much when I was young. As Lamartine wrote: "All our desires are merely memories."

My brother had a friend, a hearty young man named Alfred B———. He had a friendly face and the personality to go along with it. He was very considerate to my mother and was especially nice to me. He'd hold me on his lap, bounce me on his knees, bring me picture books, and make me little paper dolls, which I loved and collected in a box, where I arranged them by size. One day he came while I was alone with our maid. He sat down, took me in his arms, embraced me as usual, and then, taking my head in his hands, he kissed me on the lips with such fervor that I stared at him before returning his kiss. His face, usually so calm and tranquil, was completely changed. His eyes blazed and his lips quivered. When my mother came in, he calmed down. That kiss disturbed me, and when I think about it, it provokes some very strange thoughts in me even now.

I've already mentioned that my mother worked for the vaudeville theaters. Because of this, there were almost always costumes at our house to be altered or remodeled. One day Madame D—— sent over a blue satin dress with gold spangles to serve as a model for my mother to make another one in the same style. When my mother had taken all the measurements, that lovely blue dress was put in the room where we displayed the finished articles. I played for a few more moments, then, when I saw that Mama was occupied with something else, I slipped into the room. That blue satin gown had obsessed me ever since it had been brought in. I looked at it; I touched it; I took it off the mannequin; and I managed to put it on myself, even though it was too big for my little body. The gown was so long that I couldn't see my feet, but only the front caused me any difficulty. I had seen fine ladies at the theater, and I had not forgotten how they handled the trains of their gowns. So I pinned up the front of the hem, and there I was, trailing that dress, which hobbled my child's feet. I picked up Mama's fan, which had been left on the pedestal table. I fanned myself as well as I could, and thus dressed up, I looked at myself with a feeling of satisfaction in the big mirror that showed my charming reflection from head to toe.

I was absorbed in my coquettish game—which was certainly far from acting like a boy—when gales of laughter and the sound of whispers made me look around. Mama and her two assistants were laughing uproariously at this peculiarly childish flight of fancy.

"Ah, my dear child!" my mother said. "What are you doing all dressed up?"

"Mama," I replied, without moving an inch, as I was glued to the spot with embarrassment, "I'm playing 'diva.'"

My wonderful mother thought this was a charming reply and was thrilled by the idea. (I think I've already mentioned that her greatest wish had been to have a daughter.) She said, smiling and coming closer, "That's nice, but you must take off Madame D——'s gown. You might damage it." That was all she said. She described the scene in detail to Papa, who laughed a great deal about it and observed proudly, "He's astounding, that boy! He imitates everything he sees."

As much as I loved women's dresses and accessories, however, I'd burst into tears at the sight of boys' short pants. I'd put them on only if they were decorated with embroidery and lace, and my mother would laughingly say, "What a funny little boy! I ought to dress him like a girl."

My favorite books at this age were Perrault's fairy tales,[7] which everyone believed to be quite innocent, and I owe my first feelings of vanity to these charming but dangerous stories. The dazzling descriptions of palaces encrusted with gold and precious stones, of silk dresses with diamonds and silver shimmering in my eyes, made me dream and inspired a desire for wealth and a taste for the unusual in my childish brain.

When she left the rue Saint-Honoré, my mother moved to the rue de Rumford. The doctor had advised her to give up dressmaking. In 1850 the rue de Rumford was at its best; it had wonderful sidewalks and fine houses with lovely balconies decorated with gilded latticework on both sides of the street; it even had some splendid townhouses. Most of these elegant townhouses were rented to denizens of the demimonde, but they were all ladies of quality, and most of them had fine carriages.

Mama opened a perfume and accessory shop on the rue de Rumford. Many of her regular clients had promised to shop there, and a good number of them kept their word. So, like Panurge's sheep,[8] the kept women, who were our neighbors, saw the parade of fine carriages coming every day to our shop, and they too rushed to become our customers. Even though at first they barely knew my mother, she succeeded in charming them too. That was one of her gifts.

At this point in my story, anyone who is reading these pages and paying attention at all must agree that, along with the innate tendencies of my character, chance had a significant role in developing in me that love of beauty and style that grew into a passion and would later degenerate into a frenzy and cause the disorders and the missteps that mark my life. There's no man on this earth, I'm convinced, who grew up surrounded by as much feminine beauty as I did, who gazed at so many pretty women's faces leaning over his cradle, smiling at him and promising him caresses, joys, and happiness. My whole childhood was spent in an atmosphere of graciousness, delicacy, and lovely faces, and neither the passage of time nor misfortune nor the cruel disappointments of life nor the long hours of imprisonment can ever tarnish that glorious memory.

Chapter Two

The Reading Room and the Novels. The Théâtre de Montmartre. The Gentleman from the Rue de Rougemont. The Pot of Makeup.

There was a lovely reading room quite near my mother's house. My father, who loved to read, made frequent trips there. I soon followed his example, but since for me books were already the sort of friends that I held on to tightly, like unfaithful lovers, I didn't borrow them; instead, I bought them from the woman owner of a well-stocked bookshop. That lady was very fond of me; I enjoyed visiting her shop because she was so kind to me; and she let me stick my nose in every corner and leaf through the thousands of volumes arrayed on the shelves there. I would spend half the night reading novels, and the licentiousness of their pages corrupted my mind, just as it contaminated my imagination and my heart.

A concierge next door had a son who was an actor who played romantic leads at the Théâtre de Montmartre.[9] She often gave my mother tickets. Those were wonderful outings, full of pleasure for me. Sometimes I went behind the scenes rather than take my seat in the auditorium, even on the opening night. That way I saw the actors up close—those happy people in public who were often so miserable in private. I paid special attention to the actresses, who were always so elegant.

One of the actresses, whom I saw on stage often and who gave me the most gracious welcome, was a certain A——, who always played the role of the elegant, seductive young lady. She showed her kindness to me the first time she laid eyes on me when she exclaimed, "The sweet little boy, one would take him for a girl!" Then she took my hand, asking, "How old are you, little boy?"

"I'm eleven, Madame," I replied, lowering my eyes, since I could see the actors surrounding us. I thought their looks and smiles were mocking me, and they intimidated me much more than the actresses did.

"Eleven years old!" cried A——. "Tell me now, B——," she added, turning to a heavyset woman with a kindly face, who played the role of the chaperone in the troupe, "don't you think he would be lovely on stage?"

"Yes," said Madame B——, "one could, if need be, dress him as a girl and make use of him." She stroked my face and asked me, "Would you like to act, my child?"

I was just about to answer when the director called out: "On stage! On stage!"

I often went to the Théâtre de Montmartre, but rarely by myself. A young man, six years my senior, came with me most of the time. My mother had entrusted me to his care, and I was glad for his company because Frederic was very sweet to me.

A year later—at that time I was preparing for my First Communion at the beginning of January—I was walking on the boulevard to buy some gifts for my father and my dear mother. My brother and I always gave gifts to our parents on the first day of the new year and on their name days, which were close to the same day. Two or three months before this celebration, which I prized above all others, I had started to save some of the spending money that my parents gave me, and on the eve of the happy day, having around twenty-five or thirty francs, I was going shopping for my gifts, which were remarkable even then for their good taste and elegance.

On December 31, 1851, I bought my mother an orange cashmere wrap, embroidered with silk thread and highlighted with gold. Nothing was more luxurious than that shawl in its shiny white box, wrapped in gold striped paper. I was coming back home happy, walking briskly, as people do when they have done a good deed for a loved one. It was very dark, even though it was only seven o'clock in the evening. In the rue de Rougemont a well-dressed gentleman with his hands in the pockets of his overcoat walked up alongside me. If I stopped at a shop, he did too; if I crossed from one sidewalk to another, he did the same. Even though this gentleman seemed to be trustworthy, I don't know why he made me feel afraid to such an extent that I felt my legs losing all their strength and I trembled all over. All of a sudden he said to me in a harsh, brusque tone of voice, "Here's a young man to whom I'd happily give lovely gifts if he'd come with me for a moment."

And when I picked up my pace even more instead of giving him an answer, he added, "One might think, my boy, that I'm scaring you, but I'm really not very frightening."

"You don't scare me, sir, but I don't know you, and I don't know why you're following me."

"It's because I'd like to get to know you, and in a good way," he replied, lowering his voice and squeezing my arm. Then he looked at me, and I felt even more afraid.

At this point, when we were at the corner of the rue de Provence, the gentleman began to seem a bit dangerous, especially for a young boy of my age. He pressed against me in order to keep me from walking on, and I don't know what would have happened, when, at the intersection of the rue Lepelletier, I cried out with joy as I saw my friend Frederic coming toward me. I rushed toward him, saying in a halting voice, "Get rid of this man who's following me." I took his arm, hanging on like a drowning man to a life preserver. All of this only took a moment, but it was enough to cause the dapper man to vanish.

Frederic questioned me, and I told him everything. After I finished, he said, "Listen carefully, little Arthur. When you run into men who say things like this man did, you must go straight to a policeman. If you can't find one, talk to the first passerby that you see. Those men, you see, are filthy fellows! Will you promise me that?"

"Yes, Frederic," I answered. He was a decent man, that good Frederic. If I had always had him close by me, I'm sure I would have followed his good advice.

Among all the women I knew when I was growing up, there were some who didn't delude themselves about my nature. There was one in particular who found me out, and after she did, she tried with all her kindness to protect me from the dangerous tendencies that she saw in me. She was quite right to tell me that I was effeminate. One day, when I saw an enchanting little pot of theatrical makeup made of porcelain overlaid with gold filigree in the window of a perfume shop in the passage du Ham, I went in and asked, "How much?" "Six francs," the shopgirl replied. That was all the money I had, except for a few centimes, but since I didn't dare get one of those pots from my mother, who also sold them, and because dreams of the theater obsessed me, I bought it. Then I made myself up at night when everyone was asleep. I used to get out of bed to perform this lovely task, and placing a pair of candles from the mantel on each side of my mirror, I would gaze at myself with extreme pleasure.

Chapter Three

The Pension B———. The Older Students. Masturbation. My Secret. My First Attempt at Love. I Was Never Happy.

I left my dear mother with a heavy heart to go to a boarding school. Even though the school was only a few minutes away from my home and I could go back home every evening, it felt as if I was leaving my mother permanently. I was so accustomed to seeing her and hearing her that even a whole day's separation seemed as long as a century.[10]

Charles K——, that was my friend's name, spoke to me about things that I didn't understand at all, but these things attracted me, even though I couldn't say why. I think it was because of the flattery that came along with them. Charles had a sensual nature. Since he realized that words wouldn't sway me, he resorted to action.

I kept to myself, alone with the knowledge of my disgrace, but still I didn't think too much about the evil that I had committed. I only thought about doing it again and as soon as possible. Having introduced me to the pleasures of the senses, Charles had destroyed all my good tendencies. This big step I had taken was irrevocable. I was lost forever—lost in my behavior and lost in my character. Having indulged in pleasure with someone older than myself, I had drunk deeply from the source of those predilections that make a man prostitute himself not by circumstance, nor by poverty, which a substantial amount of money might alleviate; no, by starting out with a boy four years older than myself, I was destined always to play the woman's role—the role of the *mignon*—that distinct and separate type among all men with similar passions.[11]

What an abominable aberration it is that a young man feels such infinite, overpowering joy in the arms of another man! What a pleasure of the senses and of a throbbing heart when a young man seems to feel such genuine voluptuousness in responding to this unnatural love! And what pleasure for the eyes, especially the eyes, to devour someone of your own sex with the ravenous hunger of inexplicable, untranslatable looks! I'm going to try to translate these sensuous feelings that have overwhelmed me so many times and have left regret and sorrow in their wake. This sorrow could be seen so clearly on my face when the thoughts came into my mind. That change in my facial expression, the cause of which no one has ever understood, was my secret—a secret that has eaten away at my insides like a pitiless cancer devouring the flesh of the unhappy victim that it is destroying. This secret has greatly intrigued my friends, I must say, and it is only with reluctance that I expose it in this memoir, which contains my dearest, most intimate thoughts.

People have often said that morally I'm not like other men. I can only add that I'm different physically as well and that this difference has caused me pain. It is the rapidly growing ulcer that has engulfed all my happy moments and the poison that has corrupted my life from the time that I became a man. This sadness, which is so powerful in my life, is the real cause of the enjoyment that I had in concealing my sex beneath a woman's exterior.

The burning regret—the sorrow that poisons my life, that has caused so many lapses in my mind and body, and that has provoked so many feelings that no torture could equal—was that of not being made sexually like other men. Not that I was different in shape, but in proportions. No other man my age can understand the heartbreaking thoughts, the blows to the self-esteem of a young man who is less well equipped than his peers. This idea—that I was not like the others—was the starting point for all the monstrous fantasies, all the sensual pleasures, all the actions taken to appease the thirst of this painful curiosity that seized me during the hours when my blood, boiling in my veins, circulated the disorder and the violence of an overheated imagination. For me it was a painful torment, unlike anything else, and it was always followed by a return to self-awareness and a feeling of depreciation that drained away my self-esteem, as a scalpel's cut makes the heart bleed. Since the age of sixteen I've felt the agony born of that comparison. Until then I had believed that I was made like all the young boys of my age, even though I had long before been struck by the differences that I had had a chance to notice during our schoolboy games. I had attributed these differences to my friends' ages, since they were bigger, stronger, and older than I by four or five years, but I was already tormented by the comparison. A secret voice seemed to cry out inside of me, "You'll never be like that!" and I'd begin to daydream. Then I'd sigh, and then once more the hope would come back to me that the future would banish these sad forebodings. I was only about twelve years old then.

I still see Charles K——— sometimes. By seducing me Charles had to a great extent broken down the barrier that my shyness would have raised against the desires that the sight of me kindled in the mind of the Marquis de X———.

How would it otherwise have been possible for this elegant man, who kept describing his intentions and his desires to me in a manner that would have been almost completely incomprehensible to a truly naive person? How could he have made me understand what he wanted if I hadn't already been introduced to the pleasures of masturbation? But, I repeat, Charles's lessons, together with my unfortunate preoccupation regarding those secret benefits, had prepared me to accept everything in order to satisfy a passion that was incessantly stimulated by desire. My infamy was irrevocable from the day that I saw him having an erection for the first time. Then I had only one thought, only one desire: to know if all young men were equally well endowed. It seemed so extraordinary to me that I couldn't believe that it was a normal part of our nature.

Many times I've heard people discuss the question of the love of one man for another. I've taken part in rather profound debates and learned disputations on this subject that were engaged in by men of considerable wit and wisdom. Even while fearing this passion, even while deploring it as a cause of the weakening of virile energy, some of these men concluded that this passion is much more a part of our innate tendencies than it is the consequence of a precocious sexual initiation or the inevitable aftermath of debauchery or the satiety of the senses resulting from it. When we are still children, what is the first desire that we have? It's to understand how we're made, as soon as we reach maturity. That curiosity causes us to pay close attention to every aspect of our sexuality, and it also makes us willing to accommodate the demands of an older friend. Here I must add a parenthetical remark: many little boys play sexual games with each other, but for most boys, these sensual desires, which are stronger than you think at such a young age, are simply a sign of an awakening nature, an instinct of love, and the onset of a nascent virility. But although these first attempts may have something in common, the results are fortunately not always the same. Every child, every young boy who has experimented with a playmate at the age when shyness would block any approach to a woman, will forget these missteps a few years later and will become a man who has a mistress—in other words, he'll become a real man. That's the usual case. Here I'm presenting the exception. When a young adolescent complies with the request of an older, bigger boy, therein lies the danger.

My example will serve to develop this idea further—an idea that a number of *complaisants*[12] who recount details of their childhood in all frankness have caused me to consider the Gordian knot of the passion that drives them and exploits them. By pleasuring myself with an older boy, I drank at the source of the sensual joy that is passive compliance itself. The child who would one day become a paid *mignon* has always (or nearly always) had the same personality traits in his childhood: sweetness and timidity. These two traits are the basis for these young men's downfall once they reach the age of puberty. Nothing is more damaging for a young man than the dreamy impulses of a timid nature. His character becomes less bold than others'. He withdraws into himself, and he isolates himself. Then vice can flourish, and we see these pretentious, effeminate types, at the same time audacious and timid, flooding the ranks of men in our lovely city of Paris. They are shameless by temperament, cowardly by nature, greedy in their ostentatious consumption, and vain in their love of luxury. They're the kind of hermaphrodites that, although they're made like other men, don't resemble anyone else either in their mannerisms or in their speech. These strange beings have been nicknamed *tantes* in the vulgar language of the common folk; more educated people call them *petits* or *filles*; female prostitutes, who are friendly toward them, but who wish to make the distinction clear by their sex and profession, call them *tapettes*. I myself have endowed them with the more fanciful epithets *mignons* and *complaisants*.[13]

If we recognize that there are extenuating circumstances for those whose downfall was precipitated by a passion for masturbation or for pederasty,[14] we should also take into account the existence of a malleable personality already partly corrupted by the evil influence of an imagination hungry for the unknown. Likewise we should consider circumstances arising from their environment or the way in which this or that young man was brought up. It is clear that a young man who was brought up from a very early age by a stern father will not develop into a man like the ones whose lives I'm describing here. As to the adolescent who is constantly—every day and every hour—under the influence of the refined, passionate, and sentimental ideas of a loving mother—a woman who is sometimes lost in fantasy, who is always too indulgent or too weak—it's common knowledge that such early influences will instill a taste for calm, solitude, and feminine pastimes that comes from the mother's ideas and teaching. We ought to acknowledge that a mother's child-rearing, as wonderful as it is, has this dissolute side to it. As I've said, I've studied this question by frequently asking those who sell their pretty bodies, and among these bizarre and effeminate creatures I've found many who were brought up by overindulgent mothers, mainly by widows. By smothering them with their frustrated love and their thwarted affection, these mothers have combined their own maternal instincts with all the little attentions that characterize unconditional love. This solicitude at every moment, these vague fears that they surround their sons with, these anxieties that they feel when they think of him having a love affair or having a mistress when the time is right, all of this inculcates in their sons the charming, foppish behavior that ties them to their childhood homes, that keeps them permanently in a childlike state, even when they're full-grown adults. It chokes off the first impulses of nature and the expressions of love in the way the law of the senses decrees. This is how so many scandalous lives begin.

A love that turns into self-love, as Rousseau wrote, is much more dangerous for timid souls, where it remains entirely imaginary. It's even more dangerous for the young man who loses himself in amorous daydreams, which he devises as he sees fit. In his imagination he awards himself the possession of one woman or another, whom in reality he'd hardly dare to look at. This is the sort of love that kills love, because this solitary love destroys all the desires that rightly belong to real love. Yes, this timidity repels even the idea of having a woman. Men who are brought up adoring their mothers as they would their sisters and by worshiping them like untouchable beings develop a fearful restraint in their dealings with other women. This is due to the excessive love that these men feel for women.

This conclusion is drawn from certain observations related to a select population. Not all pederasts have such overwhelming reasons to excuse their vices. But the delicacy of their feelings should excuse their sexual misdeeds to a great extent, since once women are put on a pedestal, in these men's eyes they're no longer approachable. By loving them too much, these men no longer love them at all. Sexual desire turns into breathless admiration, and contemplation takes the place of lustful thoughts. By seeing those beings, who should give them joy, as creatures like angels, these men eventually stop desiring such pleasure. Their hearts reject the feelings that quiver there, and they stifle their heartbeats, as a bird handler holds back the frantic beating of the wings of a bird that he imprisons in his hands. If circumstances like these can affect young men who were raised in the usual way and who are capable of meeting the demands of even the most passionate woman in their amorous relations, how must they influence and paralyze the will of an adolescent, who would need all his wits in order to conquer his shyness and who, above and beyond that, finds himself completely helpless.

That's what happened to me. I don't want to make excuses here for my corrupt and disorderly life; I don't want to lay the blame for my situation on a general theory about an error of nature; but I do want to show that I'm neither more evil nor more perverted than many others who believe that they have the right to insult and despise me. My vices were evident at a very young age, it's true, but they were neither more powerful nor more numerous than many other men's. For a long time I didn't recognize this in myself, and for a long time, as I watched my classmates endanger themselves with risky pleasures, I remained ignorant of, or rather indifferent to, these joys. I can attest to that. If I had been put in a different situation, my life would have been better, or at least less blameworthy. When I see so many men, more talented than I was, get dragged down by their passions, to claim that I wouldn't have done the same thing if I had been as clever as they were is sheer nonsense. I haven't the slightest intention of misleading in writing this; I'm describing what I believe, what I feel, what is true, and what I've learned from lengthy and careful observation.

The story of my only sexual passion for a woman, whom I met in 1853, will support everything I've said about the timidity of men. When a young man, after an upbringing like mine, finds himself involved in a romantic encounter, even one small failure is enough to bring it rapidly to a close, especially if the man in question knows himself to be incapable of performing in the manner that most pleases experienced *coquettes*. He who has the fortitude to withstand the mockery of *coquettes* can thus overcome any obstacle, but he who does not will buckle under. So, while I was still an adolescent but already on the wrong track, I wanted to break with this life of lies and self-indulgence once and for all, since I had not yet been enslaved by my own lack of initiative or by an unbreakable habit.

To carry this out, every time I went back to my mother's house, I'd put on men's clothing, and I'd try to find someone among her women clients who would help me in my rehabilitation. My senses and my eyes were entranced by Madame C——, a small woman of at least forty years of age, who was lively and pretty. She had a youthful appearance, but was also curvy and plump. There I was, staying with my mother for a week, in order to avoid falling back under the influence of my friends once I returned to my own place. I was confident that I could overcome the past with the present, buying lovely bouquets and gifts, all of which were welcomed graciously by this woman. This woman, who was a natural flirt, was lustful, gross, and debauched by idleness; in short, she was the personification of the most brutal and repulsive vice. When I was at my mother's place, I had judged her solely by her outward appearance. She only came there to buy a few things, but she came frequently. She was attracted to me in the same way that other men appeared agreeable to her. She invited me to visit her, and I went. She kissed me; she glanced at me unmistakably; finally, one day, she led me to her unmade bed, where she undid her clothing. My heart pounded, and I felt that my body, rather than being ready for love, was completely paralyzed. My poor organs were absolutely incapable of functioning, and the more I thought of what I wanted to do, the more paralyzed I became. Madame C—— came to me, gave me two or three kisses, then removed her lacy chemise and exposed her lovely pale breasts.

"Don't I excite you?" she asked. "You're giving me such a sur-prised and unfriendly look."

"But no, you do," I replied, as if in a dream. "I find you quite beautiful."

"Well then, what are you waiting for? Don't you have any balls?"

This joke, at which any other young man might have laughed and which would have encouraged them, took me aback and actu-ally revived my feelings of regret and sadness. I dropped into an armchair and burst into tears. This woman couldn't find any words in her heart to console me, to stop my crying. She had found me out, and she despised me. I left, hiding my face in my hands. That was my first attempt at love.

When I returned to my dear mother's home, I had to invent a

lie to explain the traces of tears on my face. I told her that I had learned of the death of an acquaintance, and my mother, who was sensitive and affectionate, showered me with words of consolation from her noble heart. I sobbed in her arms so charmingly and with such feeling over the imaginary death of this unknown friend. Madame C——'s cruel joke was the final blow. That defeat, which foretold so many others for me in the future, pushed me more decisively than ever into tumultuous orgies in which I played the role of the woman, because the anecdote I've just recounted took place at a time when some who knew me still called me Pauline de Floranges, while others—newer acquaintances—nicknamed me the "Countess."

I'm approaching the time when I'll have to present myself to my readers in the first of these two identities, but I've moved forward in time in order to tell the story of my love for this forty-year-old woman. When I left Madame C——'s home, I allowed myself to sink into the depths of despair for the only time in my life. How I hated that woman who had guessed the secret of my agony and the cause of my tears! I'm not exposing the extent of my immorality here in a cynical gesture. I'm laying myself bare because I've got to be honest. What would my confessions be worth if they were glossed over? They would lack clarity as well as truth. And if I held back some of the more revolting details from a wise and objective man, how could I explain my missteps and the role that they forced me to play?

After that cruel disappointment I retreated ever deeper into the crazy dreams of my romantic imagination. I became skeptical at an age when all our beliefs are still lively and fresh. I enjoyed denying the attraction of that which I couldn't possess. I became insensitive in order to fight against my natural tenderness. My poor heart, which overflowed with affection, seemed to be open only to superficiality. I rejected my true nature in order to devise a false one that I adopted in the same way that I made up my face with a mask of red and white every day. Everyone thought that I was deficient by nature, a heartless and cold individual.

Little by little I evolved into a machine for paid pleasures, and I began to lose my critical faculties by spending time exclusively with people who lived for and by pleasure. I got drunk on the unbridled pleasures of that mad life, and when I was praised, caressed, and adored, I found myself to be happy. Vanity, finding itself satisfied or thus coddled and catered to, took the place of regret, but in order to prolong this dizzying happiness, I had to ensure that I was never alone with my thoughts, indeed never alone with myself.

This, I think, is the difference between a rich man and a poor one. When a rich man's feelings are hurt or when he no longer gets a thrill from ordinary pleasures, he can lose himself by procuring ever newer ones for himself; he can even invent some, thanks to his money. As long as I lived in the lap of luxury provided to me by some of these debauched men, I was almost happy, because a man only feels true suffering when he lives in poverty. That's the second reason that persuaded me to remain what I was. Work of all sorts disgusted me because it was monotonous and uneventful. Any serious or useful occupation would have been difficult for me. That's why I completely abandoned the study of drawing, which I had undertaken as the first step toward a serious career. I only enjoyed reading because it suited my love for oddities. I don't need to add that this balm for my spirit acted just like oil tossed on a blazing fire. I became more and more rotten. My life was a kind of intoxication . . .

When I was alone, I'd sing at the top of my lungs, because only one thing—only one desire—burned inside of me, and that was to sing professionally in a *café-concert*. It seemed to me that I'd be happy then. I was already familiar with the prestige held by the stage, and a few more steps in the wrong direction might bring me a measure of success. In short, after my first immoral act, my life has been nothing but a series of foolish mistakes, injuries, pains, and regrets.

And yet, during my imprisonment at Mazas[15] I had to smile as I listened to men who thought that they were uttering profound thoughts because they were educated and erudite. Lawyers and doctors would whisper to their colleagues, "What a strange life, what a strange young man, but he was happy, because a person with such vices doesn't feel any remorse." They'd then keep on talking at length, trying to explain something that they didn't understand.

All my past struggles have proven one thing to me: I was never happy even when I was celebrating the joys that I've chosen for myself. Every kind of prostitution is a moral degradation, a dishonorable situation, so that in order to live happily you must not even recognize it, but these thoughts have almost always been in my mind. To make a person happy, any kind of sensual abandon must lead to total forgetfulness, to an overwhelming ignorance of the abject state that you live in and to a real distaste for all that is noble and all that is uplifting. With this sort of preparation, men seeking the pleasures that I describe here don't feel any remorse, because they've no moral code, and their senses give them pleasure and relief that they enjoy fully.

As for me, was I able to achieve this forgetfulness, this tranquility? I was thin and weak, with an ambiguous sort of beauty, and my regrets always contended with the meager joys that I experienced. My sadness expressed itself in a biting and sarcastic wit. That's the way that I denied the existence of love, friendship, and even sensual pleasures. This sort of irascible personality earned me the reputation among my friends of not being able to feel anything in regard to love—as if those fantasies bought and sold by strangers could be called "love." Those fantasies, which I don't believe are in the realm of love, do have an intrinsic feeling that can, however, affect us deeply. This comes from two of the dearest joys of mankind—friendship and unconditional affection. These two things, it must be said, often flourish in the close bond between two young men who are already dreaming about love but who don't dare to put those dreams into practice.

After having denied that the noble emotion called "love" can be found in a perverse sexual attraction, a few years later I was forced to recognize its overwhelming power and undeniable reality. I had to suffer so much and in so many ways that I'm amazed that I survived the experience. Yes, unconditional affection and devoted friendship can cause a person to risk everything, to forget everything, for the happiness of the friend who is their object. At that point we have no more false vanity, no more fears of the public's ridicule or harsh words. We're willing to stand up to anything, because our body and our heart don't belong to us anymore. We give up everything, because nothing is really ours anymore; rather, everything belongs to the dear friend whom we've chosen. If that friend is a sensualist, if he has base passions, we'll lower ourselves to his level, and all the while we'll honestly believe that we're on a higher plane. In these cases there are no second thoughts. Nothing exists except for the loved one, except for the person who commands his lover's heart and holds it in thrall. Yes, in a situation like that, friendship is united with the filthiest desires, and a friend may add to another's happiness by according him sexual favors without feeling ashamed.

I had been indifferent up until that point, but from the day that I felt an emotion like the one I've just described I sacrificed everything for my passion. From that day on I understood the power and the value of the word "to love." From that moment on I suffered because of it—but I also lived.

Chapter Four

A Protector. I Become a Great Lady. The Lessons of Paula. The First Date with M———. *Tribades. Complaisants.* The Room on the Rue d'Astorg. My Second Baptism. Charles. The Countess and Prosper. Three Months at Mazas.

I must leave the innocent memories of my childhood behind and skip over about fifteen months to get to the Gordian knot—the evolution of my immoral life.

My father was the coachman and then the valet of the Marquis de X———. After his death, his son, whom I'll refer to as M———, often came to our house. My father had known him since he was a child and had that blind attachment that servants from a former age felt for their masters and their masters' children. Any wish of the young marquis was for my father a command that he wouldn't have even dreamed of not obeying immediately. The marquis seemed to have the highest regard for his father's old servant, and his kindness enchanted my father. My mother was less easily charmed; she didn't have a servant's temperament; her honest and noble heart hated any position that reinforced the superiority of the master, as well as the obsequious platitudes that went along with the servant's inferiority.

M——— was a tall, handsome man of twenty-six. At that age, and in spite of his excesses, he still retained all the splendor of his masculine attractiveness. He visited us regularly around the time when I had just had my First Communion. He had always been very friendly with me but in the way that people act with an older child. He occasionally gave me illustrated books as presents. As soon as I became an adolescent, his visits became longer and more frequent, and he grew more attentive. He obviously was trying to win my affection and often asked my parents' permission for me to ride with him in his coach. Then we'd go to the Bois de Boulogne,[16] and he'd speak to me in the way that people speak to a young lady. He'd praise the charm of my face, the expressive beauty of my eyes, the dainty size of my mouth. He'd hold me close against his body, saying, "If you wished, dear Arthur, you could be happier than a king's son, and you could have all the lovely things that you want so much."

Then, using other sweet words, he'd get me to share my secrets, and I'd tell him everything about my wild dreams and the frustration that I felt at not being a woman, since I was so ill suited for being a man. One day when he couldn't get enough of my explaining what I meant by the phrase that recurred so often in my confessions—the sad regret of being so ill suited for being a man—he said, after listening to me, "But on the contrary, that's so sweet. You're so unlike a man that it would be very easy to change you into a charming lady." "Oh! It would be delicious!" he exclaimed.

Then he explained all the plans that he had for me. He told me everything, the boundless generosity with which he'd take care of me, the money that he'd give me every month to spend as I wished—everything, including the type of pleasures that I'd have to give him. And I wasn't afraid. My passionate nature, already guilty and corrupt, didn't make me reject these propositions that would ensure my moral perdition, even if the sexual favors they entailed might lead me to a premature end.

Once M—— had revealed all this to me, he was determined to go to my parents that very day to ask permission to complete my education, so to speak. That was certainly the word for it!

I was thrilled by all the splendors that he had described to me, and my innate vanity, as well as my passionate nature, was already yearning to experience the overwhelming pleasures that he had sketched out for me. Everything that he had told me seemed so special that, with my regret dissolving into my desire, I was eager to latch on to this man, who said that he loved me like a friend and like a lover. My feminine tendencies shuddered with a mixture of emotions as I imagined myself in the arms of this handsome man who was sought after by so many women. Without a doubt it was enough to turn the head of anyone who was as vulnerable as I was.

When we got back from this coach ride, he put his case to my parents. My mother cried, and seeing her in that state, I threw myself into her arms, as I was also in tears. My poor father, who in his heart of hearts was as vain as I was, gave all the high-sounding responses that he could muster. He was enchanted by the "honor" that the dear son of his master had offered him. He explained to my mother what enormous advantages this situation would entail. M—— supported these statements with his own assurances. He told her some splendid lies! He vividly described my rare talent for drawing, and he predicted a prosperous and respectable future for me, thanks to a talent that would make my fortune and guarantee my happiness. My mother smiled. The hope that filled her poor heart effectively banished her maternal suspicions. I left, calling out to her, "Till tomorrow, my dear Mama!"

When we were alone in the carriage, M—— told me, "I think that your lovely eyes will cry no more. Tomorrow, when you go to see your beloved mother, bring her whatever gift you please, as fine as you wish. Tonight I'll give you five hundred francs, and on the first of each month, you'll get the same amount from me. Tomorrow I'm going to give you a few extra francs so that you can buy some materials for painting, since you'll have to learn a little of that in order to please your pretty mother."

"Oh yes, I'll learn," I replied, "and I thank you from the bottom of my heart."

"Don't thank me too much," M—— answered while embracing me, "just tell me a bit more about how you're going to love me the way I love you."

I blushed as he stared at me, and looking down, I told him that I loved him already.

The carriage stopped at the rue de Trevise. The marquis helped me out and ushered me into a lovely house, which was inhabited by kept women. We walked up a fine staircase, covered with a beautiful carpet, and when we got to the first floor, M—— didn't ring the bell; he simply knocked twice with the knob of his walking stick. A very polite maid answered the door.

"Is Paula in?" he asked, stroking the young hussy's cheek.

She seemed to enjoy this teasing. "Madame is always in for the marquis."

"Well then, I'm going to save you the trouble of announcing me, or should I say, us," he replied, gesturing at me.

We went into an empty sitting room. In spite of the thick carpeting, footsteps could be heard, and a lively, well-modulated voice called out from the next room, "Who's there?"

"It's me, my dear," M—— answered as he lifted up the heavy curtain in the doorway of a dressing room. He gently pushed me ahead of him, and I found myself face to face with a lovely woman.

"What? It's you, you big, bad boy!" the courtesan exclaimed happily as she threw off a velvet jacket that she had been trying on. "But I haven't seen you for almost a year! And who is this pretty boy?" she asked, walking toward me. Then she brought her pretty face close to mine, saying, "Here, my boy, we're strict about paying the toll. Kiss me! Let's have a kiss!" I gave her a big kiss. This woman, who quickly became my friend and confidante, was my first true platonic love. With her I experienced the charm of that exquisite and intimate friendship that courtesans extend only to young men who share the values of Parisian *complaisants*. From that day on Paula had won me over with her lack of pretension and her genuine gaiety.

"This young man," M—— began, seating himself between me and the lovely blonde, "is a dear friend, who has stolen my heart, and whom I want to make my mistress by changing him, with your help, into a charming courtesan."

To my great astonishment, the pretty lady didn't act at all surprised. Smiling, she looked at me and said, "That will be quite easy." And then, giving the marquis an inscrutable glance, she remarked, "So, it has recurred, has it?"

Thanks to Paula, by that very evening I had my own apartment in the building on the rue de Trevise near her own. When everything was ready, I moved in and dressed in women's clothes furnished by a dressmaker who served these ladies. As I was unaccustomed to wearing this sort of outfit, it took me a while to get dressed by myself alone in my room, so Paula told the concierge that I was just recovering from an illness and that for the next month I'd be going out very rarely. And so a maid was hired for me.

Paula gave me my first lesson. I was a little clumsy, a bit embarrassed, but I didn't seem ridiculous in the least, as my new friend and M—— observed. We christened with many glasses of champagne the new temple of love that the marquis was building. It was eleven o'clock at night when Paula left us, since she wasn't dancing that evening.

"You'll forgive me, won't you?" the marquis said. "You'll never leave me, will you? You'll love me a little, won't you?"

These sentiments were incomprehensible to me. In spite of the harm that man caused me and in spite of the loss of my whole being that he'd cause every day, my truncated nature and my changed character made me forget all of that. Since I had so often envied women when I was reading, I was able to forget, while listening to this seducer, that I was nothing more than a plaything for a debauched man whose affection for me would last only as long as I could please him. Looking at him, who was such a handsome man, so tender, so much like a dear friend brimming over with affection, I really believed what he said. I believed that he loved me. Wasn't that one hundred times easier to believe than what had happened to me just a few hours ago? So I told him that I would love him, and he seemed happy. Then he took a thousand-franc note from his wallet and placed it on my bed, saying, "Here's my wedding gift." Then he got up, put on his gloves, kissed me again, and added, "I'm going to send you to Paula. Follow her instructions well. She's a clever girl."[17]

"But," my pretty teacher said between bursts of laughter, "I am forgetting the most important thing. You don't even know your name."

"Goodness no," I replied. "He didn't think to tell me."

"Well then, my pretty, you're 'Madame Pauline de Floranges' — a sonorous and distinguished name, don't you think? I must admit that the naughty marquis had a brilliant idea, making you dress in this outfit. You wanted to become a woman, so now you are one."

The next day M—— lunched with me. He stayed for a while, playing the piano well and singing a few artistic songs tastefully. At two o'clock his carriage arrived, and I knew that he was going to take me for a ride in the park. He celebrated this first date by giving me a long Indian cashmere shawl with an orange background. I had seen others like it worn by my lovely neighbors on the rue de Rumford. As soon as we were inside the carriage, I leaned back against the cushions as prettily as I could. The marquis was thrilled by the way I took up the pose so naturally. He said over and over, "You'll beat them all in a little while. You're already their equal. You were made to be a great lady."

When we arrived in the park, the marquis took me to the Restaurant de Madrid, telling me with a smile to keep playing my part and not to be afraid of the stylish ladies whom I was going to meet there. It took some nerve, and in spite of my confidence—the confidence I had in my luxurious wardrobe—I could feel myself blanching under my pancake makeup, and my heart was thumping. There were some astonishingly elegant courtesans there, almost all of whom were accompanied by their lovers—the men who kept them. These gentlemen—mostly sons of noble families—were the marquis's friends. They came to shake his hand, to offer him a cigar, and above all to take a close look at the woman to whom he introduced them. Everyone was perfectly cordial toward me. As for the ladies, they scrutinized every detail of my wardrobe. The marquis took me back home, overjoyed with my success.

There's one thing in my life that made me so happy that it alone banished all my regrets and my sorrows, at least temporarily. Certainly during this time and even in my later years it gave me great comfort. It was the realization of my most bizarre dream, of seeming to be something that I was not. The desire to dress as a woman, to be accepted in the eyes of the world as an elegant lady, pleased me so much that, when I was able to do so, it took the sharp edge off of my regrets to such an extent that nowadays I suffer because I can no longer wear those clothes. That wardrobe gave me so much indescribable satisfaction that I owe to it the few moments of happiness that I had during my shameful career. I've always loved beauty and hated the puny constitution that nature gave me. When I dressed in men's clothes, I always looked like a boy, because I lacked the features that make a man handsome. I had broad, well-developed shoulders and a thick neck, which are the essential elements of a masculine physique, but along with them I also had puny arms, skinny, bony thighs, and . . . I won't discuss the rest. I've already described the agony that I endured because of that. I have shapely legs, a well-turned ankle, small feet, and a small, round waist, which is rather rare in a man. Women's clothes covered up all my imperfections and displayed the handful of good points that I had.

The *amateurs*,[18] especially those who appreciate the female form—and there are quite a few who will gaze at a pretty leg—will throw you a compliment as you pass by. You receive these words of praise mingled with the smell of their cigars. But what does this kind of incense matter if it appeals to your vanity and cheers you up? For me—rare bird that I am—a flattering word or a banal compliment used to thrill me, because it demonstrated to me that I had fooled a discerning judge. I, who had so desired to be a girl, had triumphed over natural law. With a great deal of patience and effort, I had succeeded in resembling the finest being in all creation—I was a *woman*! And when people talked about me, they referred to me as "the lovely, the charming Pauline." With that I was able to forget my feeble body and enjoy hours and hours of an enchanting illusion. My biggest wish was to be a great beauty, one of those charming faces that I had glimpsed in the company of some of my dissolute friends. And for almost a dozen years with the help of all sorts of makeup, with the skill that my hairdresser fixed up my abundant red hair, with the assistance of my exquisite wardrobe, and with the care that I hid my ugly hands inside made-to-order, smooth gloves, I could make my uninteresting and unfinished self into a beauty. And if not perfect in every detail, I gave a stunning, fascinating first impression. My beauty was completely artificial, but it was also striking, and it always caused a sensation, whether in the soft light of a drawing room or the harsh spotlights of a concert hall.

2. A *tribade*. From a drawing by Arthur W——, 1874. Source: Legludic, *Notes et observations*.

To be honest, in addition to the odd inclination for cross-dressing that *tribades* have,[19] I had also noticed that many of them have to do it because of a bodily defect or an ugly appearance that a woman's wardrobe cannot conceal. But virtually all of them do so because of their desire to be men. An unattractive physical appearance only made the desire to cross-dress twice as urgent, as I learned from my acquaintance with two women: A———, who made such a charming horseman, and B———, about whom people would exclaim, "She's perfect!" But the outward appearance of perfection in both cases was due to a certain lack of feminine characteristics. When a woman dresses like a man, there are two things that give her away: her thighs are too shapely and her chest is too curved. These two defects are in fact the proof of her beauty. But B——— had none of these lovely curves, and the despair that she felt at the age of fifteen was the same as the one that I felt about my small size. So she adopted men's clothes and looked ravishing in them. Even men were fooled, and women went wild over her.

It was about three years and a few months after the marquis had made me the dissolute, odd, and unique creature that I've described here. I was then sixteen years old, and it was 1854. He was still quite charming toward me, but he was less demanding. Sometimes whole weeks would pass without his spending even one night with me. I was surprised by that, but I was feeling quite comfortable with the peace and quiet that he gave me. One day he was supposed to take me to the Satory races,[20] and I waited for an entire hour, but in vain. Since I didn't want to pass up a chance to show myself off to my fellow courtesans in my new finery—which was irreproachable and of the most ravishing taste—I got into my carriage, which had been standing in front of my door since eight o'clock that morning. Still, my self-centered vanity was disturbed by an anxious feeling that I couldn't banish from my thoughts. When I was seated comfortably at the races, some regulars—friends of the marquis—came to greet me and to shake my hand. Several fashionable ladies wished me a good day, and the flower seller came as usual to offer me a spectacular bouquet of moss roses.

"Oh! You're alone," the young girl said. "Is the handsome marquis coming later? Or is he not coming at all? While you wait, here are some roses that are as fresh as your delightful wardrobe. Oh! You're always dressed so beautifully!"

"My dear," I replied to the flower seller, "I don't want a bouquet today, because I've forgotten to bring any money with me."

"Well, really, that doesn't matter, since I know you, don't I?"

As she left, I heard a man's voice calling out, "Righto! There's a woman for you. People were saying that not only wouldn't you come to Satory today, but that, like Artemis, you were crying your heart out over the loss of your great mogul."

I'm not sure exactly what I felt as I listened to that young nincompoop, who had just informed me of the total destruction of my place in society without realizing it. . . .[21]

After reading the letter that the marquis had left me, I couldn't help breaking down in tears. The money that he had left me did little to console me. I had lost the person whom I considered my stalwart supporter. Even if I didn't love him deeply, I had a great affection for him. I had become accustomed to him, and at my age I thought that the relationship would last forever. It had never occurred to me that he might abandon me some day. I read and reread his letter several times, and each time I said to myself, "What's going to happen to me?" It was an embarrassing situation, you must agree. If I went back to my parents, I'd have to tell them about the marquis's departure, and they'd have every right to wonder why a man who had promised me a high station in society would leave me so abruptly. This would set off a torrent of questions, each more difficult than the one before. I also have to confess that now that I was living a dissolute life, going back to the straight and narrow was a thought that horrified me. But what could I do? How could I resolve this situation?

Thus I made my debut in the *cafés-concerts*. The money that the marquis had given me made a spectacular performer out of a mediocre one, since I could dazzle my audience with my splendid appearance. Besides, I had a clear voice with a pleasing tone, so I sang passably well.

Every evening, along with the regulars at the *cafés-concerts*, in the front rows of the audience you'd see young women, many of whom were very pretty and beautifully dressed, showy but in good taste. These women usually came in pairs and were charming priestesses of that enormous cult that worshiped at Sappho's altar. They belonged to that strange sect, that incomprehensible love, from which men are excluded. They were the most important *tribades* in Paris.

In order to explain and understand them you must be a close friend. Otherwise you'll be shocked and surprised by their bold appearance and strange behavior. If you understand their world, you'll realize that the strangeness is due, beyond the fact that they're performers, to a certain inclination or inborn taste for the oddness that they have. Such a woman, so comfortable dressed as a man, usually has a masculine personality and masculine tastes. She speaks her mind; she's argumentative, willful, and stubborn; she's firm in her opinions; and she's intrepid in her pleasures. She plays billiards, fences capably, rides admirably, and has a loud voice with sharp, brusque overtones. Her posture and movements don't have a woman's suppleness but seem to come from a virile nature. Beyond this you might see her, in spite of herself, always being gracious toward other women, and when she's involved with a woman friend, you must agree that their friendship is very close to love.

In addition to the beauty that most of them had, there was something odd and hard to decipher in their facial features that caught the eye. It was an expression that was simultaneously sweet and anxious, tender and stern. But you'll always find these characteristic giveaways: whether their eyes are big or small, they're bold to the point of audacity and worshipful to the point of idolatry;

their mouths are prey to nervous tics, pursed in a way that incites lust and sensual acts; their smiles are charming and attractive; and sometimes they hold their lips half open, as if they were about to receive a kiss.

The other distinctive part of the audience was made up of men, who looked young and attractive. Some were endowed with a beauty that would have pleased even the most exigent women. Their actions and gestures were the exact opposite of those that I've just described. This difference attracted your attention, of course, and these personalities, who stimulated your curiosity, seemed also to do everything possible to attract attention. They sat in small groups, but they really made up one big family, you could say. If you looked closely, you might have concluded that they and the pretty ladies shared a secret code in a secret society. Their relations seemed to be based on a sort of mutual admiration.

These mincing, perfumed young men, fitted out with the finest gloves, makeup, and professionally curled hair, were the most elegant of the *complaisants*, who strolled along the great boulevards in the expensive neighborhoods. The *complaisants*, the *tapettes*, the *filles*—these are the names that they called each other—these odd creatures in general resemble females from birth. They are very docile as children and prefer quiet games, they play with dolls, they play house, they make little shrines at the heads of their beds, and all of these games greatly please their poor mothers. Yet, as they grow up, these attributes are replaced by vices, and these vices condemn them to a shameful existence for the rest of their lives.

As adolescents they've their sweet ways that charm their parents; they're as timid as young ladies, they're hesitant in their speech, they don't enjoy going out to cafés, they don't take pleasure in the distraction of horseback riding; instead, they love the theater and *cafés-concerts*, and they seek out plays that feature cross-dressing. They've an innately tender nature, a romantic imagination, and they love to chat about fashion and clothes with their mothers. Those dear ladies are very pleased with their children and tell their women friends, "My Charles is as good-natured and loving as a girl." But when their boys get to the age when they have to decide upon a profession, these good parents are really at a loss. What career is suitable for such an obedient, passive child? Certainly a boy who is disturbed and frightened by the slightest noise can't become a carpenter, a mechanic, or even a metalworker. In addition there are too many working-class men in these sorts of workshops, and thus too many bad role models about which to worry. And, on top of everything else, these jobs are simply too vulgar. A boy like this needs a more dignified situation, like that of a glove maker, a shop assistant, a hairdresser, or an engraver in a printing business. And if the boy really shows artistic talent, he can be educated to become a painter or a sculptor or at least a drawing teacher or a piano teacher. If he has a nice voice, these poor folks think that he might make his way in the theater, or he might become a poet.

Since the marquis no longer supported me financially, I had to leave my lodgings on the rue de Trevise. An apartment that rented for twenty-eight hundred francs a year wasn't suitable for a singer who only earned eight francs a night. So I moved out and began living on the rue d'Astorg. My childhood memories made me fond of this neighborhood, which was also very convenient. It was close to the cafés on the Champs-Elysées. I won't reveal anything more about my relations with La Belle Anglaise, La Charles, and La Belge,[22] except to say that they knew that I was a cross-dresser, and they agreed that I could make assignations with paying customers, just as they did, after the show.

On Thursday I had an open house at my new apartment. My place on the rue d'Astorg was certainly unpretentious. One bedroom with two windows served as the drawing room, and I made a closet into my dressing room, but the furniture of the marquis was even more striking in such a small space. My guests, both male and female, thought that I had furnished it quite well, and it's true that all the little decorative touches in these two rooms made them quite charming. The *complaisants* have a tradition of baptizing every new member of their society. My name, Pauline de Floranges, was a pseudonym, but it wasn't acceptable in my circle of friends. As we drank our champagne, La Belle Anglaise lifted her glass, stood up, and announced, "On behalf of all these young ladies, as well as our dear sisters, who are assembled here, I, Auguste D——, known as La Belle Anglaise, now baptize Arthur W—— the 'Countess.'" Then she sprinkled me with a few drops of *Clicquot*.

Everyone present at this ridiculous ceremony had stood up and watched it with absolute seriousness and a real sense of gravity. For the *tribades* and the *mignons* who were there, this was a well-known and powerful act. As for me, I thought that it was just a joke, but when D——, taking his seat again, added, "My lovely, I've dubbed you the 'Countess,' and I swear that this name will remove all traces of your real one," he was only too accurate.

My first guest was Charles B——, with whom I had a real friendship. You shouldn't assume that this comradeship, this friendship, was ever an excuse for sexual relations. No, on the contrary, with prostitutes, no matter how attractive their colleagues might be, they never feel the slightest twinge of sexual desire; they'd never even think of taking their pleasures together; they have their men for that.

La Charles was the most unbelievably passionate creature. He loved men madly and claimed to have loved them from a very young age, from childhood. A suggestive word or a pornographic image made him think of love; drawings or photographs of naked men drove him wild, and he'd masturbate while looking at them. One day he saw an album I had just finished. It was an anthology of male sexual organs, life-sized, painted in watercolors. When Charles saw this collection of 160 illustrations, his reaction was: "Oh! Countess! Countess! How naughty of you not to have said a word about this lovely selection. Let me have it for a little while." And he immediately went into the drawing room to masturbate.

La Belle Anglaise paid me a visit one day. She told me about

3. La Charles. From a drawing by Arthur W———, 1874. Source: Legludic, *Notes et observations*.

a man named Prosper, who was the one to see if I wanted work. "He'll look after you," she said, "and you'll see how nice it is to live as a couple." It was arranged that I'd meet this Prosper that very evening. After all, I really needed someone who could protect me, because the way I dressed sometimes got me into embarrassing situations. I was also bored with being alone, and I often remembered the lovely evenings that I spent with the marquis, especially when his attentiveness and his caresses made me think that I was fulfilling my most cherished desires. After he left me, I often had moments of regret and despair that brought back to me my self-loathing and my deep feelings of regret about the past.

That night, after the show, as I said good-bye to the other singers in the café where I was working, I was introduced to Prosper. He was a well-built man with a friendly face, outgoing, lively, and even-tempered. He was twenty-two years old. He escorted me home, and there I was with a lover on my hands. This was really the exact opposite of the way that I started out, since Prosper was more like a friend than a demanding master. I gave him whatever I wanted in order to keep going to the café, and he was satisfied with that.[23]

PART TWO: ENGEL

Chapter One

True Lovers. "Young Ladies." A New Protector. Beatings with Riding Crops. Conscription. In the Forty-Fourth Regiment of the Line. Permission. Deserter.

True lovers call themselves *garçons*,[24] especially when they live with *complaisants*, probably in order to distinguish themselves from their partners. A *complaisant* has a real need for company and affection. Despite the corruption that comes from such a degrading situation for a man, and despite the licentious pleasures that influence everything for those involved, there's no male prostitute who, just like his female counterpart, isn't alienated from the man who pays him. From that alienation—one step away from repulsion—necessarily comes the need to give oneself to a person who not only doesn't pay but who also gives gifts to the one he has seduced. This sort of abjection in an already abject state is nevertheless the only remedy that pederasts have to raise their self-esteem. "That guy, I love him, and I give myself to him freely!" is what they say with a sort of pride.

For the *garçon* life is easier than it is for women. It's all very calm, and there are none of those awful quarrels in which female prostitutes get embroiled so easily. A true lover, who is almost always crude and brutal with women, is exactly the opposite when he's hooked up with a *mignon*. If the *complaisant* doesn't have a maid, his boyfriend acts as his personal valet, handing him the items in his wardrobe one by one and holding the mirror while the *complaisant* is parting his hair. Because the *complaisant* hates to leave the comfort of his home, he puts off getting ready until the very last moment. Getting dressed takes a long time and is much more involved than it is for any woman, even the most flirtatious, because a male prostitute never overlooks his flaws or any other unattractive features. He concentrates intensely, putting all his effort into hiding them as he applies his makeup.

A true lover is at ease with himself; he loves his physical attractions; he preens. Why would he be any different? He knows all about his assets, and they're even more precious to him since they've guaranteed him a life of idleness and, more often than not, a life of happiness.

Professional pederasts are not all attractive—far from it. There are many who are mousy-looking, whose outward appearance is vulgar and not at all genteel, but this is where the prestige comes from, because, with serious study and research, they can achieve a look as beautiful as the appearance of those who were born with it. They can give themselves "a new face," as we say in the theater.

They enlarge their eyes with an eyeliner; they redraw their mouths with a well-practiced smile; they shape their hair with a curling iron no matter how unruly it is; and they get the most stylish coiffure. If their complexion is patchy or reddish, they can color it. Their skin might be rough with bumps or acne, but iris lotion or almond cream will make it as smooth and fine as glove leather. Even their body shapes are perfected, and any natural imperfections can miraculously be brought into line. A *fille* follows the dictates of fashion religiously and has a distinctive way of dressing, and every one of them is based on the same model. So, in 1856, the *mignons* all curled their hair into ringlets hanging as close as possible to their eyes and cascading from their temples. As for the part in their hair, it was right down the middle of the head.

Filles, who are serving sentences for a number of years in a prison, naturally have their eye on the *garçon*, who reminds them of their life as prostitutes. They take an interest in him and write to him. They hook up and become a couple. And then begins a life that is filled for each of them with fear, jealousy, and suspicion, where even the smallest misstep causes painful repercussions. You must watch out for guards who always have you under surveillance and for co-workers who aren't really what they seem to be and most of all for those who are what they seem to be, but who, having been rejected by a *fille*, are constantly on the lookout for revenge. It's impossible to understand the struggles, the sorrow, the poignant suffering that such relationships cause. A man deprived of all distractions and all sexual gratification will not only begin to masturbate while fantasizing about his lover, but he won't be able to stop thinking about seeing him or meeting him. He'll risk months in prison only to spend a brief moment together. The impediments make his desire twice as strong. All of this makes him feel discouraged, provokes in him angry outbursts, and causes him to threaten friends who are jealous of him. Prison hasn't quieted his feisty spirit; he's always ready to fight back with his words or with his fists; and he gets into fights easily. This leads to solitary confinement and suspension of rations. You have to see them, leaving their cell after a month or sometimes two, having eaten nothing but dry crusts of bread, and having abandoned themselves to their secret pleasures almost every day. In those cases the *fille* is just as she was on the outside—good-hearted and faithful. She gives all her food rations to her companion, and often she suffers on the other's behalf. In prison this is what we call "feeding." "She feeds her man," the prison guards say. When the sentence is over, the first one released waits for the other. Then he comes to meet him, or he arranges a meeting place, and they fulfill their pent-up desires.

Women who love women, *tribades*, are deeply sympathetic toward the beings that I've just described, since, like them, they have an unnatural love. They're indulgent and have a soft spot for the young men whom they call their "sisters," and that feeling is genuinely reciprocated.

The *tapette* has an affected manner of expressing himself, as ornate and bizarre as his extraordinary life. The word that he uses most frequently when he talks to his friends is "Miss," and the way that it's pronounced is unique, just like his inimitable "my dear." Nothing is more fascinating for a writer concerned with the characters of everyday life than these conversations, where the superficiality of these boys, who are already grown men, is obvious from the very first word. When two *tapettes* meet on a boulevard, the signal that they use to identify themselves is so subtle as to be virtually unnoticed by those not in the know: they lift a hand up to their collar while touching the tips of the thumb and middle finger together, making a gesture that I described when I sketched my portrait of La Belge.

"Hello, darling, how have you been? It's been ages since I've seen you."

"I've been so busy. Auguste is ill. I've arranged for my furniture to be brought in, and the workmen are so slow about it that I can hardly leave the house. Everything is topsy-turvy at my place.

4. La Belge. From a drawing by Arthur W———, 1874. Source: Legludic, *Notes et observations*.

You know how much I love my furniture. I was going to invite you on Monday, but since you're here now, well, you're invited. Oh, my dear! It will be such a fun evening. All the girls are coming. The Countess will be there; we'll have a concert; and she'll sing three songs for us."

"Oh, but my dear, are you sure the Countess will come? She has a paying engagement, and if she misses an evening, that's a loss of nine francs, eight for her salary and one as a fine. I'm not sure, but the manager might even charge a three-franc fine."

"My dear, I saw the Countess yesterday, and she has promised me that she'll come. Anyhow, she can afford to take an evening off. I'm going to pay her fifteen francs. I'm not cheap, you know. I'm doing very well, moneywise, and I can treat myself to it. You know that all the girls will be coming dressed as women, and almost all the women will be in trousers? You'll wear your *Bordelaise* outfit, won't you? You look so charming in it. I've got to see the Countess because, since I only dress that way for balls, I don't have everything I need, but the Countess will get it for me."

"Will there be any men there?"

"Oh yes, our lovers!"

One afternoon someone rang at my door. I got up and answered it. A very elegant man asked to speak to me privately. I took him to my room and told him that I was alone. He then explained that he knew Paula and that she had spoken to him about me, and if I didn't have anyone, he'd gladly be my protector, but since he recently lost a great deal of money, he could only offer me ten louis a month. He also insisted that I should be free of any other attachment and that he should be given a key to my apartment so that he could come at any time. I told him that I'd give him my answer at three o'clock the following afternoon. I was getting tired of my unsettled life where every night I had to walk the streets like a common prostitute. So I split my savings and few mementos with Prosper. He packed up, and we took leave of each other as good friends.

The next day I had a new master. And "master" is certainly the word for it because I've never been such a slave, so deprived of any fun. Monsieur de T——, my second protector, was thirty-seven years old, well built, with good manners, a handsome face, but one that was marked with an air of willful stubbornness that with the slightest provocation would turn into an insane fury. At those times he'd beat me with a riding crop that he always carried.

How many times did I think about M—— . . .

Like all cold-hearted people, this man was stingy and tight-fisted. He complained whenever he had to pay the dressmaker's bill or the hat maker. He almost never took me out with him. He didn't approve of the amount that I spent on my wardrobe. He even inventoried my pairs of gloves. But I was no longer a naive child. After three months of this miserliness, I said to him coldly, "My dear, when I accepted you as my protector, I did so on the condition that you'd fulfill my desires and cater to my whims, but you're an ill-tempered man that only an extremely forgiving person could excuse. As for me, I'm fed up with you. I've no fond feelings for a man who beats me and isolates me from my friends. I've had enough of you and of your gifts. Give me back my key and do me the favor of forgetting where I live. That's all that I want from you."

This fine man was extremely surprised! He tried to dissuade me by offering me 100 francs more and a necklace that I had wanted a little while before, but nothing worked. When he realized that he couldn't change my mind, he took my key out of his pocket, put it on a corner of the mantelpiece, put on his gloves, and left, saying, "You'll miss me."

"Never!" I exclaimed, slamming the door to my room. I started to breathe freely again. For three months this man had tormented me. I decided to go back to singing, and five days later I did. I saw my old friends, and I forgot the gloomy liaison with Monsieur de T—— amidst the frivolous pastimes and kindnesses of my friends.

There had been many wild days and many mistakes in my life. I was now twenty-one years old. But in the superficial society of which I was a part, in the role that I had adopted, people don't count the years. Instead, people pretend to forget them and the deterioration that often accompanies them. So time doesn't matter, nor does space, in this sect of those who deny their sex; I was an example of that. Though corrupted and degraded in my morals and my lifestyle, I was, in my inner self, still the same naive and loving child of earlier times. I had passionate outpourings of tenderness toward my dear mother. I felt like a child again as I spent hours at her side, reading to her from the books that she liked so much, chatting with her as if I still merited her chaste kisses. Then, back in my apartment, where everything reminded me of my shameful and abject state, I'd kneel down, weeping, lifting my impure hands up to God, but my lips no longer knew how to pray. I had a loving character, tending toward enthusiasm, and these two qualities developed a kind of courage in me that hadn't flagged, even when I faced the possibility of jail or prison. I was guilty, and I didn't wish that on anyone, save those as guilty as I was. I served my sentence with fortitude and withstood the ten years without breaking down. Even so, my firm resolve was shattered under much less serious circumstances, and I needed my mother by my side to face them.

I want to tell you about the day that I had to go to Neuilly for the conscription lottery. Since I had lived my life thus far quite removed from the everyday demands of a man's life, I feared them, and lacking the backbone to carry out the duty that others considered an occasion for loud cheers, I needed to lean on my mother's arm for support to give me courage on that seemingly endless day. I drew the number 180, so I was in the reserves. Certainly, in a year I could have saved enough to buy my way out, but being foolish and more of a spendthrift than ever, depending on promises that never materialized, the day came when I had to join my regiment. I had barely 100 francs, so I had to go. Oh! What pain I felt when I went to kiss my poor, weeping mother good-bye. I swore to her that I'd return soon. I was terrified of being a soldier and I despised the army life, but I went to my company at Melun all the same.

In spite of the favorable treatment that I got in the Forty-fourth Regiment of the Line, I never stopped feeling unhappy. I couldn't shake the thought that all I wanted to do was get out as soon as possible. I was starting down the road to desertion, and as a result I made the mistakes that caused me to commit the act that earned me ten years in prison. I was supposed to sing at a party hosted by my colonel, and I asked him for a ten-day leave to visit an uncle, whom I described as rich and who could buy me out. I got the leave, and with my heart thumping with joy, I saw my beloved Paris again. It was rainy when I arrived at the Gare du Nord at six o'clock in the morning, but to me, it seemed the most glorious day ever.

After I arrived, I threw myself into my dear, sweet mother's arms, and, weeping, I told her that I'd never go back to my regiment. The poor woman got a little frightened, but she loved me so much that she was quickly won over because she, too, desperately wanted me to escape, especially since we all know that mothers know little about military life. We had ten days to find a way out. As for me, I had long ago found one, but my dear mother, who knew nothing about it, kept searching in her mind and in her heart for a solution. I told her in that convincing manner that I put on so well to calm her down that I was quite comfortable as a woman, and rather than playing the part just when I performed, I'd become one forever. That wonderful woman, whose dearest wish had been to have a daughter, was quite pleased with my idea, and so I told her that the next day she could be the judge of my transformation. Monday at three o'clock in the afternoon a lady in mourning, who was dressed quite tastefully, rang at her door. This lady threw herself into the good woman's arms and covered her with kisses. From that moment on I no longer needed to lie to my mother.

On the twelfth day the police were on my trail. One afternoon in March I was with my mother, singing her favorite song, "The Comforts of Old Age," when someone rang at the door, and I got up to spare my mother the trouble of answering it. A handsome police officer came inside and greeted us very humbly. This poor man had, it seemed, come once before and had returned to ask my mother if she had any information about her son. My mother, who felt quite confident at the sight of my flawless disguise, told the policeman that she still hadn't heard anything and that she believed that I must have gone abroad—an idea that I backed up. The policeman looked at me several times, but on the sly and only because he thought I was attractive.

What I have to recount now is much more painful and difficult. I kept on living almost exactly as before, except that I saw my dear mother practically every day, and I treated her as well as possible because that dear lady had no one else. My father had made some bad business deals, and he was ruined. After he was declared bankrupt, he died of remorse. My mother, who had a strong and brave character, didn't let misfortune drag her down. She had served as a maid for the parents of the Marquise de K——, and the marquise attested to my mother's integrity—a trust that she certainly had earned. This lady lived in a small townhouse on the rue d'Amsterdam, but she left town five or six times a year, and she had my mother watch over the house. Every other day my mother would go there, keep an eye on the place, and air out the rooms. She could even have stayed there if she wanted.

In 1860, the Marquise de K—— left for Algiers and gave my mother the keys to her house. It was there that my mother first experienced the symptoms of the illness that would take her life. She became ill and had to stay in bed, so she occupied a bedroom on the third floor of the house. I'd come to see her and to take care of her. I was still very elegant but desperate. I had many debts and no way to pay them off. It was at this time that my poor mother passed away. I had the keys, so I snooped through everything, even breaking into the cabinets that I couldn't open. I could have easily gotten away with several thousand francs, with which I could have escaped abroad, but since I had never stolen anything, nor had any inclination to do so, I took things haphazardly. I paid off my debts, and with the rest I lost myself in my grief, since I was now alone in the world. I really didn't care if I lost my life, which had been so precious to me before. The perpetual masquerade had become overwhelming. I stayed on, nevertheless, and two months later I was arrested and sentenced to ten years in prison.

Chapter Two

The Central Prison at Poissy. Eugene R———. His Love. The Official Favor. Changing Prisons. March 3, 1866. Fontevrault. The Handsome Prisoner #598. Gustave Engel. Secret Letters. Jealousy and Pain. I Am No Longer Myself. The Songs at Vespers on Sundays. The Madness of Despair and Isolation. The Garden Cells. The Procession of Corpus Christi, 1868. The Release of Gustave Engel. July 22, 1871.

At the beginning of September 1861 at midnight I arrived, chained to another inmate, at the central prison at Poissy[25]—a house of detention, lockup, and punishment. After I went through the intake procedures, I was assigned to the "Images" workshop on the morning after my arrival. This was the nicest and most comfortable job in the prison. We cut the lace trimmings that decorate those charming religious images that we all loved so much and that young ladies still do. We also tinted writing paper, and there were some sheets decorated with watercolors of bouquets that were really works of art. My talent for drawing served me well at Poissy.

"Everything new is beautiful," as the saying goes, and everything seemed that way to me at Poissy. Everything that I saw and every face that I noticed gave me a chance to exercise my mind. Looking beneath the dull sameness of our prison garb, enlivened by only a few traces of individuality, I tried to reconstruct the life stories of the men around me, with the oddest ones providing sad or exciting chapters.

The foreman of the lace trimmers was Eugene R——, who had been sentenced to ten years in prison for embezzlement—that is, putting away a little on the side. He was twenty-seven and the type of fellow that country folk would call a "good-looker," and if he had polished his rough edges, he'd have been considered an attractive man in any context. He had an open, honest, and smiling face with lovely big eyes and a mouth that denoted passion and sensuality, but he had that cleverness typical of peasants, so he could put on a naive and placid-looking face for the chaplain and the administrators that expertly concealed his passionate tendencies. As a result the prison authorities considered him a model inmate. That was how things stood when I joined this society of assorted sinners.

Poissy was only six leagues from Paris, so some of the prisoners were Parisians, and there were representatives of every social class and type. You might have expected a few to have known the Countess at least indirectly or many others to have heard of her. No information spreads faster in prison than that of a new prisoner's background, especially when he has a strange past that arouses everyone's curiosity. I had barely been there two hours before my life story had made the rounds, passing from one inmate to another. It doesn't take much to interest men who are so isolated from life's distractions; and a small thing can fire up the imagination of young men with ideas of libertinage and dreams of passion that this life together can justify or at least explain. Those who had had unnatural sexual urges outside of prison would have more so inside, and those who had never experienced those thoughts would adopt them easily. So my arrival stirred up many thoughts and unleashed many desires. I've never been attractive, but I have certain pleasing features that make my face more striking, more charming, than that of a real beauty. Above all I was so accustomed to pleasing others that I always tried to do so in every way and in every place. While I was in the holding cells at La Roquette,[26] I had heard a lot about life in prison, and I couldn't get out of my head the marriages that were made there. I made a rational decision—a bad one, as it turned out—based on those stories. This explains why I was so cold-hearted—for which everyone has criticized me, though, I think, wrongly. But knowing that I was going to be locked up for ten years and thinking that I'd have to start from scratch once I was free again, I wanted, in order to have enough money, to earn as much as possible and to accept the gifts of food that I was offered, so as not to deplete my small savings. I did this for the whole time that I was at Poissy, and I was able to save almost everything that I earned.

When I started working in the Images workshop, suitors presented themselves, and as usual these were the youngest and best-looking ones in the place. Each one made me a proposal, and the boys really tried to win the love of this "girl," who could have as many extra rations as she wished. I was used to sizing up men and their faults, so I chose the method used by so many others. I accepted R——'s proposal.

This young man, frugal and sober, who had economized on his own needs to amass a pile of money, was generous when he wanted to make himself loved. He gave me everything that you could get or buy in that place. He wrote me a letter announcing his intentions, but this missive consisted of just two lines: "I love you! If you'll be my boyfriend and only go with me, you'll have everything you want." I accepted.

From that time on a sort of life began that I hadn't had the slightest inkling of before. R——, like all dissembling types, hid within himself a stubborn will and a violent passion that soon frightened me and left me constantly anxious. This man thought about nothing but me, was concerned about nothing but me, and watched nothing but me. I became his obsession, and his nature, after a long hibernation lasting many peaceful years, revealed itself as passionate, ardent, and tempestuous. He couldn't sleep; he followed me around like a shadow—in the courtyard, at the chapel, in the dining hall, at the workshop; everywhere I went I felt his eyes glued to me. He had unbearable fits of jealousy. Because he loved me, he made my life a torture. I couldn't speak to any young and attractive acquaintance without seeing him flinch, and afterward I'd receive a letter filled with reproaches or threats. He had the guards in the dormitory search me, and I was often punished at his urging. Jealousy had blinded him so much that he became a coward. I didn't understand this feeling, and I regretted having a relationship with him, but it was too late.

When I was finally fed up, I told him, "I don't want to have anything more to do with you. Have me punished if you wish, but I won't speak to you again." He was speechless. Then he stopped working and began to cry. The depth of his despair was so obvious that, after having a good laugh about it, the administrators told the guards to ignore the crazy actions of this poor chap, since they knew teasing him would lead to nothing good. This relationship lasted for four years and five months.

Then, since he had only eighteen more months to serve, he was released. He had made my life a real purgatory, but on the eve of his departure, despite his joy at being freed, he wept wholeheartedly and kissed my hands with real affection. He begged me not to serve out the rest of my sentence at Poissy. He knew that the Ministry of Justice allowed a first-timer to request a change of prison, and he urged me to leave. His love for me made him worry that I'd take up with another inmate, even though he wouldn't be there to see it. I told him that I'd do what he said, because in spite of myself I was touched by this friendship that had turned out so badly, making him unhappy and making me suffer so much as well. Also, he had deprived himself of comforts every day for my sake. He gave me at least 200 francs, and he really had to sacrifice to do that. Therefore, I wrote out my request to the Ministry of Justice and showed it to him. In my letter I requested a transfer to Fontevrault.[27] Poor R—— was happy, and when he left, he asked me to forgive him. "If I have made you suffer," he told me, "it's because I loved you too much . . . You see . . . You made me crazy . . ." I have sketched this story in one page, but I could have spent twenty on it, because there were so many strange incidents involved.

Hardly a week had passed after R—— was freed when one morning at five o'clock the officer in charge came to the dormitory and said to me, "Get up. You're going to Fontevrault." We get so attached to our routines in this life. Would anyone believe that, when I left that prison where I had suffered so much, I felt indescribable pangs of regret and wept as I followed that officer? A closed prison carriage was waiting for me. I arrived at Fontevrault twelve days later, on March 3, 1866. As was customary for any new prisoner, I was led first to the baths, and after I emerged from the water, a handsome young man with an admirable but pale face gave me a towel to dry off and a shirt to cover my nakedness, saying, "Take this, kid!" This tall and handsome young man was the stockroom clerk; his number was 598; he had served as the bugler for the First Riflemen; he was to become more than a brother to me. His name was Gustave Engel.

I was assigned to the shoemaking workshop, and even though my job was stitching—the least difficult task—I couldn't help comparing this situation to the one that I had left. At Poissy I was my own master; I was the head man in my workshop; people asked me for my opinion; everything that I did and everything that I made was of excellent quality; I received nothing but praise; I earned a lot; I worked with pretty and elegant things—lovely pictures framed in lace, boxes of shiny letter paper with gilding and cut-out designs, slim paintbrushes, pencils, and lovely blocks of colors. It all somehow reminded me of my hours of leisure in my past life. Here, in the dirty shoemaking workshop, I handled nothing but smelly and crude objects and tools; I had to wear a lowly leather apron teeming with fleas and smeared with filth. My vanity suffered because of it. Since I was so used to looking good, even if only in the eyes of my fellow prisoners, I felt that not only would I no longer make a good impression at Fontevrault but also

5. Gustave the Rifleman. From a drawing by Arthur W——, 1874.
Source: Legludic, *Notes et observations*.

that my tales of past glory, compared to my current situation, would bring me nothing but ridicule. In prison, just as in any other setting, or maybe even more so, you can show off, make an impression, and attract attention when the circumstances that brought you there force you to turn them to your advantage, but to do so, an inmate must have work that allows him to dress well. Now in all the prisons, the shoemaker, if he isn't the foreman or the overseer, is always dirty and badly dressed, whether he's a stitcher or a cutter. When clothes are given out, this workshop always gets the worst because, they say, "It's good enough for the shoemakers!"

After a week in the stitching job, even though I was far from satisfying the man who supervised my apprenticeship, I decided not to spend any more time in this workshop. The director, when he assigned me there, had said, "There's no suitable work for you right now, so in the meantime I'm going to place you in the shoemakers' workshop, but I won't leave you there indefinitely." Therefore, I begged him to put me somewhere else, and two hours later I was sent to the carvers in the furniture-making workshop. I sighed with relief because I had won the first round. There I'd make designs for furniture and carve the wood. This job is done standing up. Every workman has a worktable, which is put in the most brightly lit and nicest spot in the workshop. Two enormous windows lit up the workshop that I had just entered.

In the inmates' classroom I was appointed to be a monitor. As a result I got a new uniform—a jacket with a red collar that is usually worn by scribes at the Fontevrault prison. I had regained a bit of the status that I had had at Poissy, and while marching in line in the exercise yard, I could face up to the stares of the other inmates. Besides the vanity that my previous life had inculcated in me, I had another powerful incentive. Ever since I had set eyes on the rifleman, I could think of no one else but this young man. His sweet and soldierly appearance, his handsome face, and all the rumors that circulated about him had prompted feelings in me that I hadn't really understood yet but that had obsessed me continuously. We had a lot of freedom in our sleeping quarters, and I had asked my neighbor about the stockroom clerk several times, but this man, who seemed determined to curry favor with me, seemed equally bent on discouraging me in that regard. Whenever I asked him about the one whom I thought about constantly, he always replied reluctantly and with unflattering comments, such as, "The rifleman! Oh! He's a pretty bad fellow! You're wasting your time with him! He's not your type!"

Two or three other men in the workshop whom I spoke to gave me similar answers. It was clear to me that these inmates were motivated by a dislike that grew out of the jealousy inspired by the rifleman's good looks and other advantages. Meanwhile he had some bad luck that helped bring us together. He lost his position and was assigned to the shoemakers' workshop, where he used to work before becoming a stockroom clerk. People who don't want to give you good news are always eager to pass on bad news. One of the men whom I had questioned about him came to me very happy, saying, "He got busted! Ha! He can't act so uppity any more! He's back to eating black bread like the rest of us! He's going to be hungry because he's got such a big appetite! And as part of his punishment he's not even allowed to buy white bread! The director has suspended his canteen privileges for a month!"

I decided then and there to give him as many extra rations as possible. I had almost 250 francs saved, so I could pay for them. At this point all my thoughts of frugality and greed were banished. This new love, though shameful, had cleansed me. I felt such joy every morning as I wrapped up the food package to send to this new friend, whose name I didn't even know, since in prison we almost always used the numbers assigned to us. I had included a note with my first parcel in which I asked the rifleman to accept it in the spirit in which it was offered, as a friendly gesture. I also asked him his name, and he replied:

Friend,

Thank you for what you're doing for me. I'll never forget it. It's difficult to send letters from here, because there are unfriendly eyes everywhere, but I'm resourceful, and there's always a way, whether to conceal them inside a book or by some other means. My name is Gustave Engel, nicknamed the "Rifleman," because I was a bugler in the First Regiment of Riflemen. I want to thank you with all my heart, but you shouldn't deprive yourself because of me.

Here's to you!
Gustave Engel

I can't describe the joy that this note gave me. I read and reread it and never tired of saying his name, which seemed so sweet and which is, in fact, lovely and melodious. From that day on I understood the meaning of the word "to love." Oh! How well I knew then that I had never been in love before, because I had never experienced such overwhelming intoxication, such a stirring in my heart. I looked forward to every exercise period in the yard, because I'd see him there. He might smile at me. He might even talk to me. All those acts that had led to my fall and all the sacrifices committed by those who had corrupted me—how I now wanted to do them for Engel, for my dear Gustave, my friend, my brother, my everything! This affection made me cry as much as it gave me joy. I had only one will—his. And with a single word, a glance, or a smile he'd give me joy for a whole day. A letter from him put me in seventh heaven. I forgot that I was in prison, and the walls that so many others cursed I blessed, and I still love them because it was there that I learned how much devotion and self-abnegation your heart can hold for a loved one. I was glad to give everything that I had to Gustave. Our earthly happiness is a friendship or a love without limits where shared feelings merge completely. And I had never felt this sort of mutual affection before, at least not to the extent that I had yearned for it.

I wasn't a twenty-year-old anymore. If I had been free, I could have used my skills to disguise the ravages of age. My wardrobe and my makeup could have hidden several years, but in prison we're forced to be natural. Engel preferred youth, and he was surrounded by it. There were several poor kids in his atelier that had been raised, practically from childhood, in the Colonie de Mettray or the Colonie du Petit Bourg.[28] These youths were not only young, but several of them were nice, and some of them were very good-looking. In addition, in prison they had all developed a passion for masturbation and pederasty. To give themselves pleasure with a friend, especially an older one, was always their dream. They didn't hide it; they had gotten accustomed to it at such a young age that, without the upbringing and social norms to counterbalance it, they were quite open about it; they weren't at all ashamed of it. Any man, if he was at all young and not too unattractive, aroused lustful thoughts in them, which they put into words for all to hear, and frequently, very frequently, they'd indulge themselves right in front of their fellow workers. I've seen them do it, and I wasn't in a position to criticize them for it.

Since Engel was so handsome and was reputed to be extraordinarily well endowed, he was the object of desire for everyone around him. He took as much advantage of this as possible. Like all sensual men, he loved to show off as well as to get his fill of pleasure. The guards tried their best to keep everyone under surveillance, but there's always a suitable moment for those on the lookout for it.

On Sundays every writer, like every monitor, had to write letters for men who couldn't do so themselves. After a year's relationship with Engel those days became a sheer torture for me. Everyone knew about the single-minded and jealous love that I had for him and the efforts that I made to give him pleasure and joy. Those who wanted him were jealous of that, and others, who had propositioned me and been rebuffed, were even more so. So they got a kick out of making me suffer. They'd come and tell me everything that they knew about my friend, and they'd add things that they had invented. I underwent an indescribable torture—a pain as new to me as my love. I was jealous to such an extent that I revealed my unhappiness for all to see. Knowing about his constant dalliances discouraged me. My tears flowed silently and copiously, to the great glee of our mutual enemies. I spent my days alternating between extremes of joy and sadness.

Whenever I entered the dining hall, my eyes would go immediately to the table where my friend was seated. He'd wait for me to come in, nod his head in greeting, and give me one of those smiles that made my heart feel completely at ease. But sometimes, when he was preoccupied or annoyed by something, he'd forgo this daily ritual, and then the expression on my face would change immediately. I couldn't eat; I felt as if a heavy weight were pressing on my chest; and the inner voice of jealousy would murmur, "Everything they tell you is true; he doesn't care for you; he doesn't think about you." On those days when the guard would come to call the men to choir practice, I still had a little hope. If, at the beginning of mealtimes, he passed by without looking for me, oh! then despair would invade my entire being, and when the choir arrived from the chapel, if I saw that he had gone back to his workshop without making up for his two oversights, I'd be in the depths of despair. This was not an easy way to live, and now that it's all in the past, I wonder how I put up with this sort of existence for four years and seven months. But having never really had a true love, and no longer having my mother to love any more, I had put all my pent-up emotion into the feelings evoked in me by this friend, whom I might never see again. I'll never forget the emotions that our first kiss aroused in me. When I felt that beloved mouth on mine, I thought that I was going to faint with joy. The affectionate words that he said to me sounded like heavenly music to my ears. Oh! Every torment that he inflicted on me had been forgotten! Infidelity, indifference, all had been forgiven!

Engel had a voice that, if not exactly beautiful, was at least reso-

nant. The chaplain had him sing solos. At vespers he would perform the *Tantum ergo sacramentum* and the *Salutaris*.[29] Oh! So well!
My feeling for him was so strong that it had affected my nervous
system. As soon as I heard the sound of his beloved voice, my eyes
would fill with tears. "Ah!" I'd say to myself. "Is this how it is
when you're in love?" These emotions wore me out. My love for
Engel was so genuine, so devoted, that I wasn't at all ashamed of
it, and all my peers complained about it. Many of them wanted to
separate me from him; some really did care for me sincerely, but
it was a wasted effort. This love, which would endure and make
me forgive anything, had sprung up almost instantly. As soon as I
laid eyes on Engel, I fell in love with him, and eight years later, as
I write these words, I can still feel that love in the rapid beats of my
heart, where he still lives.

One day, after a quarrel with Engel—a quarrel that I had started
with my ridiculous jealousy—he wrote to me:

> I really regret getting to know you and wanting to recipro-
> cate all that you have given me. You annoy me with your
> reproaches. I found out, after coming back from chapel, that
> you've saved all my letters and that the guard wasn't able to
> get them from you this morning. I want you to give them all
> back or I'll never speak to you again in my whole life. Also,
> from this day on, I don't ever want to hear about you. You
> mean nothing to me.

This unsigned letter, cold and disdainful but well deserved on
my part, if more in spirit than in fact, made me mad with despair. I
still had his letters in a case; I carried them with me; they had never
left me; they were my only treasures. At night in the dormitory
under the flickering lamp light I'd unfold them carefully, I'd kiss
his signature, and I'd read them again and again. In the evening
during the exercise period I gave this precious hoard to Edward
B—— for safekeeping, asking him to hold them for me. He prom-

ised that he'd do so, but he was smarter than I was, and after a few days he burned them all.

After my class I went up the stairs of the workshop and asked the guard to take me to the director. Since I needed a reason to leave the workshop, I said that I wouldn't work any longer and that I didn't want to stay in the general prison population. I had made a firm decision. I wanted to get away from Engel, not because I didn't love him anymore but because I loved him too much, and I hoped to cure myself by putting some distance between us. We were both unhappy. By getting myself locked up in isolation, I'd allow him to live freely, and I wouldn't have to suffer any more from hearing about his infidelities.

When an inmate refuses to work and asks for isolation, he incurs a one-month penalty. He has to sleep on the bare floor and eat only dry bread. I was allowed one hour to stroll in the little garden, away from the cell blocks. This was in May 1868. Nature was green and blooming. I gazed at the foliage for a long time, but the budding beauty only redoubled my sadness.

Corpus Christi, which is a very holy day, was celebrated at Fontevrault in an unforgettable way. Magnificent portable altars were built. Then each workshop, preceded by its banner, would make a procession to each station of the cross, while the prison band played. Engel led the bugles and other brass instruments. On that day, when I was reading and walking in the garden, I heard the sound of music. I listened mechanically, because you pay no attention to time when you're living the way I did. Reading helped me to forget a little. I was almost happy, and on that day my thoughts were far removed from Engel when suddenly the sound of that familiar voice reached me. The performers, who were marching along the loop of the road that bordered my garden, had just stopped by the wall, and I heard my friend say, "Let's rest a bit, kids, because it's damned hot today." The book I was holding in my hands slipped as I clasped my hands together in a despairing gesture; my knees gave way; and I fell on the ground, crying out,

"Engel, my dear Engel!" Tears streamed down in a torrent that can only come from a truly heart-felt pain. The musicians left. I went back to my cell and started mentally reviewing every incident in that overwhelming love. I recalled all the letters that he had written to me—those precious letters that I had hoped to find again some day.

On March 10, 1870, Engel was released. The night before, just to see him one last time, I went to the doctor's, because each inmate had to bathe before his departure. Engel squeezed my hand, told me that he'd never forget me, and gave me a few trinkets of the sort that an inmate was allowed to give as presents. The things that he gave me were quite worthless, but I treasured them more than anything else I owned. On that day Engel gave me his badge with the number that was used instead of a name and that each inmate wore on his sleeve. This simple number, 598, spoke volumes to me and was precious to me because my friend had touched it every day. He also gave me the pencil that he had used to write to me for the last time. Long ago he had given me more valuable things. On other occasions he had sent me locks of his hair, blond and silky; I meant to put these dear strands in a locket once I was free.

On July 22, 1871, I was released.

Autobiographies as Case Studies

Doctors and Patients

In the second half of the nineteenth century much of the discussion in print about male homosexuality in France took place in a medical context — in articles in medical journals, chapters in scholarly treatises, or papers presented to learned societies. Physicians encountered the men about whom they wrote as patients in their private clinical practices or as inmates in the course of their work in asylums, hospitals, and prisons. They recorded their observations and amassed documentary evidence for studies of sexual deviance, which they would use when they served as expert witnesses in court cases dealing with sexual assaults, public offenses against decency, or other criminal offenses. The seven prominent French physicians whose works are excerpted in this section—Ambroise Tardieu, Jean-Martin Charcot, Valentin Magnan, Paul Garnier, André Antheaume, Léon Parrot, and Alexandre Lacassagne—practiced and published in the fields of forensic medicine and neurology, and it is in this context that they addressed questions of same-sex sexual attraction. Their scholarly writings reflected this concentration on the criminally insane (as they diagnosed their patients), but their presumed audience of medical colleagues included general readers as well—men and women who were eager to learn more about the developing field of sexology. It was a "hot new research agenda," as Vernon Rosario, one of the leading historians of French medicine in the nineteenth century, has noted.[1]

Dr. Ambroise Tardieu was the leading medical expert on "pederasty" (the term most commonly used at the time for male same-sex sexuality) in France in the middle of the nineteenth century. Attached to La Riboisière Hospital in Paris, he was frequently called upon to give his expert opinion on cases dealing with rape, sexual assault, or public offenses against decency. In 1857 he published many of his findings in *Etude médico-légale sur les attentats aux moeurs*, which earned him the professorship of forensic studies at the Faculty of Medicine in Paris. Until his death in 1879 he continued to revise his work, usually by adding new materials from the cases in which he had become involved. His Neo-Lamarckian belief that habitual actions caused perceptible changes in physical characteristics led him to describe and categorize the visible signs of active and passive sodomy for the benefit of other doctors and criminal justice authorities. In his writings he detailed not only the physical deformities, localized irritations, and venereal diseases believed to be associated with this kind of sexual behavior, but he also described what he believed to be the shape and size of the active sodomite's penis and the passive sodomite's anus.[2]

Tardieu did not restrict himself, however, to simply describing the physical signs of pederasty. He also believed that the trained expert could detect a habitual pederast through certain exterior attributes, such as his inevitable effeminacy. In his opinion, these external features were symbolic of the internal "moral perversions," "intellectual weaknesses," and "affective faculties" of men who were attracted to other men.[3] As Rosario has put it: "This effeminacy constituted a clear, fixed psychological and ontological marker of pederasty for Tardieu."[4] Tardieu also believed that these mental and moral failings easily led such men into the dangerous world of criminality. The typical pederast, Tardieu emphasized, was capable of shrewd manipulations and terrible acts of violence. He frequently engaged in petty thefts, grand larcenies, or blackmail schemes, and as Tardieu pointed out in a section analyzing the defendants in several sensational murder trials, violence often accompanied these criminal activities. Not only was the pederast a health risk to himself and his partners, but he was also a danger to society.[5]

Tardieu based these conclusions on his study of numerous cases of sexual assault that came before him in his capacity as the leading medical expert on sexual crimes during the Second Empire. In the early part of his career, he usually restricted himself to physical observations. However, as he continued to revise his work in light of new cases that had come to his attention, he began to include additional information in his case studies, such as family histories, biographical notes, reported conversations, and in some cases written statements. Most of these statements were autobiographical in nature, but they were frequently not narrative in structure.

The account included in this section, "My Confession," is not a conventional autobiographical narrative. It offers no family history; it does not discuss the author's childhood or adolescence; nor does it include many details about the anonymous author, except for the introductory note by Tardieu. He explained that the "confession" had been "obtained during the criminal investigation of a serious charge of blackmail" in 1845. The short first-person account focuses on describing the writer's feelings for four different men—his four "loves," as he describes them. Tardieu prefaced the account by claiming that it exemplified the expressions of passion that he had encountered in his extensive reading of pederasts' letters. He also noted, as if in passing, that distinctive features in the discourse of same-sex attraction, while strikingly similar to expressions of "true" or "genuine" love, merely replicated or simulated that of heterosexuals. These features were "curious" and "strange," he insisted, but they could not achieve the same level of authenticity as those of heterosexual love. According to Tardieu, the anonymous writer's exuberance in recalling his feelings revealed his total lack of guilt, and this attitude led Tardieu to assert that the man had lost all rational understanding of his actions.[6]

Despite Tardieu's professional stature and the success that his analyses had achieved in France, his ideas were strongly opposed by German medical experts. In 1852 Dr. Johann Ludwig Casper claimed that same-sex sexuality was an in-born trait in certain men, but was an acquired vice in others. His younger colleague, Dr. Karl Westphal, published an even more influential article entitled "Die konträre Sexualempfindung" in 1869. In it he described same-sex sexuality as a hereditary condition that frequently manifested itself as a form of insanity, and as such it was not really a matter for the criminal justice system but for the medical profession, especially its psychiatric division. In the decades that followed, this view and the term "sexual inversion" became better known throughout Western European medical circles as Westphal's work was read and debated by French, Italian, and English experts.[7]

Many scholars of the history of sexuality have been quick to dismiss the influence of Tardieu and his studies as full of "all kinds of misinformation."[8] Instead, they have focused on the work of his German contemporaries Casper and Westphal and their interpretation of same-sex sexuality as an innate factor of human psychology. However, Tardieu and his disciples remained the leading authorities in France on pederasty well into the 1880s, and as Robert A. Nye, another leading historian of medicine in nineteenth-century France, has pointed out: "The older notion of 'sex' [as opposed to the modern notion of 'sexuality'] persisted in French science and medicine for a far longer time than elsewhere."[9] In other words, the physiological explanations for same-sex sexual behavior continued to have a profound influence upon the French medical examiners who dealt with cases of sexual assault or public offenses against decency. Nevertheless, at the very beginning of the 1880s, Tardieu's successor at the Faculty of Medicine in Paris, Dr. Paul Brouardel, challenged his findings by claiming that he was unable to detect the physical signs of pederasty as described by his predecessor.[10]

Two other doctors, Jean-Martin Charcot and Valentin Magnan,

following closely upon the work of their German colleagues, offered the French medical establishment another interpretation of same-sex sexual behavior in their study, "Inversion of the Sexual Instinct," which they published in 1882.[11] Charcot and Magnan criticized Tardieu for seeing same-sex sexual behavior as vice. For them it was "a neuropathic or psychopathic state of the deepest kind."[12] They based their interpretation on the case of a thirty-one-year-old man, whose autobiography we have translated in this study. From a very early age, this man had displayed a desire to see men and boys naked; he also had hysterical attacks and masturbatory habits during his adolescence; and he developed an interest in female clothing as an adult. In their analysis of his background, they found a family history of mental illnesses. They noted that his mother had an exaggerated sense of religiosity; his grandfather lacked equilibrium in the conduct of his life; and his great-grandmother was an eccentric, very friendly to strangers, but mean and acerbic to family members. They concluded that the patient's family history contained evidence of hereditary degeneration. They framed their patient's account of same-sex attraction with descriptions of the treatments that they had attempted, which included counseling the young man to engage in heterosexual intercourse and prescribing doses of a strong sedative.[13] In the second part of their article they connected this case with four additional cases of men obsessed with buttocks, boot nails, night bonnets, and white aprons. Later on, in 1887, Alfred Binet would reclassify these kinds of sexual obsessions as "erotic fetishism."[14] However, for Charcot and Magnan these five different cases all formed a unique pathological condition that was marked by obsessive-compulsive behavior and hereditary mental illnesses.[15]

The topic of fetishism was later picked up by Dr. Paul Garnier, another medical expert, in the 1890s. His first study, entitled *La Folie à Paris: Etude statistique, clinique et médico-légale*, included the case study of Gustave L——, a man who had an obsessive fascination with working-class men's clothes and the men who wore them. He had been arrested and charged with the attempted murder of "his partner in pederasty." Garnier prefaced the account with a brief physical description of the accused, who was "of medium stature and normal physical development," and whose family history contained a number of telling signs of a "degenerate inheritance" in which close male relatives suffered from epilepsy, had been committed to insane asylums, or showed signs of other "mental illnesses." Gustave L——'s story is, for the most part, recounted by the doctor, and the apparent question-and-answer elicitation of the patient's medical and sexual history was transformed into a cohesive, third-person description, frequently interrupted by a long, direct quotation from Gustave L——. This style has the effect of distancing the reader from the subject. The man's medical history was interwoven with his life story, and thus details, such as Gustave L——'s memory of incidents of bed-wetting in adolescence, were linked to the emergence of his "very strange [erotic] propensities." Garnier concluded that the criminal charges against him should be dropped due to his mental instability. He reached this conclusion for many reasons, but mainly because of Gustave L——'s agitation when talking about his obsessive jealousy.[16]

Garnier published another study, *Les Fétichistes: Pervertis et invertis sexuels: Observations médico-légales*, where he presented the case of Gustave L—— once again, but he also included another case—that of Louis X——, who had been arrested in the Bois de Vincennes in Paris after exposing himself to a worker there. Here, too, Garnier prefaced the man's story with an examination of the twenty-six-year-old's antecedents—"a rich family with numerous indications of mental instability"—and he interspersed the account of Louis X——'s sexual history with brief diagnostic asides. The account of the patient's sexual behavior and proclivities was especially detailed and graphic, since the doctor quoted Louis X——'s "autobiographical notes" directly. Garnier theorized that Louis X—— was not only a "true born invert" but a fetishist as well, since he had developed a fixation on men who wore shiny, highly polished boots and pursued these men in public streets and parks. Furthermore, the patient described his use of a dildo to masturbate himself while fantasizing about these young men in boots. The doctor concluded that Louis X—— suffered from hereditary degeneration and needed to be treated by the medical profession, not punished by the criminal justice system.[17]

Building upon the work of Charcot and Magnan, Drs. Antheaume and Parrot presented the case of an eighteen-year-old man by the name of Antonio, who was confined at the request of his father to the Charenton asylum after an unsuccessful suicide attempt. At the time the young man had mailed a note to his parents, in which he explained his current state of unhappiness as the result of his love of boys. His father handed this suicide note over to his doctors, who published it, along with Antonio's account of his life, in a medical journal. This chronologically organized autobiography had been written, as his doctors explained, a few days into Antonio's confinement after the patient got over his "reticence and quasi-feminine shyness" about discussing his sexuality. It was accompanied by a notebook that Antonio had "filled with sketches related to his homosexual tendency." The sketchbook, however, was mentioned, but not shown, because the doctors presented only brief selections of the autobiography—"only the most typical passages," as they explained.[18] Consequently, Antonio's story consisted of writings in different genres addressed at different times to different readers.

Like Antonio, Charles Double produced his writings under duress; he wrote them while in prison after being tried and convicted for the murder of his mother. He had been sentenced to death, but his sentence was commuted to a life sentence at hard labor in the prison colony at Cayenne in French Guiana. Between the months of November 1904 and February 1905, while in the Saint Paul prison in Lyon waiting to be shipped out, he filled several notebooks with his writings at the request of Dr. Alexandre Lacassagne, a physician and expert in forensic medicine. Lacassagne began his medical career in the military hospitals of France and Algeria; in 1880 he was offered the professorship in forensic medicine at the medical school in Lyon, where he taught until his death in 1924. Throughout his career he wrote and spoke on topics as disparate as tattoos, infanticide, serial killers, sexual deviance, capital punishment, and suicide. In 1896 he founded the journal *Archives d'anthropologie criminelle*, which became the leading voice for a new theory of criminal behavior.[19]

Lacassagne challenged the theoretical position of Cesare Lombroso, the famous Italian criminologist, whose concept of the "born" criminal with atavistic traits had gained widespread acceptance throughout Europe.[20] Although Lacassagne also acknowledged a hereditary component in the origins of crime, he understood that component in Lamarckian terms as the inheritance of acquired characteristics, thus placing emphasis on the social environment as the medium in which criminal tendencies were nurtured and developed.[21] As part of his research agenda, he planned to write a study on the lives of criminals entitled *Le Livre des vies coupables*, using the autobiographies of convicted murderers. Adopting a technique that had been practiced for decades by French physicians of the mentally ill, Lacassagne chose a small number of inmates, including Double, asked them to write their life stories, gave them writing materials, and requested that they pay particular attention to their motives and their states of mind. After these men completed their notebooks, Lacassagne collected them, read them, and annotated them. He claimed that they added significantly to his theory on the origins of crime. Although he was a prolific writer on all kinds of medical and criminal subjects, he never published this book on the autobiographies of criminals. Instead, he gave the notebooks, along with the rest of his papers, to the Bibliothèque municipale de Lyon.[22]

Double was clearly affected by the circumstances of his imprisonment and medical treatment. Because his primary reader was a medical criminologist, he used legal, medical, and psychological terms to promote his own analyses and to dispute the theories and diagnoses of the experts. He took care to structure his account of his crime as a legal brief arguing in his own defense and condemning a cruel society that had no place for men like him. However, he also stressed what he perceived as his unique predicament, explaining his psychology in terms of a contradiction between his "feminine" and "masculine" characteristics. He filled four notebooks with his writings, putting a warning note on the cover of each one: "To be read by medical doctors only." The final notebook ended with a personal appeal to Lacassagne: "Charles Double recommends himself very respectfully to Dr. Lacassagne. He would be very grateful if he could write a letter of recommendation on his behalf to the medical doctors in charge of the prisoners at Saint-Martin-de-Ré in Guiana."

The life stories in this section have one attribute in common — they were collected and intended for publication by medical professionals. All seven of these doctors used observations, case studies, and fragments of autobiographies as evidence for their own theoretical positions in the etiology and classification of sexual deviance. As scientists, they sought to collect a variety of examples, to classify them into coherent systems, to identify alleged problems, and to propose methods of treatment. Their questioning of patients about their upbringing, their sexual awakening, their erotic fantasies, and their adult sexual encounters provided the fragmentary and highly subjective accounts in this section. Today it is not possible to know which stories (or which segments of these stories) were told freely and which ones were coerced, although we must agree that in the context of a man's pending criminal trial, incarceration, or internment, freedom was an elusive concept. Nevertheless, as Harry Oosterhuis has argued in his study of Richard von Krafft-Ebing and his patients, telling one's life story could be an opportunity to impose meaning on a person's conduct, and shaping a narrative around the confession or around the explication of one's sexuality could be a means of constructing one's own understanding of these often inchoate experiences.[23] With this caveat in mind, we believe that reading these case studies will give contemporary students and scholars not only a glimpse of various aspects of these men's lives, but also an insight into the preconceptions and practices of some of the most prominent figures in French medicine in the second half of the nineteenth century.

Loves by Anonymous

In Dr. Ambroise Tardieu's *A Medical and Legal Study on Assaults against Morality* (1867)

I have frequently had the opportunity to read the letters of self-confessed pederasts, and I have noticed that they employ the most passionate language, the strangest nicknames, and the most intense images borrowed from true love.

I can give an example of one that will not be the least curious in my current study. I will reproduce it in its entirety. It is entitled "My Confession," and it was obtained during the criminal investigation of a serious charge of blackmail at the beginning of 1845.

FIRST LOVE

The first man that I loved! Oh! How to explain how I loved him! How to describe the delicious shiver of my senses when I heard his voice and the happiness that I experienced in stealing a look at his features and the tender care that I took in making a smile appear on his lips! I must admit that he was the first being who made my heart beat faster every day, who always filled my dreams with pleasing images, and who opened up to me a whole new life; from then on all the happiness that I had came from him, all my feelings were for him, everything I did I did for him. Each of his words came vibrating through my whole being like a tender melody. His look, calm and smiling, seemed to reflect the sweet joys in the depths of my heart. I thought that it was this delight that the angels must feel.

Also, next to him, I felt as if all the other emotions in life faded into insignificance. What were they to me but prejudices imposed by law and habit! What was there for me in the pleasures of society or the triumphs of pride! How many times did I avoid my childhood friends in order to be near him! Oh! For him, what on this earth would I not have done! What would I not have asked from heaven! And what rival affection could have conquered my soul!

SECOND LOVE

Must I say it, though? The three years of my first infatuation were hardly over when another love came into my heart. No power of will could have fought against the spark kindled in me by a being who didn't have a claim on my memory, but whose candid face awakened in me a thousand charming hopes. He had big blue eyes, and I loved to contemplate their tender depths. And when his head lay upon my shoulder, when his lips happened to say my name, sealing the first pact of our frank friendship, I said to myself: "Here, too, will I experience the happiness of being loved!"

THIRD LOVE

How is it that after a certain time a gentle boy with a pale complexion and black eyes came into my life? I truly cannot say. . . Still, since my pen wants to tell the truth and my heart is obliged to reveal its secrets, I must confess that this new passion wasn't merely one of those thrilling episodes that happen in the life of a man, like a shooting star that streaks across the sky without disturbing the celestial harmony. My young lover found a place in my soul, and in order to keep him there I lavished on him my most intimate caresses. I loved to watch the awakening of his first feelings, to have him describe to me alone the burgeoning of his senses. I could never have resisted him. I'd have gone mad!

Oh! If I could wrap myself in an enigma, what would I still have to tell you? If I could conceal in the depths of my soul this last weakness of nature, then I'd stop the account of my first loves at this mystic number of three! But, alas, destinies are great and inexplicable. And I must, despite myself, finish by telling you that I fell in love with a child who seemed to have fallen from the heavens above. He was as beautiful as the little cherubs whom we see suspended in air holding the ends of the Virgin's veil away from her face. His mouth, so small, had one of those smiles that could almost have made Eve swoon, if it was thus that the devil tempted her. In his eyes was a sensuous innocence that made everything possible and everything forgivable. Lovely and gracious, submissive to my whims, attentive to my desires, he overwhelmed me with sweet looks and charming caresses. To see him was to love him . . . and that is why I loved him.

And yet, if you really want to understand, if you really want to know how I loved them all, how they loved me, and how we lived together, then lift the curtain that hides this sight . . . It's one of those incomprehensible mysteries that nature alone reveals.

There are cases like this one in which it is difficult not to recognize in pederasts a genuinely unhealthy perversion of the moral sense. To see the profound degradation, the revolting filthiness of individuals apparently distinguished by education and wealth who seek and consort with other men, one would be seriously tempted to believe that their senses and their reason have been impaired. And one can hardly doubt it once one has collected all the evidence, such as those facts, which I have received from a judge, the Honorable Counselor C. Busserolles, who has invested an equal amount of cleverness and energy in pursuing cases against pederasts. These facts I cannot conceal. One of these men, who fell

from an elevated social position to the lowest depths of depravation, used to lure street urchins to his place; he would kneel down
before them and kiss their feet with passionate submissiveness, and
then he would ask them for the most despicable pleasures. Another
experienced a unique pleasure in being brutally kicked by the lowest sort of person. What can one make of such horrors if not attribute them to the saddest and most shameful form of madness?

Observation 1 by Anonymous

In Dr. Jean-Martin Charcot and Dr. Valentin
Magnan's *Inversion of the Sexual Instinct* (1881)

The perversion of the sexual instinct is associated with many mental conditions from the childish obscenities of an old man in the throes of dementia to the appalling desecrations of corpses performed by certain impulsive madmen. A large collection of facts exists that, far from defining a particular condition, describes only the symptoms of different illnesses, revealing the weakness or the perversion of the moral or emotional faculties of an individual.

Nevertheless, we are not here to consider perversions of the sexual instinct, which are often traceable to mental illnesses in general, but to examine a specific mental phenomenon, where a sexual attraction for the same sex is manifested to the exclusion of the other sex—an odd but inescapable fact of our civilization.

Without a doubt, since antiquity we have found traces of this unnatural love, and many examples of friendship from our pagan past have been based on such shameful promiscuities. Nevertheless, these cases are clearly nothing more than the degrading consequences of the relaxation of the moral standards of our time in a profoundly vice-ridden society.

Evidence of these types of absolutely morbid personalities has been reported by various authors. Still, before getting to the heart of the matter, we would like to report on a case that by its simplicity, its clarity, and the high degree of intelligence manifested by its subject sketches out with clearly defined contours against the background of dark shadows the chief characteristics of this unusually morbid tendency.

Neuropathic tendency of ancestors; disparity between father's and mother's ages. Inversion of the sexual instinct: voluptuous sensations from childhood; since puberty occasional ejaculation at the sight of a naked man or a statue of a nude man, or the obsessive memory of these images, a naked woman leaving the subject indifferent. From five to eight a tendency to steal. A habit of masturbation until the age of twenty-two. Hysterical attacks starting at the age of fifteen.

Here is the patient's own account of the bizarre symptoms that he experienced and what he described as his sensuality:

> My sensuality manifested itself since the age of six by a violent desire to see boys my own age and older men naked. This desire wasn't difficult to satisfy, since my parents lived near some barracks, where the soldiers weren't embarrassed to let their private parts be seen. One day (I was maybe only eight years old) I saw a soldier masturbating. I imitated him, and I achieved, from the pleasure of my imagination that was fixated on this soldier, the physical sensations of a very strong tickle. I continued to give myself this pleasure, always by exciting my imagination through the remembrance of naked men.
>
> My parents left N—— in order to establish themselves in B——. There I saw soldiers going to bathe in a little creek, which was very picturesque. They bathed completely naked. In order to be able to satisfy myself, I pretended to go and sit by the edge of this creek and to draw the landscape. In this manner I watched the soldiers without seeming to look at them.
>
> Toward the age of fifteen puberty arrived, and my masturbation gave me much more satisfaction. Besides, I achieved an erection and its consequences as much through my imagination as through my actions. It happened more than once that, at the mere sight of a man's member, I'd get an erection, have an amorous convulsion, and experience the loss of sperm. During

the night my imagination worked overtime and led to the same results.

I stopped masturbating completely at the age of twenty, but I was never able, despite all my efforts, to stop the excitement of my imagination. Young, handsome, and strong men always provoked a powerful emotion in me. A beautiful statue of a nude man produced the same effect. The *Apollo Belvedere* in the Louvre made a big impression on me.[1] When I encountered a man whose youth and beauty provoked my passion, I was tempted to please him. If I had given free reign to my sentiments, I'd have offered him all possible kindnesses. I'd have invited him to my home; I'd have written to him on perfumed paper; I'd have brought him flowers; I'd have given him gifts; and I'd have deprived myself of many things in order to please him. I never did allow myself to go that far, but I felt very strongly that I was capable of doing so.

I really must conquer this desire that I've experienced. I know how to control the feelings I've just spoken of, but I'm unable to control love itself. Luckily, this love doesn't overwhelm me constantly. I work—and my studies are a great help to me in resisting my sensual thoughts—but often my sensuality overwhelms me, and in the middle of a very thorough examination of a question I'm interrupted by the sudden vision of a naked man in my imagination. I've always fought against this sensuality as much as I could. I was able to prevent many acts that I felt compelled to commit, but I never succeeded in extinguishing this sensuality. The supreme satisfaction of this sensuality has never been anything but the sight of a naked man and, above all, of a man's penis. I've never felt the desire to penetrate a man or to be the sexual object of another man. To look at the genitals of a handsome and strong man has always been the greatest sensual delight for me.

As far as women are concerned, as beautiful as they are, they've never awakened the slightest desire in me. I've tried to love a woman, hoping to arrive at some natural ideas, but despite her beauty and her efforts, I was left completely indifferent, and my erection, so easy for me at the sight of a man, didn't even begin. Never has a woman provoked in me the smallest amount of sensuality.

I adore feminine outfits. I love to look at a woman who is well dressed, because I say to myself that I'd like to be a woman in order to dress so well. At the age of seventeen I dressed as a woman for carnival, and I felt an incredible pleasure in wearing a wig, putting on a low-cut dress, and trailing my skirts on the floor as I walked. Until the age of twenty-two I took great pleasure in dressing up a doll. I'd still find that pleasurable today. Women are astonished to find me so well informed about the good taste of their outfits and to hear me speak so knowledgeably of such things as if I were a woman myself.

The love that I feel for a man passes quickly. Whenever another man appears who is more handsome in my eyes, the thought of the one who preceded him disappears. The nocturnal emissions no longer seem to be as frequent as they were several months ago. It has been more than three weeks since I had one, but I continue to have my usual dreams, and I still desire to see nothing but naked men.

Such are the details of his situation that the patient himself describes, fully aware of the aspects of the obsession from which he cannot free himself.

This sick person, what is he?

Physically speaking, this man, aged thirty-one, is dark, tall, well built, with a normally shaped skull, bright eyes, an energetic- and intelligent-looking face, despite a slight overbite of the lower jaw and two rather large, oversized ears. He has a thick moustache, whose fullness gives his face a certain military look. He stands up straight; his walk is firm, even a little stiff; and he has no trace of femininity. In other respects, his sexual organs are normally developed, with hair growth in the pubic area; and his testicles and penis are shaped normally without any trace of an anomaly. There is no sign of hypospadia.[2]

Regarding his intelligence, he is a cultured man, well educated, and quite erudite. He has consistently been gainfully employed, and he has always been at the top of his class. After a rigorous program of classical studies at the university, he quickly ascended the academic ranks, so that by the age of thirty he had achieved the position of professor in a department of a university. He is a lover of fine art, especially of music, and he is particularly fond of Chopin, Gounod, Delibes, and Massenet, finding in these composers the sentimental elements that please him. He also finds the poetry of Victor Hugo and the descriptions of nature by George Sand to be especially charming.

He is kind, a bit effusive, with an easy manner, and he considers himself happy when he can help his friends or do good deeds for the less fortunate in society.

If we examine his pathological history, we will certainly notice shadows in the apparently homogeneous background of this well-developed person. First of all, his family history reveals a great disparity between the father's age, who married at forty-nine, and the mother's, who was only eighteen. It is true that, on the father's side, the uncles and aunts, and even the father himself, lived to an advanced age without any trace of nervous ailments. As for the mother's family, the grandfather showed evidence of an unbalanced life without this condition actually leading to a diagnosis of insanity, but it does reveal the unhealthy tendencies that one finds in individuals who are predisposed to mental illnesses. Even though he was a notary in his little village, he led a somewhat irregular life. He was acquainted with some of the well-known artistic figures of his day, including Malibran, who was his friend,[3] and he entertained them in his home. But he neglected his duties, and finally he was obliged to give them up. His grandfather's mother had been known for her eccentricity; she was very friendly to strangers, but at home she was mean and vicious. The mother, whose purity of morals combined an exaggerated religious piety with a strong penchant for fashion, went out of her way to show herself off at festive occasions and large public events.

During his childhood he had scarlet fever and whooping cough, which were cured without any complications. From the age of five to eight the patient had a well-documented tendency to steal, taking without any remorse pens, pencils, and other objects from his schoolmates and teachers, which he then took home, but he did not keep them. One day he stole an inkpot that contained red ink from his tutor's desk, and just as he was walking through the doorway into the classroom, the inkpot fell out of his pocket and broke, spilling the liquid that exposed his crime. Terribly upset by this unfortunate accident, he renounced thievery from that moment on.

The nervous tendencies of our patient revealed themselves not only in psychic difficulties and moral aberrations but also in convulsive seizures from a very young age. To judge from the symptoms that preceded these attacks, from their duration, and from the benign character of their aftermath, which did not interfere with his going immediately back to his work, the attacks are closer to hysteria than to epilepsy. These episodes began when he was fifteen. At first they were very rare, but they increased in frequency in 1869 and 1870. They began with a state of mental excitement, which would distract the patient, not allowing him to concentrate on a single thought and preventing him from paying attention to anything. They also made him say things that he never intended. It seemed to him that what he wanted to express was replaced by another idea before he even had time to say it. In other words, thoughts multiplied so rapidly that he had no control over them. In addition, he knew full well that he was in this state while it was happening.

These mental phenomena were accompanied by incessant blinking. His problems began at the time he woke up either during the night or in the early morning, especially between seven and eight o'clock. When he was forewarned of these attacks, he would stay in bed, or if he was out of bed, he would hurry back to lie down so that he would not be overcome by the attacks while away from home. These precursory events usually lasted a rather long period of time and would rarely stop there, and afterward he would simply fall into a deep sleep. When the attacks came, the usual course of events was that they would occur in the morning, but at different times. One day, for example, the attack happened in the afternoon after a profound emotional crisis.

According to one relative, who is in close contact with the patient, when an attack comes, the patient cries out, loses consciousness, and becomes rigid; then his limbs shake, his eyes roll, and he clenches his jaws; and if one did not place a wet cloth between his upper and lower teeth, he would bite his lips and tongue almost every time, which did happen sometimes, despite the precautions taken. Foam appears on his lips and his face is drowned in sweat. After the attack, he falls into a deep sleep. A second attack may follow the first approximately three hours later, and then a third approximately three hours after that, and sometimes even a fourth one. These four attacks take place over a day and a half. The day after the cycle begins, around noon, the mental agitation and the blinking will stop. A profound feeling of exhaustion always follows the attack, and the patient has a hearty appetite and even feels hungry. For two or three days afterward his urine is reddish and thick. He feels a bit depressed, especially when those around him are disturbed by his attacks and their recurrence. Nevertheless, his mind is clear, and he can apply himself to serious work, as if nothing had happened. These attacks began in 1865. Before that time no one recalled any incidents of convulsions. For the first few years the attacks were few and far between, more than a year apart. In 1869 and 1870 they became more and more frequent. Since 1870 an attack has occurred every three months or every two months or even every three weeks.

A habit that sometimes tends to be exacerbated after the attacks is the need to count and recount flowers, stripes, nails, and squares, in a word, the insignificant details on a tapestry, screen, ceiling, or any other kind of decorative element. The convulsions do not seem to have had any influence on his mental problems. In fact, it was after these episodes that his mental problems began, and they have not changed, despite the increasing frequency of the attacks during the last several years.

According to the testimony cited above, which was written by the patient last June, he feels himself to be completely enslaved by his abnormal desires. This moral tendency has distinctly changed during the time of his treatment. Already in August he said that he had noticed that the sight of a woman no longer left him indifferent. In September, following our advice, he tried to substitute the image of a woman in his memory for the image of a naked man, which had so obsessed him in the past. He tried to do so several times, but he had to exert a great force of will to divert his imagination from his desired object. Finally, at the beginning of September, having noticed less resistance in summoning up the image of a woman in his consciousness and having even experienced a bit of satisfaction from admiring her in his mind's eye, he made another effort, in which he was victorious. He was able on several occasions, without forcing himself, to have sexual relations with a woman, proving that he could experience the normal feelings of sensual pleasure. The effect on his moral well-being was excellent. He experienced a respite from his obsession for several days, but having to leave Paris and having to use only his reason to fight against his obsession, he felt, as he put it, that his thoughts were becoming fixated once again on his unnatural desires.

In addition to the physical and moral treatment that we have given to the patient, we also used hydrotherapy in the form of cold-water jets and cold showers, and we administered potassium bromide,[4] which has diminished the intensity and the duration of his attacks, but not their frequency.

Autobiographical Notes by Gustave L——

In Dr. Paul Garnier's *Madness in Paris* (1890)

L——, Gustave, thirty-two years old, a domestic servant charged with the attempted murder of Monsieur X——, his partner in pederasty, whom he had accused of infidelity for a long time, is a man of medium stature and of normal physical development. However, at birth he inherited the most deplorable tendencies. His father died in an insane asylum. He had a brother, who died during the Franco-Prussian War and who, we were told, suffered from epilepsy. In addition, a first cousin was stricken with a mental ailment.

The childhood of L—— is said to have been exempt from serious illness, but his temperament was nervous, and his character was impressionable and unstable. In 1878 he had his first attack of epilepsy. At this time he was performing his military service, but his well-attested neurosis made him unfit for service and earned him his release. Was it really at this time that he began to show the first manifestations of epilepsy? We think instead that epilepsy had appeared at an earlier date. In fact, L—— urinated frequently in bed during his adolescence, and it is necessary, without a doubt, to attribute his involuntary and unconscious micturitions to these nocturnal crises. Whatever it may be, it is important to note that the person charged has experienced strange propensities from a very young age, on which we must now focus our attention.

At the age of ten L—— noticed for the first time that, when a man embraced him, the touch of the man's beard against his cheek left him with a strange sensation. He was troubled and overwhelmed by a voluptuous emotion. "I remember," he says, "that this titillated me in the most enjoyable way in the world, and since then I sought occasions to renew this pleasure again and again. Soon it was the sight of a man urinating that aroused me. I did all I could to see his genitals, and when I succeeded in doing so, I was prey to a great excitation that impelled me to masturbate."

This tendency did not take long to become more obvious. At the age of thirteen he would persist in gazing at certain men who pleased him. These men were workers with a masculine appearance who were dressed in their work clothes. "Well filled-out overalls," L—— remarked, "have always been my fancy." He achieved orgasms through the simple mental representation of a man to whom he assigned attributes that charmed him. During the little time that he served under the flag, he was able to determine that military uniforms left him indifferent. It is only the overalls of a worker that move and attract him. We insist deliberately and for good reason on specializing the appetite, which has, in similar situations, a value of primary significance. In effect, we find there the fixed character of a pathological impulse with its inexorable tyranny.

Also, as in the majority of similar cases, cohabitation with women is more than relegated to the background. L—— did not experience any desire for normal sexual relations. Without going so far as feeling actual repulsion, he is, at the very least, indifferent. He has even had some casual mistresses, but it was, as he acknowledges, in order to increase his bragging rights with his friends and to do as they did. To enable us to make a better judgment about the strange sexual aberrations that L—— has come to have, we are reproducing some excerpts from the notes that we took. Their cynicism would be revolting if one lost sight of his pathological perversion and associated it only with the evidence of a shameful and degrading vice.

Regarding the mistress that he had, he wrote the following:

This woman had a great deal of consideration for me, and I was very grateful to her for it, but to tell the truth, it wasn't on her account that I saw her and that I maintained relations with her. It was for the *lover* that she had. I'd have paid dearly to be loved by the man whom she no longer loved and whom I adored with all the strength of my being, even though he never suspected it. I was happy to compete with him on his own turf. I took satisfaction—I, a young man of twenty-three—with this woman of forty-six in thinking of this man dressed in his overalls. In my intimate relations it was always he whom I had before my eyes; it was with him that I imagined myself to be; and it was only with the *idea* that I had of him at that moment that I achieved satisfaction.

Nevertheless, the patient soon left this woman in order to search out "handsome workers," to use his expression. He was frequently absent from all the households where he worked as a domestic servant, and he was always fired after a short time. One evening on the Champs-Elysées, L———, in search of a man dressed in overalls, encountered someone for whom he soon avowed an ardent passion. He recounts in enthusiastic terms the practices of mutual masturbation and pederasty that he performed with this individual. From this time on he had but one exclusive desire, one single preoccupation: to be constantly with the man he could no longer do without.

"Since that time," he told us, "I was prey to a real obsession. I felt that I was madly in love with him and that I couldn't live without him. I became extremely jealous. Having realized that he went with women, I felt as if my heart were being squeezed in a vice. I'd have killed the woman who took him from me and who snatched him from my life. My torments were so violent that I developed jaundice and became sick."

After having told us the story of his reproaches to the unfaithful man, of his jealous quarrels, of the alternating ruptures and reconciliations with his "lover," he cried out emphatically:

Ah! dear and sad memories! I embraced this beautiful body, this pretty face where not one wrinkle appeared, this mouth, so fresh and made for kisses, these beautiful eyes that I adored, these cheeks so sweet, this perfect skin! How all of this cried out for vengeance! How I should have cursed this ardent friendship that ruined my life! And yet I still loved him!

Terrible memories! May you be banished from my thoughts so that I may drink my fill of this cup of forgetfulness. Your indifference made me suffer like a martyr. I, who had forgotten everything for you, had neglected my future! Finally it was a lost cause. I've preached long enough in the desert . . . I'd have liked to have disfigured you, but I didn't succeed . . . So much better for you . . . I'm happy about it. Enjoy life. As for me, I have no more future. My end is in sight . . . God alone will justify me in my intolerable existence. Ah! adored countenance! May you find as much affection elsewhere . . . but never . . . I bid you farewell, dear, dear adored Louis. My thoughts are of you alone and for you alone I wish to live. Your memory has taken root in my heart and is watered by my tears.

For several weeks L——, who was absolutely consumed by his strange and unhealthy passion and was prey to all the torments of an intolerable jealousy, underwent a sort of moral crisis, attested to by all the records of the investigation. He no longer slept; he was overexcited if he found himself in the presence of "his Louis"; he pleaded with him to give him affection; and he warned him that he would no longer be able to control himself if he was abandoned. One day at X——'s place he was completely overwhelmed and alarmed. He threatened him with a loaded revolver with which he had armed himself.

"I was in despair," he said. "I'd have preferred a knife thrust to his indifference . . . It was finished. I saw it clearly . . . He no longer wanted me. I wrote him letters in which I told him that I was going to die, and I had, in fact, thought of hanging myself plenty of times. I threatened him with revenge. Finally I made a drastic decision. I decided to damage this pretty face that I had loved so much and that had given itself to others. On the day when I pursued him with a razor with the intention of slashing his face, of disfiguring him instead of killing him, I had two glasses of absinthe in order to stimulate myself and to give me the necessary courage . . . ," and so on, and so on.

L—— is a pederast. Far from denying his shameful habits, he confesses them with a complacent lustfulness of language. Nevertheless, we believe that we are able to say that he is a pederast of a different sort. If the revolting practices in which he indulged are, in a general way, the products of degrading passions, it is only fair to observe that certain aberrations of the sexual sense are truly in the domain of pathology. The more one applies oneself to the close study of individuals who offer us examples of sexual perversion and sexual inversion, and when one reconstructs their entire life story without overlooking their hereditary antecedents, the more one can be sure that in many cases these moral anomalies lead straight to a defect, to a state of moral degeneration. It was thus that Tardieu made his presentation when he wrote about pederasts: "There should be more serious attention given to the mental state of certain individuals convicted of pederasty in whom the moral perversion could degenerate into madness." Moreover, the inversion of the sexual sense is an episodic syndrome. Today it is described among the functional irregularities that distinguish hereditary degeneracies, as established in the excellent work of Charcot, Magnan, Brouardel, Lombroso, Krafft-Ebing, Tarnovskii, and others.

A child of eight or nine who experiences a voluptuous curiosity for male nudity, who feels a unique satisfaction when the hairs of a beard brush against his cheeks, and who is pursued a little later by the captivating and obsessive idea of a young man dressed in overalls is something other than a vicious child. One is right to say that he is a being hereditarily predisposed to moral deviations. Such penchants, appearing so suddenly at an age when they could not be the product of the influence of vice, reveal a pathological impulse.

L——, with his strange excitements, his agonizing and morbid jealousies, and his crises of despair, is a delinquent individual, enslaved by the yoke of irresistible obsessions. Truly defective in intelligence in his manner of judging things, he is in addition suffering from a grave neurosis, and in this regard it is not irrelevant to note in passing that pederasty is frequently found in these epileptics. The epileptic variety of this unnatural tendency has already been noted in the medical literature.

Gustave L——, who presents a curious example of the amorous jealousy of the homosexual,[1] benefited from the withdrawal of the criminal charges against him. He was remanded to the civil authorities and interned in a mental asylum in order to be treated at the same time for his epilepsy, his mental debility, and his tendency toward melancholia into which his unrequited love drove him.

Autobiographical Notes by Louis X———

In Dr. Paul Garnier's *The Fetishists* (1895)

Louis X———, twenty-six years old, is a man of letters and belongs to a rich family with numerous indications of mental instability, principally on the maternal side. One of his mother's brothers committed suicide; they say that it was during a bout of brain fever, but it is more likely that alcohol played the greater role in this crisis. Another brother, having suffered grave and repeated convulsions in his childhood, has always been considered mentally unbalanced, an eccentric, even though he is well educated and very intelligent. They cite this rather bizarre fact about him: in 1848, having entered the Tuileries with the insurgents,[1] he stole a small piece of cloth torn off a piece of furniture, but soon, overcome by remorse, he went without delay to the tomb of his father in order to beg forgiveness for his theft. His mother considered him a madman. Though the hereditary defect is less pronounced on the other side of his family, the intemperate habits of Louis X———'s father should be taken into account. One last fact to point out relating to this heredity is that one cousin was confined to the asylum of Ville-Evrard.[2]

To us Louis X——— seemed to be a perfectly well brought-up man, used to the contact of elegant and select society. He was very well groomed in his appearance and in the care of his whole body. He gave us the impression of a sophisticated young man in everything that has to do with fashion and grooming. Dressed in shoes polished to the most brilliant shine, he wears a pince-nez for reasons of style, he claims, rather than out of necessity, because his sight is sufficiently good, and he replaces it with a monocle when, as he says, he wants to make an impression. His deportment is calm; his gestures are sober and reserved; his voice, in its monotonous intonations, is sweet and not very virile. Tall, svelte, he has hair and a beard that are golden blond in color. His hands are manicured like those of a woman who devotes hours to this extremely meticulous upkeep. His fingernails are the object of a veritable cult and are kept at an extraordinary length that would be incompatible with any manual occupation.

The exterior of Louis X——'s body reveals only one structural anomaly. On the right-hand side of the head and face, the temple and parietal bump are more prominent than on the other side, and underneath them is a sort of fissure from front to back as if the parts have been hollowed out by a sharp instrument. The roof of the month is arched.

The accused has always enjoyed excellent health, but from an early age he attracted attention because of the anomalies of his moral organization. He has always had a timid character, not very demonstrative. "No one has ever seen him laugh," his brother told us. Because he enjoyed being alone, he used to spend the greater part of his time inside his room. He displayed a love of paradox and was inclined to irony and scorn. Except for that, he had never been subject to serious criticism either at home or at school. His behavior was normal, due to passivity rather than a desire to earn praise.

His habits were bizarre. He had some manias that are comical. Very meticulous in the care that he devotes to his grooming—and this ever since the age of twelve or thirteen—he would anoint his face with pomade and then powder it, handling the mirror the entire time like an extremely coquettish woman. When he is out in the country, he takes the most meticulous and ridiculous precautions to protect his complexion from the ardor of the sun. His brother has often found him in the morning immobile in his bed in a grotesque position with his head under the covers in order, he says, not to "burn" his pillow. But soon phenomena of the most important sort appeared, caused by the exaggerated care he gave to his person—phenomena of a sexual type, whose evolution we can follow from their first appearance to this day thanks to the autobiographical notes that the accused has written upon our request.

At the age of thirteen Louis X———, boarding at the *lycée* of X———, began to engage in masturbation through imitation, he says. He sought out the touch of his friends, and it was, above all, when he went home to his family, where he enjoyed the greatest freedom, that he abandoned himself to solitary practices. Since that time he has not been able to achieve orgasm by onanism, except through the contemplation of polished boots, to which he was instinctively drawn, even as a child. Outside of manual masturbation, all other onanistic acts inspired in X——— nothing but profound disgust. Thus he arrived at the age of seventeen feeling no inclination or attraction for women.

Well educated and studious, he passed his baccalaureate brilliantly enough, and he soon began the study of law, without being able to interest himself in it very much. Because he was attracted to literature, he resolved to devote himself to it and to make it his career. His first attempts were completely unsuccessful. Then came a year of military service, which diverted him from his lack of success. At this time, encouraged by his comrades, who teased him about his girlish timidity, he attempted to have sexual relations for the first time. Coitus leaving him cold, he soon returned to his habit of onanism.

In 1887, his service having ended, X——— returned to his family. He went back to work, and while preparing for his law degree, he wrote two novels that went unnoticed. He distracted himself from his literary disappointments by reading the works of classical authors, but his choice fell particularly on those who concentrated on the descriptions of sexual aberrations and of relations against nature. Martial, Petronius, and Aristophanes were, and still are, his favorite authors.[3]

By that time he was twenty-two years old and felt vague desires for passive pederasty for the first time. One day, during one of his promenades in the Bois de Vincennes,[4] he was about to satisfy them when a circumstance outside his control intervened. From that moment on he had the greatest pleasure in thinking about the young men of his own age in the streets, especially when they had a pleasant face and were well dressed. Clothing had a great deal of importance in his eyes, but his pleasure increased prodigiously when they were wearing polished shoes. He took note of those young men who had the greatest charm for him, and returning home, he would masturbate by evoking their images. From this time onward an uninterrupted series of incidents began to occur for Louis X—— in which the culture of letters and the unhealthy search for the strangest ideal took a wrong turn.

Having received his law degree, X——, in order to please his family, applied for a job in a large insurance company. While waiting for a response, he told his family that he had accepted a job as a clerk in a lawyer's office, even though he had no intention of performing such functions, which he considered well below his worth. He was even convinced that it would not be long before he made a name for himself in literature. During a period of four years he maintained the illusion of this bizarre notion for his family. He pointed out the lawyer's office where he said he went every day, but he never actually went there. He heaped subterfuge upon subterfuge in order to sidetrack the vigilance of his older brother and his mother, giving them details on what happened at the office, on the dullness of his work, and so on. He used to tell his family that the plays he wrote were in rehearsals and that he had to deal with such and such theater director. Each day he left his house regularly, but he spent the time of his supposed internship at the lawyer's office in various visits to museums, in the Bois de Meudon,[5] where he collected beetles, and principally in the Bois de Vincennes. In his wanderings, crisscrossed by various misadventures—thefts and assaults of which he was the victim—Louis X—— pursued without respite but always unsuccessfully what he called his ideal. He painted the following portrait of his life:

I would have liked to have a friend a little younger than myself, handsome, well educated, and elegant (I've already mentioned the importance that clothing has for me). We'd spend several hours together each day, talking about literature, philosophy, and so on. In the meantime we'd caress each other and masturbate each other. But I wouldn't have wanted at all to ask him to engage in pederasty with me. I'd have feared that the disgusting details that make up this habit would alter our friendship. On the other hand, I'd have liked to be possessed at least once by another man in order to know what it is like. None of these dreams would be realized.

Discouraged by the lack of success of his literary work, tormented by the dread of the imminent discovery of his accumulated lies, troubled profoundly by the inability to realize his pederastic dreams—which were belied by the more or less laughable incidents that he experienced and which fled from him like a mirage—he used to return home nervously excited and in a bad state, tormented by a tenacious frontal migraine.

He searched constantly for a way to satisfy the passion that dominated him, and one day he decided to substitute a wooden dildo for a male organ, since he could not get the desired contact. In the end he bought a dildo of a certain size, but the dimensions were so big that it hurt him. He then chose another one of medium size. Here is how he proceeded with its introduction (we are copying exactly the passage from his memoirs that relates to the different phases of this strange maneuver):

In the course of December 1893 I bought a dildo and tried to introduce it into my anus with vaseline ointment. Since I didn't have the courage to become involved with a man, I told myself that it was necessary for me to experience at least the sensation of this act, which I thought of constantly and which I didn't know yet. With my knees bent, dressed in a pair of pink silk underpants, which I had purchased long before, I placed the dildo covered with vaseline before my anus. I took care to put a small piece of old linen underneath so as not to soil my underpants. Then, all the while holding the dildo with my left hand, I pushed it up in order to catch it with my anus. With my right hand I held my underpants. At that moment I had a semierection. Once the dildo entered my anus, the preparatory work was finished; the real pleasure was about to begin for me. Masturbating myself with my right hand, I made every effort to push the dildo out. When I came, I pushed it back in with my left hand, and this I did six, eight, ten, or twelve times. I achieved a slight increase in pleasure when I managed to introduce the dildo with one thrust without using much effort. After trying to prevent ejaculation as long as possible, I made up my mind to do it quickly, after having taken out the dildo one last time and holding it tightly between my buttocks.

I've just described the facts. Now here are my sensations during the act. They're extremely complex and were much less clear than those during my masturbatory experiences in the preceding years. However, I always achieved a double pleasure. On the one hand, these entrances and exits of the dildo in my anus gave me the sensation of a male organ doing the same work of entering and exiting, and this male organ I connected in my imagination with the body and face of young men between twenty and twenty-five years of age whom I had encountered in the last few months and who had the greatest charm for me because of their figure, their costume, their male appearance, and their polished boots. Their images appeared to me successively four, five, or six times, but I was careful to hold in reserve one of the most seductive ones for my final push at the moment of ejaculation. And on the other hand, I imagined that these young men with their polished boots had pederastic relations with me and masturbated me at the same time.

In the course of the last few years, I've been haunted by two ideas: (1) to find a young man of eighteen to nineteen years of age who would want to associate his life with mine, both erotically and intellectually, and with whom I'd exchange masturbatory experiences without pederasty; (2) to find a man between twenty and twenty-five who would want to make me experience what passive pederasty is all about. But in the end the first idea of this friend, who in my mind would take care of almost all my erotic dreams, faded into the background and diminished in importance in favor of the second idea. Always looking for beauty of face and elegance of clothing, in my imagination I no longer evoked the gracefulness of the ephebe but the virility of the adult male.

These strange proceedings did not suffice for X———. In search of new discoveries to stimulate his perverted sensuality, he began to write on the wall of public urinals, especially in the last two on the avenue de Vincennes. With absolute regularity—the stereotypical inscription was always the same—the phrase began invariably as: "I lend my ass to handsome men with polished boots" and terminated with disgusting promises. In writing those phrases, which were the same every time, X——— always got an erection, his eyes gazing at his own polished boots.

We have already noted the fetishistic cult that Louis X——— professed for polished boots, but it is necessary to describe the evidence of this obsession more completely. Since the age of sixteen or seventeen X——— enjoyed looking at young men, but especially those with polished boots. In the street, instead of looking at the face, he began to cast his eyes at the feet. "The triple combination of shiny shoes, an elegant outfit, and an agreeable face on a young man ravished me," he wrote, "and provoked an erection." On the public thoroughfares he took pleasure in looking at the brilliant boots of soldiers.

He felt the most intense sensual satisfaction in contemplating the polished boots displayed in the shoemakers' shops and would station himself there for hours. For several years he went out of his way to see the shoes displayed in shop windows on the boulevards. It was with difficulty that he tore himself away from this contemplation—the source of a genuine sensual intoxication for him. The more brilliant they were, the more subjugated he was, and at home he dreamed that he had stolen them.

However, it was not until the end of 1893 that this attraction reached the height of intensity. X—— announces it with a certain solemnity in his autobiography. He passionately wanted to buy polished boots, but different considerations always stopped him. His obsession led him toward the military school, where he had frequent occasions to contemplate polished boots. He watched for the officers who were passing by, and then he followed in their footsteps for several moments, his gaze fixed on their boots. Finally, powerless to satisfy his love for polished boots in this fashion, he decided to buy them. This decision gave him a thrill, like that of possessing a lover:

"I brought them back to my place," he wrote,

with enormous agitation. My heart was beating violently. I shut myself up in my room in order to enjoy my new acquisitions at my leisure. I put them underneath my pink silk underwear. My sexual excitement was at its height. "At last I have them!" I repeated to myself. In the evening, as I lay down to sleep, I placed the boots on my night stand, well exposed to the light of my lamp. I could not stop looking at them, and my sexual enthusiasm kept me constantly erect. The following morning I contemplated them again for a long time before deciding to go out. Since that moment I've taken my boots every day out of the carton where they've been placed, and I've looked at them for a very long time.

One must say that X—— took attentive and jealous care of his shoes. One day the maid, while making up his room, misplaced them. He was extremely distressed, and from that moment on he made sure to place them in a cupboard, to which he kept the key. Each day it was a pleasure for him to take them out of this cupboard to clean them. He wiped them with infinite care, neglecting nothing in order to make them even more brilliant. Afterward he displayed them in the sunlight of the window in order to enjoy their full radiance. He admired them; he was fascinated by the sight of them; they brought him to orgasmic spasms.

X——, who had until then hesitated to go out with his boots, resolved—with such emotion!—to walk in the Bois de Vincennes with his shiny boots. "I went out, dressed in a riding outfit," he recounts in his notes,

> with my polished boots. Surely, I told myself, I'd be noticed in this outfit, desired either by the adult man or the young man whom I had been dreaming about for such a long time. And just so, that day nothing, absolutely nothing, happened. I returned home extremely agitated; I couldn't even eat. However, in the streets a lot of people turned around to look at my boots. But since these people were not at all those whom I desired, this gave me no pleasure at all.
>
> Nevertheless, I must confess that when I got home, I noticed that, despite the precautions I took while walking, one of my boots had a slight crack across the toe. This saddened me, like the sight of the first wrinkle on the face of a beloved friend. Henceforth I kept them at my place.

The sight of polished boots did not only produce erections in X——, but sexual orgasms as well. Their odor, to a lesser degree, awakened a similar excitement. He sniffed them; their perfume was extremely pleasing to him. Their touch also had a great attraction for him and gave him exquisite sensations. In the morning in his bed he pressed them against his thighs, all the while trying to moderate his ardor, as if he was afraid of harming them.

Of his relations with his polished boots X—— drew the following portrait, whose obscenity, as revolting as it may be in itself, must not cause us to forget, however, that we find here evidence of a pathological obsession:

I put on my pink silk underwear and my boots; I climb up on two chairs, my legs apart; and I open gently the door of my armoire with its mirror in order to see myself from behind, thanks to the reflection of the mirror on the mantelpiece. In masturbating myself, I keep my eyes firmly fixed on my buttocks, my thighs, and above all on my boots. At that moment I'd like to be able to make love to myself, to abandon myself to touching my whole body, whose image I could see in the mirror. The sight of my boots causes me to overstimulate myself so much that I could dispense more often than not with introducing the dildo in my anus. My goal was to project my semen into one of the openings of my boots, and when I succeeded in that, it was the height of pleasure. On other occasions, at the point of ejaculation, I slapped my buttocks, my thighs, and my anus with one of my boots, all the while keeping my gaze on the other boot in the light that was reflected in the mirror. But nearly always I placed each of them on a chair near the window, inclined in such a way that they'd shine the most, and at a certain distance so that I could try, as I put it, to reach them with my semen. This operation, because of the excessive pleasure that it gave me, induced a sensation of triumph and victory in me when the seminal liquid splashed against my boots.

Last June X—— finally believed that he would reach his desired goal of engaging in passive pederasty. He met a young bicyclist who pleased him in the Bois de Vincennes. Misinterpreting the look of this stranger, he imagined that he was making advances toward him. His desires were so inflamed, his heart beat with such force, his emotions were so intense that he thought that he saw the young man cast his eyes on his polished boots. Without a doubt he desired him as much as he himself wished for his caresses. In a paroxysm of excitement, he displayed his genital organ, but his disappointment was great when he saw the young man turn away from him with indifference. The only result of X——'s demonstration was to provoke the indignation of a roadworker, who had him arrested.

It is indisputable that the conduct of the accused is evidence against him and gives him, at least at first, the appearance of a vicious person tormented by his shameful appetites. Must he thus be considered a vulgar sodomite little deserving of pity and, as such, subject to legal prosecution?[6] That is not our opinion, because a doctor's duty is to analyze what is really underneath such appearances.

Once he achieves a certain age, a man feels awakening in himself instincts that push him toward having a relationship with a woman and toward the search for pleasures in the intimate union of the sexes, which results in the perpetuation of the species. Instead of these heterosexual relations, X——, a true born invert, has been tempted since his childhood by relations against nature only in the exclusive form of passive pederasty—active pederasty having absolutely no attraction for him. Furthermore, he is haunted by an ideal type; without this ideal man his homosexual appetites are not aroused; his entire morbid being yearns for him; and he ceaselessly searches for him, without ever encountering him. If he believes at times to have found him, he is quickly disabused, and especially during the last few years his existence has been nothing but a long series of disappointing illusions. Only his polished boots have not let him down; they have always induced the sexual excitement that the sight of and contact with a woman has not succeeded in stimulating in him.

We are bound to say that X——'s onanism is not the usual kind of onanism. The ordinary masturbator attains a voluptuous paroxysm by physical processes to which he frequently joins a psychic excitement made up of the erotic mental representations that pro-voke an orgasm. Nevertheless, when the excitement of the sexual sense is not possible except through the intervention of an object (e.g., a white apron, a handkerchief, a nightcap, shoe tacks, pig-tails, or polished boots), the situation is simply a clear type of mor-bid obsession that can only manifest itself in a degenerate, in a sick person who is affected by a full psycho-physiological deviation, culminating in this case as inversion of the sexual instinct. Louis X——, from the hereditary point of view, offers in his strange moral individuality anomalies that we only encounter in diseased patients marked with degeneration. And what is even more pecu-liar is that this concept, in which pederasty, onanism, and literature constitute a trilogy, is one without which X—— cannot achieve complete satisfaction. Such a concept can only be born in a sick mind with multiple aberrations from which irresistible impulses flow.

6. "Before dying, I will read a few pages from *Dédé*." Antonio. Source: Achille Essebac, *Dédé* (Paris: Ambert, 1901).

Letter to My Parents and *My Autobiography* by Antonio

In Dr. André Antheaume and Dr. Léon Parrot's
A Case of Sexual Inversion (1905)

The patient who is the subject of this article has been confined to the clinic of one of the authors after a suicide attempt that occurred under rather special circumstances. He is an adolescent, eighteen years old, whose family had recently sent him to Germany to study with a teacher. He had not revealed any obvious mental disturbance until one day at the beginning of last February when he fired a shot into in his right temple in plain view on Bonn's public promenade. Luckily the bullet went through his temple and produced only entrance and exit wounds that were not serious. Nevertheless, a great public outcry was heard, and the wounded man was taken to the hospital. Then, a few days later, his father arrived, having just received the letter cited below:

Written at E——— on January 31, 1905

Dear Papa, dear Mama, dear Family,

By the time you receive this letter, I'll have already departed for that eternal sleep, or I'll not be far from it. In any case, it'll be too late to prevent me from dying.

I'm committing suicide!

Life is bearable, however painful, for certain individuals; the ambition or the desire to have a better situation at a later time, "hope," in other words, keeps most men alive. Other men, the greatest number of them, however miserably they live, cling to life because for them it's strewn with sexual delights that make them forget the sad moments.

I'm not ambitious. I don't love women.

I love . . . yes, I love . . . something reprehensible . . . something forbidden . . . something that society treats as immoral and infamous . . . I love young and beautiful boys . . . I'm a pederast . . . I desire them passionately . . . but my desire can't be realized without facing the threat of dishonor and degradation.

And nevertheless, I'm more pure in this love than all the young people that I know who are always running after girls . . . those girls whom I abhor.

Today I'm eighteen years old. Judging the future by the past, I envision the future as *good* if I love women or as *ignoble* if I love boys . . . I don't want to belong to women . . . Therefore . . . I must die!

At this moment of supreme anguish I wish to make my confession to this world—the cause of my death.

When I was nine, a priest loved me. When I was fourteen, a young man of eighteen adored me. At fifteen, I loved with a hidden love a child of eleven whom I had seen in the street and who fulfilled my dream.

This child, I learned later, was named Hector. The love that I had for Hector couldn't be satisfied because of this contemptible human morality. I decided to destroy myself morally by entering a monastery. That's the reason why I didn't take my examinations and why I didn't hesitate to come to France. In France all the young boys whom I saw, if they were handsome, were for me the subjects of new desires. Therefore, I left for Switzerland in order to enter the teaching order of the Dominicans, without realizing that I was throwing myself into the lion's mouth by wanting to teach the beings whom humanity has forbidden me to love.

You sent me to Germany, and I saw . . . yes, I saw . . . in the midst of the grief of my exile . . . that my ideal couldn't be realized in Germany any more than in any other place.

I am, therefore, making the decision to kill myself. Forgive me! Forgive me a thousand times for the pain my death will cause you. I approach this decision deliberately, and I contemplate it with a smile on my lips. I've never done harm to anyone. I've sinned only solitarily in thinking about "them." I die a virgin in regard to the women whom I detest, and I also die a virgin in regard to the boys whom I adore! My flesh is pure. My hair will not have been touched by any hand, neither by those whom I detest nor by those little hands of the children whom I love.

I'll be leaving for Cologne or Bonn. I've bought a little revolver as childlike as my soul. I'll fire one of its pretty little bullets, and I'll die happy in thinking about my ideal, whom God will lay to rest, if He is good, and whom He'll make slumber by my side forever.

If you wish to retrieve my body, it will be either at the cathedral in Cologne or in Bonn. Cologne and Bonn were the cities where Dédé lived—a character in a novel that was my only consolation in these last times. Dédé was another Hector.[1]

Before dying, I'll read a few pages about Dédé. Then, with my ideal in my mind's eye, with the name of Hector on my lips, I will die . . .

Farewell, my dear parents. Thank you . . . thank you for having cared for me . . . Mama, I love you. I love you all.

Your son,
Antonio

P.S. My final wish is to be interred next to Maurice and buried in a child's grave.

P.S. It is done. I'm going to this death, the end of all torments. I hope to find in eternal sleep the divine dreams that will accompany it.

God is good . . . He will forgive me.

Please leave on my little finger, which is still very childlike, the ring that my mother gave me . . .

I believe that I'm mad! But no! I'm reasoning this out very coldly. I desire pretty little boys, whom the false human morality prevents me from loving purely. With my suicide I hope to realize my dream. I'll find Plato, Anacreon, and all the Greeks who were pederasts,[2] just like me, with their respective lovers in the next world.

> Farewell to all.
> Pray for me.
> Antonio

We should note that this suicide attempt, which was preceded by sending the above letter, had been undertaken in a rather theatrical context. Antonio had taken a bath, sprinkled himself with perfume, and then held a bouquet and the "uranian" novel *Dédé* in his left hand.[3] Inside the book were two fairly mediocre sonnets that he had written and dedicated to the young man Hector, who was the object of his love.

After these incidents, the patient's father had him committed to the National Asylum at Charenton. One of the authors noticed immediately the despair and stunned surprise of the father, who considered his son an insane person because of the suicide attempt and a dissolute individual because of his sexual obsessions, which had just been revealed to him for the first time in the letter that we have reproduced here.

In the past, people close to him, especially his grandmother, had noticed that during his childhood the young man preferred the company of girls and girls' games to the exclusion of boys' games. During his adolescence people were struck by his concern with his appearance and clothing, by a certain effeminacy, and by an excessive shyness around young women, which was exactly the opposite of his behavior in earlier years. However, his family did not suspect any kind of serious deviation in the development of his genital instinct.

When he was committed to the asylum, Antonio protested against this measure, arguing that he had been of sound mind when he attempted suicide. This eighteen-year-old adolescent is tall (five feet six inches) and gives the impression of a young man who is very concerned with his personal appearance. His outward appearance reveals a certain effeminacy and an eagerness to please. His brown hair is long and curly; his face, with a normal development of facial hair, is carefully shaved; and his gait and mannerisms are more feminine than masculine.

A number of congenital physical malformations are present: facial asymmetry, badly spaced teeth, abnormal position of wisdom teeth, steeply arched palate, misshapen and unsymmetrical ears. However, there is nothing anomalous about the genitals, and the hair, which has developed normally on his face, is equally well distributed on the legs and in the pubic area. An examination of his reflexes revealed nothing unusual, and neural sensitivity is present in all the usual sites, except for a slight hypersensitivity at the scrotum and the perineum. No defects exist in his visual abilities, nor in his ability to distinguish colors, smells, or flavors.

When he was questioned about his uranism, Antonio was reticent and revealed an almost feminine prudery. Nevertheless, after a few days he chose to make a complete confession and gave us a notebook filled with sketches related to his homosexual tendency and an interesting autobiography. One can discern much from these documents about the unhealthy nature of the sexual obsessions that plagued him for several years. Below are the most representative sections of his autobiography:

AGE SIX

At age six I was really a girl as much in the physical sense as in the moral sense. What was this due to? Was it due to the fact that up until then I lived with my mother and my maids? Was it due to the fact that I had little girls as playmates, whose mothers came to visit my mother? I don't know. What I remember very well is that, if I had to choose between a boy and a girl, I'd prefer to play with a girl, and it often happened that I'd dress up as a girl and play either "tea party" or "visit" and all of those games that were peculiar to girls.

At an even younger age, at the age of four, it seems that I had a foolish passion for dolls.

AGES SEVEN TO EIGHT

Soon my life changed. I had to learn to read and write. At first my parents enrolled me in a little school where there were boys between five and ten years old. I swear that I suffered greatly because of them. They called me 'girl,' and they made me feel ashamed because I had feminine habits.

AGES NINE TO TEN

For family reasons, and for my education as well, I was sent out to board with priests at a Catholic school. Right away I gained the respect of all my teachers, and I withdrew even further from the rest of the students at school. In vain, during recess, certain little boys invited me to play at their games—I always refused. I preferred to be with my teachers, to spend time with them, to let myself be caressed by them, and so on.

AGES ELEVEN TO TWELVE

Nevertheless, my face and my body, to my great disappointment, were always the object of ridicule for the other boys:

"Hey, girl!" "You've got the face of a girl!" "Someone made a mistake! Someone put you in pants instead of a dress!" What could I do in the face of such taunts!

AGE THIRTEEN

It was at this time that I made a trip to France. The exercise, the change in scenery, the sojourns that we made in foreign lands, all contributed to emboldening me a bit and to developing me physically.

I had lost almost all the physical characteristics of a girl; my features were becoming more masculine; my body was no longer feminine; later the down that comes with puberty came to cast a shadow over my upper lip . . . Something very curious happened to me, whose origins I couldn't explain. I wanted to love someone, it seemed to me, but above all I wanted to be loved. And upon my return from my travels, when I was ready to return to boarding school, my only problem was the difficulty of choice. The older boys (and I remember that there were plenty of handsome ones) pleased me more than the younger ones. One of them in particular, a big, strong boy of seventeen, fell in love with me (or at least he seemed to), and I must have encouraged him, because I loved him even more. What happiness I felt in my whole being when we were seated next to each other on the same bench. He always told me, when he saw the hateful (or maybe jealous) looks that the others directed at me: 'Don't be afraid! I'm here to defend you!' With great care I kept the little notes that he passed to me underneath the benches when a suspicious teacher used to separate us in class. Unfortunately, there was another boy my age who was certainly more beautiful than I and whom my older friend made some significant advances to. Ah! But when I saw this, I made certain that I left him in the evening without even shaking his hand. This poor boy was expelled from school, for what reason I don't know, and I never saw him again.

It was then that a friend taught me how to excite myself under the pretext that it was useful in the development of my virility. My first solitary excitements occurred while thinking about the 'older' ones. I imagined that I was in their arms and that they were kissing me. The memory of my 'seventeen-year-old lover' (if I can use that term, although I can't think of any other) came back to me time and time again.

Other young men, even gentlemen of my acquaintance, appeared to me in my nightly dreams. This is not surprising, it seems to me, since at puberty many young boys, especially precocious ones, have completely feminine passions for their teachers and their friends. But I was not precocious, since only at the age of fourteen, for the first time and to my great surprise, did I see coming out of me the seminal liquid of males.

AGE FOURTEEN TO FIFTEEN

I then had several friends, among them a young boy who was rather vicious. He often made unsavory propositions to me, which I rejected, not from disgust but for so-called morality's sake.

AGE SIXTEEN

Toward the end of my fifteenth year and at the beginning of my sixteenth I was taken by a foolish passion for a young boy of eleven or twelve. He was fine, sweet, tender, and gracious. I loved him passionately throughout the year but without letting him know it. I looked for him during his walks in the streets, and I followed him as long as possible. At the sight of him I turned pale, my legs weakened, my throat tightened up, and it was impossible for me to say a word. Just to see him was enough. I loved him as much as a mother loves her child. I wanted to caress him, to take care of him, to press him to my heart. And sometimes this completely pure maternal instinct was mixed with carnal desire. Sometimes, alone in my room, I felt carried away by unreal dreams. It seemed as if I saw him naked, as if I felt him brush against my skin; I gazed at him as one contemplates a painting. But soon I was seized by an intense passion; desire assailed me, and I got excited just by thinking of him. He—he alone!—occupied my brain during almost an entire year, but he was not the first one whom I had so desired. Several young boys had already attracted my attention, but the memory of them never lasted more than a week. He—he alone!—was the first one whom I truly loved.

My role vis-à-vis this object of my passion was thus dramatically opposed to the one that I had before puberty. At that time I loved like a woman. I wanted to be loved, to be enveloped by the love and the protection of the "older" one. I'd have consented to anything that he wanted. I'd have been the woman in the relationship—passive in coitus. After puberty, on the other hand, my desires were for children younger and weaker than myself. In my love for them there was also a desire for protection, but this time exercised by me, and I'd have been the man in the sexual relationship.

AGE SEVENTEEN

By chance, when I read *The Inferno* by Dante, an unfamiliar word aroused my curiosity; this word was "sodomite." I conducted some research, in the course of which I discovered the word "pederast." I was happy to have found a word that applied to my case. It was then that I began to read a series of ancient and modern works dealing with the same subject. I was glad to see that I was not a monstrous exception. If these readings encouraged me to persist in my love of boys with the glorious examples that they furnished me, they didn't create that tendency, which clearly existed in me from a much earlier time. I had an absolutely natural curiosity to know everything that related to my case and to read the stories of others who were inverts like myself.

The company of little girls and young ladies no longer attracted me at all, and never were my senses aroused by the sight of a beautiful woman. I treated them as friends, but they disgusted me whenever I thought about sexual relations with them. The conversation of my friends bored and shocked me when they spoke about their gallant adventures with women, about their hopes, and so on. I always slipped away quickly.

I've always had a repugnance for vigorous exercise and sports. I prefer quiet pleasures, daydreams, drawings, and paintings. I have several albums filled with drawings that I made of beautiful little boys. I love music and the arts very much, and among paintings and statues I prefer those that depict handsome men to those that depict beautiful women. I also love literature, and I've recently begun to write a novel about a uranist. After all, I don't see any dishonor in being an invert. Several illustrious men whose works I admire have been inverts. I protest against the miserable human morality that condemns the practices of homosexual love in our time. It hasn't always been condemned, since it was certainly accepted by the Greeks and the Romans.

Those are the sections we have chosen to present from this autobiography; it ends with the theme of justification, which is a typical subject with uranists. Here are some additional pieces of information that we have gathered regarding the hereditary and personal influences of the patient:

Progenitors: His father is forty-five and his mother is forty-two. Both are in good health and do not reveal any abnormalities. His grandfather, on the father's side, died of diabetes at the age of seventy-seven; on the mother's side, the grandmother died of complications from rheumatic heart disease at sixty-four. A great-uncle suffered from kidney stones, and an aunt has chronic rheumatism. No epileptics nor anyone else prone to seizures exists in the family.

Personal history: He was born of a full-term pregnancy, but the birth was difficult, and forceps had to be used. During childhood he suffered from whooping cough, measles, and scarlet fever. At the age of ten he had jaundice, which caused great concern, and at eleven he had swollen glands without inflammation of the testicles.

Cases like this one are not unusual in nonmedical literature, but since the number of inverts that enter mental asylums is limited, it is rare for a psychiatric doctor to see inversion in an eighteen-year-old and under such authentic circumstances that the reliability of the diagnosis can be confirmed.

In a study he published in 1898, entitled *Sex Crimes and Sexual Perversions*, Thoinot, who was guided by the work of Westphal—which was disseminated in France by Ritti, beginning in 1878—and further inspired by the work of Magnan, Garnier, Krafft-Ebing, Moll, Chevalier, Raffalovich, Laupts, and so on, correctly finds that sexual inversion, or uranism (Ulrichs's term), has the following pathological characteristics:

1. the anomaly is manifest from the first stirrings of the sexual instinct, in other words, showing the congenital characteristics of inversion;
2. sexual attraction toward persons of the same sex (homosexual attraction) with a varying, yet always distinct, repulsion toward the other sex;
3. normal anatomy and normal functioning of the genitals during inverted sexual acts;
4. full awareness of the abnormal condition, which nevertheless remains out of the control of the patient's will like an obsession or a compulsion;
5. the presence of a number of degenerative symptoms, variable in quantity and severity.

If we examine the clinical records that we have presented here, we find the fundamental characteristics of sexual inversion, or uranism, but with a few particularities that should be highlighted.

The first point to bring up is the ease with which the patient was able to hide this pathological condition from his family, who were concerned and worried about his health and searching for a solution to this enigma. He had done this for four years, ever since his abnormal sexual instinct had awakened and he had become aware of his anomaly. An extraordinary circumstance, like the farewell letter that he sent on the eve of his suicide attempt, was necessary to reveal his condition.

Another peculiarity is related to Antonio's uranian emotional love. Since puberty—in other words, since his sexual instinct was awakened abnormally (homosexual tendency)—this adolescent has reacted emotionally following the pattern of "the caricature of normal love," as Krafft-Ebing called it, but he has not satisfied his passion physically with the object of his inverted love. Since we are talking about a disturbed person suffering from hyperesthesia, his emotional love has been violent; the patient loved with an impassioned intensity and exuberance that is perhaps so strong that no physical satisfaction could have been achieved.

Like others of his kind, Antonio has had "erotically inverted" dreams many times, but a curious fact is that his dreams concern either children or adolescents. This is interesting because love directed at children is rare among uranists, even when the uranist is an adolescent. In general Krafft-Ebing's dictum is correct: "A person who desires a child, a little boy, is a libertine, a vice-ridden invert, and not a uranist." Here, however, is the exception to the rule.

Another exception to the rule is that before puberty Antonio primarily loved people older than himself and submitted to their caresses passively, but after puberty his homosexual desire was aroused only by adolescents and children to the exclusion of adults. This exception, to which Antonio did not attach much importance, merits our attention because it reveals that in his dreams and day-dreams this invert does not want to be passive, to be possessed by his inverted love object; on the contrary, he wants to be active and to possess his beloved, as if the beloved were a woman with whom he could have intercrural coitus. This tendency is so rare among sexual inverts that certain writers believe that it is a symptom that can be used in forensic medicine to distinguish inversion caused by vice from the morbid inversion of hereditary degenerates.

Finally, one last observation is related to the clear consciousness that the patient has of his pathological condition and the intensity of his sexual obsession. A sexual psychopathology of extreme intensity imposes itself on his consciousness, changing his outward appearance, his tastes, and his personality, and allowing the idea of suicide to take hold and to grow stronger until the act is accomplished.

What is the etiology of this inversion?

If we examine Antonio's heredity, it tells us nothing; only arthritis can be blamed, and we all know how imprecise that can be. Looking at his personal history, we find nothing that explains the anomaly in the development of his sexual instincts, so here we are really in the realm of hypothesis. In *Psychopathia sexualis*, Krafft-Ebing discusses the origin of uranism in this way: "The cause here can only be found in an abnormality of core internal conditions, in an abnormal psychosexual tendency. This tendency is related to anatomical and organic causes that are still unknown. As in almost all of those cases the invert has various neuropathic defects, and these defects can be correlated with hereditary degenerate conditions. From a clinical perspective we can consider this aberration of psychosexual feelings to be a symptom of organic degeneration. This perverse sexuality occurs spontaneously and without any external motivation at any time in the development of a person's sexual life; it is an individual manifestation of an abnormal degeneration of the *vita sexualis*, and thus we recognize it as a congenital condition."

This is the case with the patient under review. Apart from the fact that the hereditary cause is unclear, it seems that most of the evidence supports the hypothesis of an organic degeneration, since this patient suffers from both a functional anomaly and a number of congenital physical malformations.

7. Photographic portraits of Charles Double. Source: MS 5366, Fonds Lacassagne. Courtesy: Bibliothèque municipale de Lyon.

Mental Hermaphrodite and Other Autobiographical Writings

By Charles Double (1905)

THE CHARACTERISTIC MENTAL AND PSYCHOLOGICAL
STATE OF A PARRICIDE INVERT

The investigating magistrate, Monsieur Ihler, told me during the interrogations I underwent in his office that my feelings and psychology could never be examined carefully enough. He had understood that the heart of someone as special as I am, like that of certain women, was so deep, so complex, and that it contained nuances and fluctuations of feelings, desires, and tendencies that were so varied and so changeable that sustained and undivided attention and observation of the smallest details were indispensable to make a precise and correct analysis of it. If you want to examine and understand my crime accurately, you must acknowledge first that two completely distinct and different selves coexisted in me: one that was instinctive and natural and another that was rational and religious. These two beings lived side by side, always at war with each other. My religious self watched and studied my instinctive self exactly the way a doctor would examine and watch over a patient that he wanted to cure of a disease and its painful crises. My instinctive self is very bad, but not all bad; it has also some good in it. Absolute evil doesn't exist here on earth. As I've said, my instinctive self had this distinction: it is deeply and essentially feminine; I've all the flaws and all the qualities of feminine hearts. Not only do I replicate them, but I exaggerate and accentuate them naturally: in shrewdness, duplicity, pride, vanity, jealousy, love of luxury, resentment, malice, stubbornness, and tenderness toward males; in the need to love and be loved; in anger, arrogance, disdain, and impressionability; in the highly developed and morbid sensitivity; in all that (and I'm forgetting some) I surpass many women, and I'm more of a woman than they are. I have intuition, intelligence, subtlety, expensive and refined tastes to a far greater degree than my mother, which even made her envy me.

As for my rational and religious self, it's neither an abstraction nor a fantasy. It has a very distinct vitality and expression. It's locked in perpetual combat with my *instinctive* self, but unfortunately it's often vanquished. Nevertheless, I'm not a brute or a thoughtless creature. Even though I'm a parricide and a criminal, I've a very clear and precise notion of good and evil. I've a finely tuned moral sense and a conscience that allows me, when the opportunity arises, to concede points even to those whom my accidental and unfortunate lapses have elevated over me as judges and masters.

Having put it that way, I can therefore say that I've a dual personality, and you must keep that in mind if you're going to judge me fairly without illusions or preconceptions. One of the greatest torments of my life has been to recognize how few people can really understand the painful mystery of sexual inversion and of mental hermaphrodism. I read a book, whose author's name I don't recall, that states that the most respected doctors in Paris don't agree about this very odd subject. Some believe that inverts are mentally ill; others don't see it that way. Some say, "This is a mentally unbalanced man." I believe that this term is absolutely incorrect; those who use it have certainly not understood the degree of femininity in the psyche of an invert; they haven't dug deep enough to realize that the appearance of an invert's masculinity is just a misleading mask, like a false façade, like a mocking jest, like an insulting challenge that covers up the very distinct feminine reality of his psychic makeup. To me the term *femme monstre*[1] seems closer to the truth, but I think Casper found exactly the right word when he so aptly coined the expression "mental hermaphrodite."

From the moment of his birth an invert is a freak of nature, a reject, a marginalized being unlike anyone else, an object of study and surprise for science. Society doesn't accept such creatures; it rejects them, condemns them without even examining them. Those who say that I can do women's work are arguing falsely and unjustly; a real woman would find a place in society, but in order to find a place in accordance with his nature an invert needs tolerance, pity, and protection that society generally doesn't extend to him. When I was younger, I could survive. I took menial jobs that suited my special mentality. I earned fifty, seventy, or eighty francs a month, and I lived on that at home with my mother. At Belley, at Croix de l'Ain, I earned a hundred francs, but in fact the work I was doing wasn't worth more than fifty. I owe the rest to the generosity of my employer, who rewarded me for the outward probity of my behavior.

When I was thirty years old, everyone told me: "Now that you're a man, you have to make it on your own. All your friends who are the same age as you have good jobs." And they gave me jobs that demanded the full complement of a man's mental abilities. My poor woman's brain got dizzy and dazzled. I swear in good conscience that I made superhuman efforts to find a reasonable source of income, but I couldn't find any, because society doesn't accept inverts. If, when they're infants, we don't feed them to the pigs, as is done in China, it's only because we know we've other ways, more polite and less brutal, to get rid of them.

I was born with my soul filled with terror. With the foresight and intuition that is peculiar to frail creatures, I had a secret premonition that my life would be marked by a great disaster. I felt that my sensual, impetuous, and proud soul needed to be broken and humiliated. I foresaw that in order to remain true to myself at a key moment in my life, I'd have to commit a terrible deed and to undergo cruel sacrifices, and if I didn't have the courage to meet this challenge, I'd sink to the lowest depths of depravity.

Beings like me don't understand compromise or half measures

or the golden mean. To be an angel or a devil, to slither through the stinking furrows of illicit and shameful pleasures, to leap into the air and float aloft in the pure and luminous ether of the highest altitudes, that's the fate of poor, infirm people like me. When I was very young, it was predicted that I'd never be ordinary. Alas! I distinguished myself through evil. I was told that I'd be either a scoundrel or a saint. Alas! On the night of April 4, 1903, I discovered that the route to sainthood is too narrow, too difficult to traverse, and I became the worst of scoundrel. To achieve my hopeless dreams of pleasure, love, and glory, to escape suffering, poverty, and humiliation, to avoid a joyless and humble life I silenced my inborn decency and rationality. I rejected the voice of my conscience and my personal honor that protested: "You're a monster." I suppressed the instinctive and intense feeling of horror that the thought of a crime inspired in me because of my feminine weakness. I overcame the last barriers of decency and of nature. I armed myself with an awful courage against myself, and I sought in the deepest recesses of my corrupt and deviate being the inhuman, demonic strength to commit the most atrocious and repugnant crime!

People have said, and no doubt will keep saying for a long time, that I was an example of a great criminal. In this case, the word "criminal" is incorrect. It would be more accurate to say that I was an example of a great malefactor. The word "criminal" suggests an innate or unhealthy propensity for crime, a particular way of thinking that wants and accepts crime. It seems to imply the absence of any horror or revulsion regarding the commission of a crime. There's nothing like that in me. From the time I was twenty-eight years old I realized that crime might help me escape from poverty and prevent the complete destruction of my beautiful dreams, but even while considering that possibility, my sensibility, that of an imaginative, delicate, and nervous woman, shuddered at the mere thought of such an act. I told myself that someone with a weak and nervous constitution like mine was not capable of such a savage and atrocious deed, and I flattered myself into believing that I could find other, less violent ways to prevent my being cheated out of my inheritance. It was with a shaky arm, a trembling hand, an anguished heart, shuddering with horror at the thought of the pain I was inflicting on her, that I decided to shoot my mother after several minutes of internal debate and awful moral anguish.

On the night of April 4, 1903, the two different selves that made up my personality, as described at the beginning of this chapter, each spoke to me in turn. "Charles," my natural and instinctive self said, "if you keep on being weak and indecisive, if you don't want to finish this, if you don't do away with your mother, you'll have nothing but poverty and suffering for the rest of your life. Now that you're an adult, you can't support yourself in society. Your mother might live for another twenty years. Sickness and old age will gobble up her life savings, and she won't leave you anything. There's no more hope of happiness for you. Say good-bye to joy. Don't think about that intoxicating thrill that suffuses your soul when the virile glance of an adored lover meets your gaze. Forget about the fine luxuries that you want to surround yourself with and about those wonderful trips to Greece and Italy. All of this is no more than a fruitless dream. You've been daydreaming too long. Go ahead and wake up in prison with the other pathetic beggars. Or go on the road with a troupe of vagabonds, suffering from hunger, thirst, cold, and fevers. Some day God in his heaven will reward you for your suffering."

"Charles," my rational and religious self said, "look at your sick, weak, aged mother, bent under the weight of her years. You've extinguished the last traces of tender feelings she had for you in her heart. She doesn't want to do anything more for you. Don't disturb the old age of this poor widow. Let her rest quietly, peacefully, in her modest home. You don't deserve a place there. Go away, you rootless vagabond. You'll suffer on the open road, but your mother will be at peace, and God can only bless a son who's able to suffer a little to give his mother some peace in her final years. Would you dare to threaten the life of the person who carried you in her womb, the one who unsparingly gave you the precious gifts of sweetness and kindness that are only found in a mother's heart, just to spare yourself the pain of hunger, poverty, humiliation, and loneliness?"

This was the battle that was waged in my soul on the evening of April 4, 1903. Oh! How dark, terrifying, and cruel was that struggle between good and evil. I felt as if I had arrived at the grimmest moment of my life, of which those vague forebodings had given me glimpses when I was a teenager. I knew I had a choice between hurling myself upward toward the pinnacle of sacrifice, suffering, and abnegation or falling shamefully back down into the depths of unspeakable criminal egoism. I experienced two or three minutes of awful hesitation. All the feelings I've just described were swirling chaotically in my brain. In vain I told myself that my mother had been too strict with me, that I didn't deserve to be excluded by society and my family for the rest of my life, that the life of sacrifice that people expected of me was beyond my moral resources. I was still unable to decide once and for all to shoot my poor mother. Such a crime made me feel an overwhelming horror that I couldn't overcome. (This horror and this persistent reluctance to commit the crime should exclude any idea of an innate morbid motivation.) Hesitantly, in terrible distress, I saw the ghastly and skeletal ghost of Misery trying to drag me into her hideous kingdom. I pictured in my mind's eye my mother leading a calm and independent life while I, her son, a pauper, struggled from one prison to another. Jealousy and spite gnawed at my heart, but they still weren't strong enough to overcome the conscious repugnance I had against committing such a crime. I'd much rather be the con man than the mark, I thought inwardly. And finally, almost haltingly, I shot my mother, believing I had killed her outright.

She toppled over, sitting down on the landing of the stairs on the first floor, dropping the lamp she was holding in her left hand and letting out a faint cry. I thought that my revolver had a bullet in the chamber, but it had only a blank. I didn't know that for sure until the police investigation. So my mother hadn't been wounded at all; it was only the fright and the sound of the shot that knocked her off her feet. If at that time I had realized that my revolver was loaded only with blanks, I wouldn't have struck her, and if I had been sure she'd have kept quiet about that attempt on her life, I wouldn't have had the courage to continue.

After she fell, she began letting out such piercing screams that I thought the neighbors would come, mob me, and drag me brutally to prison. At that time I believed I had at least wounded her very seriously with my revolver, and hoping to stop her from screaming and to ensure my being left alone, I plunged three fingers of my left hand into her mouth. But I was so horrified at being reduced to such awful acts that I couldn't force myself to keep them there, because I was sure I was hurting her. My mother began to scream more persistently, and maddened by my fear that the neighbors or the police would come, I had to convince myself to put my fingers back in her mouth in spite of the instinctive horror and revulsion I felt at doing this. I had fired only one shot; two witnesses had heard the shot and had testified to it. So it's a mistake to say that I shot my mother six times.

I can't recall what my mother did with her arms and legs during those atrocious minutes, but I know she summoned up extraordinary energy and force from her torso. A painful, awful battle took place between us on the landing of the staircase, which was very narrow. During this fight my mother fell on her back onto the stairs, and she dragged me with her. As she slid on her back down the stairs, legs first, I slid kneeling next to her, fingers still in her mouth. The steps of the staircase scraped my knees. At the bottom of the stairs my mother sprawled out on the floor. I suffered awfully thinking about how I was making her suffer by keeping my fingers in her mouth, and I really wanted to find a way to end it quickly.

After firing my revolver once, I had thrown the weapon into

a room off the landing on the first floor. I thought it was loaded. Besides, it was so difficult to fire the first shot that I didn't even think of using it to finish my criminal deed. Anyway, it would have been useless, because the investigation proved that it only had blanks. To shorten this horrible suffering, I decided to hold her nostrils closed and to suffocate her to death. I didn't try to strangle her; her neck showed no traces of injury. Closing off her mouth and nose caused a pulmonary hemorrhage that resulted in her death.

It was this hemorrhage and a lesion in the lungs that led the autopsy report to state that the death might have been caused by a noncriminal act. Her body also had few traces of struggle or violence; there was one scrape on her left hand. By holding her nostrils closed, it appeared that I had pressed a bit hard on her face. The doctors, when discussing the slight marks that my fingers left on her face, said that they could have been the result of force. All in all their report was neither very persuasive nor conclusive regarding my culpability, and if I had known that before the investigation, it might have given me a chance to convince people that my mother had died as a result of the emotions she felt when she saw I was stealing her share of the bonds.

The doctors said that death occurred ten minutes after the airways were obstructed. A witness had heard my mother's screams without knowing exactly where they came from, and she claimed that the incident lasted half an hour. This witness, a young woman, surely must be mistaken. I told the assizes court that the incident lasted twenty minutes in order to avoid any dispute, but I really don't remember. It seems to me that I wouldn't be able to drag out such an awful torture for so long. The doctors are the only ones who were right when they estimated that the whole thing lasted ten minutes.

Here, exactly, are the feelings that disturbed my soul immediately after I committed the crime: an indescribable anguish, terror, and an unspeakable horror of myself because of the terrible crime that I committed with such a diabolical perversity and because of its seriousness, of which I was well aware. These feelings, like a veil of indistinct and incurable sadness, completely enveloped my soul. I used to tell myself as an excuse for my cowardice that my mother had led me and pushed me to commit this crime by her excessive strictness and stubbornness. The filial love that I believed I had extinguished in myself forever surged up in me against my will from the depths of my being at that solemn and mournful time. Nature, whom I had just provoked with the most outrageous challenge and with the most ironic and disrespectful disdain—flattering myself into believing that I could snuff out its powerful cry—awoke in me. Nervous tears burned my eyes, and I felt an immense emptiness inside me, a sadness that nothing could overcome. Standing before her dead body, I felt that my mother's soul floated above her earthly remains, and a mysterious and disturbing dialogue began between us. Her sepulchral voice said to me: "It was useless to kill me, to assassinate me, to try to hate me. I am, I was, and I will always be your mother. I carried you in my womb, and I surrounded you with tenderness. I've just left you, and you already miss me. It's useless for you to try to hate me. Love is often very close to hate. You didn't succeed in escaping from me by killing my body. I'll always be beside you. I'll soon be avenged by your regret and the emptiness that I'm going to leave in your life. You've snuffed out my life, but I'll live again, more beautiful and better loved, in your memory, in your fervent worship of my memory, in the delayed homage and pious tears that you'll shed for the woman who did what she could for you while she was alive."

And then in one of those unhappy reversals that are only too frequent in unbalanced characters like my own, from the depths of my being, came savage cries of egoism, the cries of an insolent, sardonic triumph, of a conceited and vindictive woman against a despised rival. This is the egoism and fierce savagery of a poor, humiliated, and rejected woman against a happy, financially well-off, and independent woman. I did feel all the emotions that I'm describing here. I'm not making them up or exaggerating anything. The human soul is changeable and mobile like the sea. My soul resembles a harp whose too taut strings vibrate in harmonious or unharmonious chords under the sway of positive or negative emotions.

I took with me thirty or thirty-two thousand francs' worth of bonds from my mother's house. I found only two hundred francs in cash, but that didn't prevent me from fleeing to Cairo, believing that I'd be safe there. I went back to Paris to cash in my bonds. I saw Courgibet there again, and I took him with me to Brittany to the seaside. This was during Holy Week of 1903. There, confronted by the majesty of the ocean, I was overcome again by the painful anguish, the searing sadness of that gaping emptiness that I had felt standing next to my mother's corpse. Oh! That poor dead woman was beginning to get her revenge. My nights were disturbed by the memory of the awful torment I had inflicted on her. I couldn't forgive myself for my cruelty. I wasn't able to stifle my feelings of unease and regret despite the pleasures with which I surrounded myself. I held back painful sobs in the midst of the distractions of Paris.

The lovely weather and charms of May helped to banish my sorrow. I feverishly enjoyed the greenery and the light of springtime. I fell madly in love with Courgibet, but his character flaws soon changed that to aversion. After having kept him because of love, I kept him because of charity, as expiation, and in the spirit of penitence, hoping that the good I did for him, the money I spent on him, would help me make retribution for my enormous misdeeds.

I've asked myself sometimes if my instincts of a woman in love, eager for pleasure and luxury, were strong enough in themselves to cause me to commit this crime. In all good conscience I think I can say no. I'd have told myself that the exquisite and rare pleasures that I desired were not worth committing a parricide. As delectable as they might be, at such a price it would be better to do without.

It's also clear that if I had found a way to support myself adequately and securely in Paris, I wouldn't have come to Belley to kill my mother, even if she had disinherited me. In that case I'd have hung her and murdered her in effigy a thousand times, but that would have been all.

Certain people who don't understand the changeability and mobility of my impulsive personality have asked me what state of mind I was in when I left Paris on April 4, 1903, to visit my mother. So here, exactly, are the different psychological states I experienced. At this point my foolish love for Courgibet still had a powerful hold on my heart, and it made me forget all the gloomy worries that the prospect of being disinherited had brought to my mind. I left Paris with the idea of asking for money to go and see Courgibet again. In the intensity of my love I even told myself that I'd give up my rights to my mother's estate in exchange for a payment of a thousand francs. My overheated imagination told me that if my mother refused to give me the money, oh well, then I'd kill her, but all of that was in my overworked imagination. I was absolutely incapable of killing my mother for Courgibet. I started out by asking my mother for money. She refused, but if I had insisted, I'd have gotten it. Far from Paris, far from Courgibet's beautiful eyes, my foolish love sputtered out like a dying ember. My thoughts went in another direction. I told myself that I was foolish to sacrifice my future for Courgibet. I realized that my mother would give me some money, but that it wouldn't be the last time, and that she would flee to another country to get away from my obsessions. Because I saw a bleak future for myself, I was determined to explain all of this to her and be done with it, no matter what happened.

Secular materialists, who only believe in nature, the alpha and omega of all matter, who believe that human life is the only fate of man, who systematically deny that a supernatural influence for good and evil rules the fate of mortals, are struck dumb with surprise when confronted by certain monstrous crimes. Without a doubt nature creates horrifying moral monsters; she creates more of them than we realize, but we must not forget that the vicious depths of human nature are exploited and stimulated by supernatural spirits that are much stronger in will and intelligence than we are. These evil spirits, crafty and sly, tempt man by manipulating his greed and weaknesses. And they don't have any other objective than to drive man to perdition. Rational men may scoff at this, but this doctrine is that of the church, and it's the most plausible one to explain certain atrocities that reveal the influence of mysterious evil forces.

From a legal perspective my sexual inversion is the unassailable part of my defense. You can reply to all those who wish to condemn me: "He's an invert, a weak, sick, and abnormal creature who, unable to find his rightful position in society, was trapped in a desperate situation. Such a crime can only be the work of a sick, unbalanced, and abnormal man." Under our system of human justice there's no cause, no matter how awful it is, that can't be defended. You can always find excuses, evasions, or extenuating circumstances to present your failures in a better light.

But under the scrutiny of the ultimate judge, whose absolute, divine, infallible justice examines hearts and consciences without pity, I couldn't bring up my inversion as an excuse. Although society doesn't recognize a role or a social utility for inverts, God himself has given them a mission. God has a special fondness for these rejects that the world regards with disgust, and when they courageously embrace a life of self-abnegation and humiliation for which their birth has inexorably marked them, he gives them joys of a superior type and consolations that the common man will never experience and that surpass the attractions of everyday earthly pleasures. Angel or devil: that's the motto of the invert.

To understand the genesis of my fall, to sketch out clearly its special attributes—so as not to be classified with those vulgar brutes who have no conscience or moral sense, who kill without really knowing what they're doing, who have an extremely limited moral responsibility—I have to delve into very intimate psychological questions and to lift a corner of the veil behind which people try to hide the ugly aspects of the human conscience. If, by acting thus, I've increased the overwhelming torrent of scorn that is submerging my honor, it can no longer hurt me. After the painful events that ended my mother's life and that destroyed my hopes for happiness in this world, I've become quite indifferent to worldly matters. What does a bigger or smaller amount of suffering and scorn matter to me? Whether you take me for a fool or a fanatic, I'm going to direct all my thoughts and feelings toward the eternal. To him who has lost everything, God still remains. When you can expect nothing but scorn and insults on earth, it's comforting to lift your heart and eyes toward heaven.

To claim to find tendencies or natural and unhealthy impulses in me to commit crimes would be to judge me falsely and to defame me completely. The most detailed and intrusive medical examinations would never be able to reach such a conclusion. It would be equally untrue to say that I'm a criminal, because the word "criminal" implies a certain inborn tendency, a certain tolerance for the idea of crime. You must limit yourself to the word "malefactor." For a long time I had been telling myself that only a crime would save me from poverty, but I felt such an instinctive repulsion about resorting to it that I kept trying to think of and find another way. On April 4, 1903, when I saw that this crime was unavoidable in order to escape from poverty and to avoid being arrested, I yielded to it, completely dead in my soul, as if I were yielding to a shockingly difficult task for which I was not suited. Even while I was engaged in my criminal act, I made extraordinary and superhuman efforts to still the voice of nature and the sensibility that cried out inside me, but I told myself that to escape from poverty and from being arrested I had to go through with it, come what may.

I've always hated quarrels, fights, and violence, but on the night of April 4 I was like a nervous and delicate young woman who, trembling and shuddering, had to perform a cannibal's task in order to avoid an even greater danger. As on the stage of a theater, where the actors are not themselves but the characters whose roles they play for that brief interlude, that night the fear of poverty and of being arrested had created for a moment in me a new character completely different from what I was in reality. And once its awful role was over, the temporary character disappeared, leaving in its place a reality of only tenderness, kindness, and sensitivity. This is one of the most interesting and odd aspects of my sad case: that a person who has within him all the feminine tenderness, kindness, and fragility was motivated by the circumstances that I've described to be like people with the worst sort of brutality, cynicism, barbarism, and cruelty.

It would be a grave error to compare me to or equate me with notorious murderers. In good as in evil I must keep my very special and distinct individuality. Many of those who achieve notoriety through crime are men who are endowed with all the virile energy, all the impetuous temperament of males. Others with a special personality and makeup have an innate inclination toward murder. They kill by instinct. Despite this, they can be quite guilty, because their brains and their consciences must warn them more or less loudly that their instinct is wrong and that they must change. My case is nothing like that. My sexual inversion caused me unheard-of difficulties. It led me inexorably to a crisis point, to that criminogenic condition that's called misery, but it didn't force me overtly to commit a crime or to cause suffering. I could have recovered from that critical state with the help of exceptional virtue and courage. I failed at that noble task, and I gave in to the monstrous emotions that slumbered in the depths of my feminine heart.

Crimes committed by certain people can be explained simply by the natural morbid drives that are inherent in their physical development. In others, usually in weak individuals, the root cause of crime is psychic, and the full explanation for their crime is found in the perfidy of their hearts. Despite the misleading outward appearance of my personality, it's appropriate to repeat the police detective's time-honored saying: "*Cherchez la femme!*"

Therefore, a doctor would be unable to perform a forensic examination on me that focuses specifically and *exclusively* on the medical issues, but a psychologist could do some poignantly interesting studies on the fickleness and profound perversity of feminine hearts like mine.

Criminal women with a weak character who plan a crime commonly use poison. They know full well that they can't cope with violent scenes. I embody this extraordinary type of criminal woman who has a very weak character, who is sensitive to the horror of blood and murder, and who, pressured by the danger she must avoid, succeeds in completely overcoming her strong repugnance to crime by assuming a temporary personality as a fierce, brutal, and pitiless assassin who takes the place of her very tender, sensitive, feminine personality.

I have to tell the story of an experience that was rather insignificant in itself but will provide overwhelming support for my statement that I'm a mental hermaphrodite. In Geneva, during the summer of 1900, I met an eighteen-year-old boy from a good family. Some of his tastes and mannerisms were a bit feminine, but he knew he had to assume the male role when he was among women. This young man had picked up vicious habits at school and continued to engage in them for profit with foreigners passing through Geneva, but the payment he asked for his favors was simply to send him postcards to add to his collection. When I returned home to France, I sent him postcards every day for three months, and I chose the loveliest ones. To make his collection interesting, I'd write delicate verses, literary excerpts, and philosophic, moral, and religious quotations on them in my finest handwriting. I was careful to avoid any quotation that expressed love and passion too explicitly. The young man was thrilled, and he told his parents, who didn't know me, that he had met a young Frenchman who collected postcards and that he was exchanging Swiss cards for

French ones. At first his mother took him at his word, but one fine day she told him unequivocally that he was lying, that these cards were sent by a woman, that everything about them—their good taste, the artful choices in the selection of cards and literature, especially the high-minded quotations, the handwriting—betrayed a feminine correspondent. And he could never persuade her that a man was sending them. That fine lady wasn't wrong; it was a woman's mind and heart, lost, homeless, out of place in a man's body.

People have asked me how being imprisoned in solitary confinement, the punishment to which I was condemned, affected a special medical case like mine. In my opinion it's even more dangerous for a temperament like mine than the stimulations of the jail's general population, even with perverts and degenerates. In my cell I'm still the great female lover (I must use these words to be truthful), the passionate woman, the sensitive, morbidly impressionable, and unique creature that I've always been. Lacking external stimulation, I delve into detailed and accurate recollections of my happiness in love in the past. With the help of my powerful imagination I can conjure up memories of loves that are much more irresistible and exciting than those that I could encounter on the outside in real life. Like a neurotic and highly romantic woman I imagine virile men who conform perfectly to my ideal. In my mind's eye I can see a parade of all my past lovers, all the men I've possessed and all those I've desired, with perfect clarity, with the vehement ardor of passion that borders on madness, without ever being able to possess them. I live in the middle of a romance novel. What I really want, and the experts at the assizes recognized this, is mental, emotional, and sentimental excitement. Foremost for me is the kind of psychic and sensual intoxication that I alone can truly understand and enjoy because of my especially sensitive character. Nevertheless, since I'm not purely a mind but also have a body and a soul, I have to admit that, after having experienced the finest, most delicate, and most ethereal feelings for a man, like those that develop in the heart of the most innocent, delicate, and pure young virgins, I experience an abrupt transition to the most earthly animal appetites and the most carnal practices.

Still there are some men—I say "some" because you shouldn't assume it could be just anyone—who, out of the blue with the charm of the unexpected, have provoked platonic feelings in me, who have affected my psychic self to such an extent, who have fostered such intoxicating emotions and feelings, and who have elevated me to and kept me in such stirring and intoxicating regions of the most vivid spiritual love that I've forgotten the secondary attraction of sexual relations. The body doesn't play a part in these types of unions. Everything is psychic. Even words and gestures are unnecessary. Hearts speak to each other simply by being close together. Eyes enhance the mute eloquence of the hearts that merge, harmonize, complete each other, mingle their emotional and mental lives, and join their greatest differences in one harmonious whole.

In these circumstances sexual relations would only take away the freshness from such an intimate, spiritual love story. But I must also say that in the deep blue of love's sky my poor mortal eyes have been dazzled and enchanted by the light of brilliant stars whose rays have touched off blazes of love in my heart and simultaneously burned and laid waste to it. I've had to suffer the horrifying and secret torments of Tantalus[2] and endure the stigma of despised and misunderstood love. Yes, I've encountered those whom I've worshiped and feared simultaneously; those who, by their very presence, have unknowingly exercised a powerful fascination over my sick organism, an irresistible attraction; those whose amorous passions and excitements are more suited to a demon than a human being; those who have stirred an exhilaration and a nymphomania whose intensity has surpassed even those observed in the most passionate women. In the presence of those men I was giddy, I was mad, I was intoxicated the way others are from whiskey or opium, but my desire and my intoxication were more refined and delicious. With those men my psychic faculties were heightened, sharpened in ecstasy and rapture. At these moments I'd lose track of time and of events. I'd reach an intensity of psychic amorous pleasure that surpasses all description. My sensitive psychic appetite was excited to an unimaginable degree. I told myself that if I could succeed in possessing one of those men, he might eventually be affected by the mad passion he inspired in me, and I'd finally get an affectionate word or glance from him.

If I had experienced the joy of shared and inclusive love with those men, I'd have achieved heaven on earth, and all my wishes for happiness would have been fulfilled and surpassed. But a kind of fate decreed that those men, whose friendship and possession would have brought me such rare, such exquisite, such other-worldly sentimental and amorous fulfillment, those men, I repeat, only understood love with women. In their eyes pederasty was the vilest crime. They thought death wasn't a sufficient punishment for it. Not only were they unmoved by the idolatrous cult that they inspired in me, not only did they fail to see me as a poor freakish woman who would have been consoled and thrilled by the illusion of love accorded to her through pity, but they saw in me nothing more than a deranged person. And thus it was perfectly clear to me that I only inspired disgust, horror, and hatred that reached the heights of abhorrence and that I'd have put my very life in danger at times if I had tried to share with them the extraordinary feelings I had toward them.

Since I've tried to reveal the mental aberrations that pervade me in all their horror, I must admit that the men who excited me in that way to an unimaginable degree were quite simply none other than pimps and thugs. I felt a searing, jealous rage when I saw them with their women, and I'd have suffered all the abjection, the servitude, the shame to be recognized as a woman by them. If only I knew how to atone for the disgrace of my outward appearance with the ardor of my devotion! Oh! The inevitable capriciousness, sensitivity, and morbid weakness that is found in a woman! Despite all the precautions and protective measures you can take against it, this natural law seems to rule strictly, to govern and issue its edicts in the world!

I knew a young lady who was born into a very ancient and noble family. She had received an excellent education in the convent. She married an honorable, intelligent man, who earned twenty-five thousand francs a year as the director of a big factory and who had an outstanding status among the bourgeoisie in the region. His wife was the picture of elegance, delicacy, and sensitivity. She was as graceful and as brilliant as a hummingbird. Tortured by suspicions, the husband pretended to go on a trip and came back suddenly one night when he found his wife in the arms of his manservant, a stunning fellow, as robust as an oak tree, whose big, dark eyes revealed a strong soul undaunted by vain fears. Madame had thought it natural to lean on this buck. Light, mobile, fluttering like swan's down in the breeze, her agitated and trembling soul had sought peace and tranquility in the solid rock of a truly manly heart. Oh! Feminine hearts! Who will ever know your strange and deep recesses? Only attentive observers and perceptive psychologists who can interpret and see life clearly would dare to claim that incidents of this sort are relatively infrequent!

In the first report he wrote about me in 1902 Dr. Boyer said that I loved men for their beauty, their strength, and their intelligence. That's true, but it doesn't clearly explain the mental and sexual anomaly that I suffer from. I really like men who are talented, witty, educated, and intelligent. I'm very glad to enjoy their company, but the feelings they inspire in me never go beyond friendship and admiration for their abilities, not for their bodies. Abilities, wit, education, intelligence, physical beauty, muscular strength, all of these alone have never evoked in me feelings of love for these men.

My illness and my particular morbid condition can be summed up in this way: Why, throughout all my life, have my tastes and inclinations always been in perfect alignment with those of neurotic, weak, passionate women? Why have I always sighed, like them, after the same lovers? Why are my psychic and emotional temperament and my amorous nature more strongly felt than the feelings and amorous emotions of women when I possess or see the men whom they love or lust after? Why is it that, when a man attracts women's attentions, he also, without exception, attracts my own? Why do I feel an attraction for these thugs, these pimps, these good-for-nothings that is even more lustful, crazy, and wild than that of those unhappy women who descend to the utmost degree of abjection to be loved by these men? Why am I so horribly jealous of these women, envying the feelings and the erotic delirium that they achieve in their sexual relations with these men? And why is it that I still tell myself that my emotional makeup would make me feel more intense ecstasy and emotions than these women feel if only I had their lovers and were loved by them?

A doctor making a forensic examination of me, using only medical criteria, would try to find innate morbid, criminal drives within me that were intrinsic to my condition, my temperament, and my organism. In response I can say that I've a very strong, inborn, instinctive, and persistent aversion to committing a crime. I've never even killed a chicken, and I made a superhuman effort to bring myself to commit the crime that I did. But if the medical doctor were also a psychologist, if he wanted to study carefully certain tendencies and emotions of my heart, he'd find deep down in my psyche not a habitual inclination for criminality but a latent reservoir of perfidy, habitually suppressed by my religious self. As an egotistical woman who loves luxury, and not finding in myself any honest means to achieve it, the idea of robbery and of crime frequently tempted my heart, but it didn't obsess me. As soon as the thought occurred to me, it would be immediately banished by the ever vigilant influence of my moral and religious self. In addition, it knew it would find my weak, extremely nervous, and sensitive personality a powerless and clumsy accomplice. These guilty thoughts and feelings pierced my consciousness like lightning bolts, and even though they recurred frequently, they invariably produced an immediate impression of horror and revulsion, which was never weakened by repetition and familiarity. A sincere psychological analysis doesn't let me pass over these evil thoughts and feelings in silence, but I've the right to present them as they appeared to me and as I reacted to them. Besides, nothing is more delicate and scrupulous than these psychological analyses of a feminine heart.

Written on January 20, 1905.

MENTAL HERMAPHRODITE

During the assizes trial, the medical experts honestly had to swear that I was a distinct type of sexual invert and that I had a psychosexual personality of the opposite sex. This pronouncement was very important to me, and if it hadn't been made by authorities as important as the eminent doctors of the medical faculty, it would surely have amused a certain number of people. People find it hard to believe that such anomalies can exist. Nature, which is often so beautiful and admirable in its creations, seems in the case of sexual inversion to have achieved the last word in barbarism, cruelty, and unreason. Nevertheless, mental hermaphrodites do exist. I'm an exact and complete example. I've met a large number of people afflicted by this anomaly to a degree at least equal to mine, and in the restricted scope of my life experience I've known a great many normally very effeminate people who denied their external sex, for whom a masculine physical makeup was as painful to endure as the dress of Dejanire was heavy on Hercules' shoulders,[3] and who only wanted to exchange their body's masculine exterior for womanly shapes more congruent with their mental femininity.

Ever since I was old enough I've delved into and examined my physical being from all angles. I've not been able to find any masculine instinct or inclination there. The masculine habits that I've adopted because of my physique I've adopted against my heart and my mind. These habits went against the grain of my thoughts and my emotions. Like a very sensual woman, I'm capricious, headstrong, and frivolous. Loving calm and tranquility, I'm naturally endowed with the instinct and the desire for all sorts of luxury, elegance, and refinement. Having love, adoration, and admiration for all masculine attitudes, I'm ignorant of erotic things, tormented by a need for devotion to these absolutely pure, masculine attitudes and I need a little esteem and attention from them. But on the other hand, I'm cold, haughty, and disdainful of all that's weak and effeminate. I become intoxicated to the point of ecstasy by a virile soul whose gaze reveals these male attributes. This is what I am, despite persistent efforts to make myself virile. What social role could a person play who is so bizarrely constituted? Isn't he unmistakably destined for nothing but rejection, impotence, and failure? Society has only a disdainful pity, a scornful intolerance for him. If this person is born poor, will he not find dangers, difficulties, and battles that are especially noble and painful along his way? How will he stand the absolute deprivation of rare, exquisite, delicious, intoxicating pleasures that he's drawn to with so much desire? If he's poor, such a person will have to enlist so much moral energy to stay virtuous and honest that he'll be an unsung and obscure hero and martyr recognized only by God.

If the invert is born rich, his fate naturally will be less unhappy. He can afford to treat himself to the illusions of friendship, love, and consideration. He'll never get the real thing, but he can buy the deceptive appearances of them. He'll never receive the same amount of consideration that society gives quite naturally to those men and women who are able to start and raise a family. The rich invert will easily find servile favors and indulgences, self-interested flattery and admiration. With his money, he'll find lovers and husbands, but what bizarre, eccentric, and strange unions! The marriages are only agreed on because of Madame's fortune, where Madame is a woman who looks like a man, where Madame plays the part of a deformed, ugly, but wealthy young lady, where, in order to compensate for her unattractive exterior, Madame is obliged to demonstrate toward her husband a devotion, a self-sacrifice, whose self-denigration is almost ridiculous and a servitude so humble that it doesn't allow for any dignity or self-respect.

A well-educated invert from a good family will seek poorly educated lovers from a vulgar social stratum. He'll feel the wildest passions, an insane love, an idolatry, a servitude, an incomprehensible need for devotion for certain well-built, muscular country boys who are a bit brutish and for certain bucks who lack any finer feelings. To the invert these vulgar fellows, who hardly merit a glance from others, will seem to be heroes and demigods. The invert will be fascinated, charmed, deliciously attracted, enchanted, beside himself in their presence. A fellow with a distinctly virile musculature and a masculine psyche can with only a glance incite lustful thoughts in the mind of the invert and provoke a mad, excessive love in his heart. The look and presence of certain pimps have attracted and excited me so suddenly at times that I couldn't break the spell. I could try to summon up all my logical faculties to come to my rescue, but in vain. I was attracted, fascinated, bewitched, and I'd have compromised my reputation and my fortune to be able to possess and caress a virile pimp with very masculine looks.

Not only does society reject and relegate inverts to the lowest level, but with that sense of injustice and partiality that it uses with the poor, the insignificant, the disinherited, and the weak, it treats inverts as dangerous individuals and claims it's threatened by their perverted instincts. Society has no more to fear from the abnormal instincts of inverts than it does from the equally abnormal instincts of a large number of perverse women, who regard love and men as no more than instruments of pleasure and greed, who know how to escape the risks and burdens of maternity by methods and tricks unknown to the stupid male. If conjugal modesty and marital chastity exist, so do conjugal and marital libertinage, and that is, people say, the most shameful of all. To violate nature's laws with a woman, to use a woman other than for reproductive intercourse and with intentions other than to perpetuate the race, is to abandon oneself to a degradation that's at least as shameful as pederastic degradation. I know that the world has different moral standards and considers these abominations to be admirable, that you can do all you want with a woman as long as you're discreet, and that, intoxicated with lust and exquisite obscene acts, you can still hold up your head proudly and consider yourself less abased than those poor unbalanced and unhappy beings whose sexual deformation has made them unfit for heterosexual intercourse!

IMPRESSIONS OF A CONDEMNED MAN

Despite the perfectly natural horror that the proximity of a shameful punishment can provoke in a weak and impressionable character like mine, I contemplated my day in the assizes court without too much fear. Since the day of my arrest my moral self had suffered such painful disillusionment and humiliations and had received such painful shocks that I somehow became indifferent to living or dying. I tried to harden myself against the pain. I sought refuge from that suffering in an ardent mysticism and a stoic impassiveness in turn.

On my day in court I suffered greatly from being served up as fodder for the spectators' brutal curiosity and the public's ignorant and unjust reactions. Since I was accustomed to finding supreme and infallible justice only in God, I wasn't terribly impressed by the pretentious, overblown gravity of human justice. I've always been able to discern its gaps, faults, and shadows, and this has stopped me from according it sincere admiration and deep respect. I suffered especially when seeing that the court was incapable of pinpointing the exact root and delineating clearly the essential attributes of the crime I had the misfortune to commit. The judge, the prosecutor, and the experts all described me as a common criminal headed inexorably into criminality, because I was impoverished and needed money to support an absurd love affair. That description of the situation couldn't be further from the truth.

I'm glad to be able to tell the whole truth. The more or less questionable and convincing pieces of evidence in the case against me certainly show that I became the murderer of my mother, but they leave in the shadows the motives that impelled me to commit this horrific deed. It is said that when a particularly fine perfume goes bad, it emits an especially noxious smell. The same is true in moral questions. Some people are called to a higher sense of morality. When they sin, their error is graver and their misdeeds are more scandalous. Unhappy are they who are called to live on the highest moral plane but who don't know how. With God's help and with the energy of their own will they can reach the summit. They'll tumble from boulder to boulder, from ravine to ravine, down to the lowest depths of vice and crime. When I was twelve years old, a highly intelligent and well-educated priest told me after a confession I made to him: "My little friend, you are destined to be either a scoundrel or a saint."

My sexual inversion and my psychological feminism played a key role in the execution of my crime. Inverts aren't men; they constitute a kind of third sex. As I mentioned elsewhere, they're exactly like amorous and passionate women in their tastes, inclinations, and desires. Very frequently their psychological feminism and their lust for very masculine men are even stronger and more pronounced than women's are. I've also said that I was the mental and psychological twin of my mother. People should consider carefully the difficult and unusual situation of a person who looks like a man but who replicates the attitudes one finds in his mother. To all outward appearances my relations with my mother were those of a son with his mother, but in reality, because of the mental anomaly I suffer from, we lived together like two women. I likened it to the life of servitude and labor I led in the world. I didn't hate my mother for it; in fact, I loved her, not with a spontaneous, instinctive, thoughtless affection, but with logical and considerate feelings. Despite our little spats and differences of opinion, I loved her because she was good for me, because my mind told me if she was strict with me, it was for my own good. Still I have to admit that I didn't love her instinctively, but instead I loved her because my reason taught me that I should. My initial impulse is always bad, but thoughtfulness and logic correct it.

As an invert I had no social worth. I couldn't even hope for decent employment, and I had a lot of trouble supporting myself even at a minimal level. I yearned for amorous relationships with very masculine, low-level pimps and workingmen. I'd have liked to be rich in order to smother them with attention, care, and devotion, and in exchange to get from them the kind of love they felt for their mistresses. I told myself that, since I was only a kind of *femme monstre*, they'd in the end come to love me as a woman because of the tenderness and delicacy of my devotion to them. The idea of killing my mother to bring about one of these amorous relationships never occurred to me, even though they'd require a certain amount of money. I never asked my mother to bankrupt herself for me. I thought it was only natural that she should enjoy her money, but since my earliest childhood, without wishing her dead, I comforted myself with the thought that I was her heir, that I'd have a certain amount of capital, and that with the help of that capital I'd be able to get from certain men the kind of attention, sexual favors, reciprocal feelings, and emotional, sentimental, and amorous bliss that my character of a woman in love desired. I didn't have a specific man in mind as such. I had met many, and only the lack of money had prevented our "marriage," but I was sure that, once I had money, I'd only have to go out into the street to find dozens who would suit me.

These were the plans and dreams of happiness that I had concocted. I carefully hid them from my mother, but she was too clever not to have guessed them. She knew that basically I was just a girl in love, the victim of an overactive imagination and temperament. She foresaw accurately that the first good-looking guy that came along would control me and get whatever he wished from me, and she used all her resources of willpower and brainpower to prevent any and all sexual relations with men now and in the future. By doing so, she stabbed me right in the heart.

When I was twenty-five years old, my mother let me know that since I was so flighty, so unreasonable, she wouldn't leave me her meager fortune after her death. I was deeply embittered by that. From that time on I had an overwhelming urge to rob her to prevent this injustice from happening, but a feeling of duty made me reject these evil thoughts. At that time I was employed and was able to support myself somehow. Every now and then the thought of a crime occurred to me, but it seemed so horrible to me that I didn't consider it. I saw it as a figment of my morbid imagination.

Another misfortune was added to the prospect of being disinherited. My weak nerves and fragile mental state made me quit the Crédit Lyonnais.[4] I could no longer compete with colleagues my own age; my intellectual and physical strength was too inferior. If at that moment I had met a compassionate person who could find me a job, no matter how humble, that would have rescued me from dishonor and crime, but an invert like me with no important connections just can't find employment. I made heroic efforts to find a job as a waiter in a café or a restaurant, as a clerk in a grocer's store, so that I wouldn't starve, but I couldn't find anything. Everywhere I went I was told I had too much education and intelligence for these modest jobs. All these failures, all these disappointments, embittered my character. I deeply despised a society where honest work was so difficult to find for the disinherited, the weak, and the crippled—in other words, for people like me. Anger and resentment filled my soul. Realizing that I couldn't find any work despite the efforts I made, I asked my mother for the five or six thousand francs that my father had left me. To forget my troubles I started to lead a dissolute life. My companions took half of what I had. I asked my mother for help, and she was good enough to lend me another eighteen hundred francs. My family was obsessed by my inversion, and fearing a scandal, they wanted me to go abroad to live in New York or Madagascar. I was quite insulted when I found out that my family had these kinds of plans for me. I thought of myself as a sick person, and because of that I thought I deserved more consideration.

In April 1903, being at the end of my rope and no longer having any hope of finding a job, I'd have gladly gotten myself arrested for vagrancy or for insulting the authorities (the thought of stealing disgusted me) in order to escape from my abysmal poverty. I'd have certainly been reduced to that, but my mother had always told me that she'd disinherit me if I ever went to prison. That alone kept me from trying to get myself arrested in Paris. Then I went to my mother's house on April 4, 1903. I went there more to get a promise from her that I wouldn't be completely disinherited than to ask her for money. For almost two years I had harassed her with requests for money, and I knew that couldn't go on. I really want to emphasize that, when I went to my mother's house, I had lost all hope of finding a job. Every place I tried I was told I was too abnormal, too strange, too useless to be accepted anywhere. So I had only one last chance left: to get myself imprisoned to avoid absolute misery and to wait for my mother to pass away from natural causes to get what was left of my inheritance. I'd certainly have preferred it if my mother had accepted that course of events, but she saw things completely differently. She claimed that I could easily support myself, that she no longer had to take care of me, that I couldn't count on the inheritance. I did what I could to dissuade her, to make her understand the problems I had finding work. She was unshakeable and persisted in her idea of disinheriting me.

The foolish expenditures I had made in 1902 led my mother to believe that her wealth would be frittered away if she left it to me. That was the basis of her obstinate determination to disinherit me after my last spree in February 1902. If I could have guaranteed her that I wouldn't throw away her money, she'd surely have left it to me. My mother was wrong in believing that I'd have wasted her money as I had wasted the six thousand francs I had inherited from my father. I might have spent one or two thousand francs with lovers who attracted me, but I'd certainly have saved a small bit of capital. If I wasted the thirty or thirty-two thousand francs that I stole from my mother, it was because the police would have tracked me down if I had kept the stolen bonds. If I was arrested, I didn't want them to find any money on me.

Thus I pictured myself mired in abysmal poverty for the rest of my life. This crime, which horrified me, seemed inevitable to me to save a portion of my family inheritance. I really believed that my mother was going to abandon me forever. That's what gave me the awful courage to kill her. People have tried to assert that I was a blood-thirsty creature, a born killer, but nothing could be further from the truth. This crime tormented me horribly. Being as nervous, sensitive, and impressionable as I was, I sometimes wonder how I was able to go through with it.

I left the scene of the crime filled with horror, suffering from having made the poor woman suffer so much. She had always been good to me, but she hadn't understood that my sexual inversion and my mental feminism didn't allow me to play the social role of a man with a normal constitution. And this made it hard for me to find a position.

I'd have liked to keep the thirty or thirty-two thousand francs worth of bonds that I took from my mother's house, but by keeping them I'd have delivered myself into the hands of the police, because they had the serial numbers. In cashing them in I must have lost half their value. I traveled around simply to escape the police. I wandered here and there, not really knowing where I was headed, frightening myself and expecting at any moment to be arrested. I willingly wasted the money I had gotten from cashing in the bonds so that human justice wouldn't take it away, and when I was penniless, I became a prisoner, indifferent to the fate that awaited me.

I've a lot to complain about the magistrate who interrogated me.

I know nothing is more unbearable than the detestable procedural frame of mind that drives magistrates. They don't judge—they accuse, they debate, they cleverly defame people by force of habit and routine. I'd have preferred to describe my crime the way I've done it here. That was impossible because the investigating magistrate, Monsieur Ihler, was bent on bringing in that damned Courgibet and never wanted to accept that it was my fear of being disinherited that led me to commit the crime.

My mother, my aunt, and all the members of my family were so obsessed with my instincts as an invert that they decided I should get no inheritance in order to be forced to work. They thought work would provide a welcome diversion from my unhealthy tendencies, and if I had an income and a life of leisure, it would encourage my penchant for abnormal love affairs. My family has never understood that I had a hard time getting a job because of my very special personality and that it was very difficult for me to keep a job, especially an enjoyable, well-paying one.

On the other hand, I have kept a very grateful memory of the attorney, Monsieur Moemod, who built a defense for an unpopular defendant like me with boundless talent, wit, tact, and taste. During the oral arguments he alone was able to move me as he described to the jury my mother's ghost, who actually came out of the kindness of her loving mother's heart to plead for mercy for me. My lawyer's argument was so eloquent; he explained it so clearly. Although I wasn't insane, I wasn't fully endowed with all the mental capacities appropriate to my sex. Consequently, people in the courtroom thought I'd be sentenced only to forced labor, but the jury had been shaken in its convictions. In the jury room the foreman of the jury told the judge that he didn't see any extenuating circumstances in my case, but despite this he considered the death penalty to be excessive. To reconcile this, the judge instructed the jury to condemn me to death but to recommend a reprieve, which would be accepted favorably by the prosecutor and the judge.

Thus I was condemned to death at midday on October 27, 1904.

I strongly resented the shame of being condemned in front of a huge crowd, which filled the courthouse and the street, but I wasn't afraid, because a secret intuition told me I wouldn't be executed. I left the assizes courtroom showing no emotion and was taken to the prison warden's office. Painful impressions were in store for me there.

Ever since my arrest it has been extremely difficult for me to tolerate being with and being touched by prison guards. They're very decent people, but they're so vulgar, so insistent on rules that contact with them is odious to me. They think they're obligated to reprimand you constantly. I'm only a parricide and a convict, but despite that I believe I've a more refined conscience and a greater sense of morality than many prison guards. They put handcuffs on me and led me down several corridors to a cold, gloomy cell. I was seized by an awful feeling of anguish and fear. I thought that after the painful emotions of that evening they were going to lock me up there for the rest of the night with no light or heat. Fortunately, the guards lit the lamp and the stove, and they watched over me. The next morning I felt much better. They brought me a lovely book, and I found in it some very interesting observations about George Sand's visit to Majorca and about Madame Miolan-Carvalho,[5] as well as some charming verses. It was enough to turn my thoughts and my imagination to daydreams.

I state it without bragging: I didn't suffer during the fifty-seven days I spent waiting for the commutation of my sentence. The guards assigned to my cell can attest to the fact that I was neither depressed nor afraid. I had become indifferent to life and death. Among the various emotions I experienced the one that recurred most persistently was the firm conviction that I'd be pardoned. I based that certainty on the following reason: by sacrificing the fortune I had stolen from my mother in order to escape the police (if I hadn't feared the police, I'd have held on to that fortune), I had made the biggest sacrifice that I was capable of. For a character like me, to live in poverty would be an everlasting moral martyrdom. I thought that, since my life had become so sad, no one would want to take it away from me. If I had held on to that fortune and my hope of happiness in the world, I'd have been less convinced about my fate, and I'd have thought that the life that was to be cut short could still bring me happiness. But today all's well that ends well. I'm going to try to live, to drink deeply of the shame and the pain, and thus to merit a better life in the future.

My days of captivity in my cell passed by one after the other in peaceful uniformity. Only the changing of the guards broke the monotony. The days were foggy and dark. I told myself that perhaps I might never see the lovely days of spring again. The thought of being put to death on a cold winter morning in December didn't appeal to me at all. It seemed to me that I'd face up to death better if it came to me on the dawn of a spring morning, when nature unleashes its smiles and displays all its riches. I got a great deal of satisfaction going back to events of my past years, reliving in my memory my childhood, my youth, my adolescence with its disappointments and its joys. I couldn't help realizing that I hadn't lacked happiness in my life, but that I didn't know how to find it, because I had sought it in the false pleasures of pride and in the satisfying of ambition, instead of being content with the humble, simple joys that were available to me. I dreamed, I thought about my mother, who was so good even in her strictness. I remembered the wonderful care with which she surrounded me, and I rued the fatal chain of circumstances that caused a deep split between us. I imagined I saw her watching my downfall, my humiliation, and the secret torments of my heart from a better world and showering down on me words of compassion and forgiveness. I hoped that in the cradle of immortality, her eyes, illuminated by the pure clarity of eternal life, would better recognize the problems and the suffering that my diseased and abnormal temperament had created in me here below, and that my suffering would now lead me near to her in eternal peace.

I was very angry to have become an object of public curiosity.

Many people think that a man condemned to death is an extraordinary being, that he can't walk, eat, drink, or sleep like everyone else, that he must cry all day long. Finally my pardon came. There were plenty of disappointed people at Bourg-en-Bresse.[6] Many were counting on the fun of watching an execution. When the police officers were bringing me to Lyon, the crowd filled the train station at Bourg. Spectators bought platform tickets and came to stare at me from the train's vestibule. I really didn't think I was as odd a spectacle as that.

I've said that during the fifty-seven days following my sentencing I didn't feel any real terror. I was sustained by the conviction that I wouldn't be put to death. That conviction wasn't at all certain, and there were moments when I had to acknowledge the possibility of the death penalty. Even during those moments I didn't experience violent emotions or real terror. I played hide and seek with death and told myself that I'd have plenty of time to worry about it when I was sure of the penalty. If I had been executed, I'd certainly have performed my religious rites fervently. I told myself that the pain of death would be the beginning of expiation. I didn't presume that I'd go straight to heaven after my death. I expected a more or less extended period of rather rigorous expiation, but since I had confessed and was repentant, I was sure that once my expiation in the afterlife was accomplished, I'd be granted what we believers call everlasting grace. This thought cheered me tremendously, because one cause of great distress for believers is the uncertainty we have regarding the way we'll die. For a Christian, to die after a good confession and having repented your sins is a guarantee of achieving everlasting peace and eternal grace, after an expiation in the afterlife proportional to the severity of your sins.

I didn't have any nightmares or painful dreams. The memory of the scene of my horrific crime didn't resurface to disturb me. My conscience told me more eloquently than any of the courts on earth that I was overwhelmingly guilty, but this didn't stop me from keeping far from me the horrible sight of blood and death that impotently haunted my brain without contributing to my moral betterment. The memory of my mother never came to me as an implacable, harsh judge, dressed up like the phantom of justice. I knew that my mother was a devout woman, a good, strong Christian, and I've never doubted that religion instilled in the depths of her heart, even during her torments as a martyr, feelings of mercy and forgiveness for her cruel and unnatural son. Christians forgive their executioners. My mother was too much of a Christian to betray that tradition, and she gave God the task of avenging her. This has never prevented me from realizing that I owe to the memory of my mother an exemplary expiation and reparation.

It's quite probable that, since I know my own temperament so well, if I had been visited by Deibler,[7] I'd have been overcome by a great trembling when catching sight of him. It would have been hard for me to pretend that I'd walk bravely to my death. You must not forget that I'm an invert. That means I've a brain and a nervous system whose sensitivity, impressionability, and delicacy are more than feminine. During the preparations for the solemn occasion it was certainly likely that my soul would be frozen and petrified with anguish and fear. Weak and nervous temperaments feel the torment of instinctive, uncontrollable fear and the terror of death more than others. These feelings would have filled me with such a violent intensity that I'd have been powerless. I'd have fainted, and the guillotine would have merely cut off the head of a corpse.

The guards who kept watch over me at Bourg told me about condemned prisoners they had guarded. But they were all men, completely virile, having the full complement of masculine abilities that men have, and they couldn't be compared to me. These condemned prisoners would certainly have been braver than I'd have been facing the guillotine, but they'd have displayed much less calm and detachment than I did during the fifty to sixty days before my sentence was commuted to forced labor. People told me about a man named Maroyer,[8] who was condemned to death at the same time as Vacher,[9] but who was then pardoned. Around the fiftieth day the poor guy had been worrying so much that his hair was visibly turning white. The prison chaplain told me about Carron,[10] who was rather a braggart during his first few days, but who visibly shrank as the fatal day came near. These individuals were men, and I, unluckily for myself, am not a man. Or I'm a particular kind of man. I don't resemble my sex, and I must repeat over and over that psychically I'm a woman.

PART THREE

Literature, Medicine, and Self-Expression

The Novel of an Invert

In the late 1880s the well-known author Emile Zola received several letters from a young Italian man who hoped that details from his life story would provide the naturalist novelist with the raw materials for a well-rounded fictional portrait of a man who was sexually attracted to other men. Zola was "struck by the great physiological and social interest that it offered," but he chose not to use the materials or even to respond to the young man directly. Instead, he decided to send the collection to his friend Dr. Georges Saint-Paul, an expert in forensic medicine, whose particular interest was sexual anomalies. Saint-Paul gave the letters the ironic title "The Novel of an Invert" and published them in a medical journal, *Archives d'anthropologie criminelle*, where they appeared in segments, like a serial novel, in the years 1894 and 1895.[1] Later, in 1896, he included them as the first chapter in a book entitled *Tares et poisons: Perversion et perversités sexuelles*, where he contrasted this case of "inversion" with Oscar Wilde's case of "perversion."[2] Strangely enough, the anonymous author of these letters bought Saint-Paul's medical treatise, read his own autobiographical letters, and then wrote directly to the doctor.[3] Consequently, *The Novel of an Invert* is an exceptional series of documents. It shows how literature and medicine helped shape the sexual identity of one man in ways that were quite original.

The anonymous author of these letters decided to write to Zola because he considered him "the greatest novelist of our times," a courageous and insightful man "who depicts all the oddities, all the infamies, and all the maladies that afflict mankind so powerfully." In particular, the letter writer singled out male and female characters in Zola's oeuvre that had a particular emotional resonance for him, but he expressed dissatisfaction with the depiction of one such character, the servant Baptiste in *La Curée*, who was fired for his affair with another man. The autobiographer felt that Baptiste was "ignoble because the debauchery in which he engaged has nothing to do with love," and he challenged Zola to make use of the sort of desires described graphically in his letters in order to address "one of the most frightful vices that dishonors mankind" in the late nineteenth century. It was a subject that up until that time, he claimed, "no novelist has dared to dramatize in a literary work."

Zola was an obvious recipient for these letters because his series, collectively known as *Les Rougons-Macquarts*, traced two branches of the same family—the legitimate Rougons and the illegitimate Macquarts—over several generations. Described by Zola himself as "the natural and social history of a family under the Second Empire," the novels show how greed, lust, alcoholism, and mental illnesses operated in the worlds of high finance, politics, commerce, prostitution, mines, and other milieus. Drawing upon the theories of Dr. Claude Bernard on scientific methodology,[4] Zola wrote these books as if the art of novel writing was a kind of experiment in which characters were set into an environment to see how their hereditary traits played out. He was also influenced by the degeneration theory of Dr. Bénédict-Augustin Morel.[5] Given the novels' avowedly scientific exploration of men's and women's degenerate traits in a variety of environments, as well as the paucity of homosexuals among them, it is no wonder that the letter writer hoped that Zola would be interested in his family antecedents, his upbringing, and the details of his sexual awakening and maturation. Perhaps, the autobiographer thought, Zola would find his own theories of sexuality and identity useful.[6]

At the time that he posed his challenge to Zola the anonymous author was a young man of about twenty-three years of age from an "illustrious family." In his letters he wrote about his sexual experiences and feelings of attraction to certain types of men. He also described the physical and sexual repulsion that he felt toward women, although he maintained close friendships with some women. Detailed accounts of his childhood, his religious inclinations, his artistic tastes, and the intense emotions that had overwhelmed and haunted him at times rounded out the narrative, along with moments of elation, feelings of self-hatred, thoughts of suicide, and a sense of dissatisfaction with his biological sex. "I could have made an adorable and adoring woman," he mused while inventorying for Zola the charms of his physical appearance. Other sections trace his family tree and openly express class snobbery toward servants and the poor, as well as antisemitism regarding his Jewish mother, her family, and especially her "race." Still other passages reveal the young man's attitude toward what he called his "fate" or "punishment." "Nature made me" is a typical assertion of his belief that his sexual orientation is innate and inescapable.

Despite the insistence with which the "invert" exercised his persuasive and narrative skills to highlight the literary value of his life story, the letters were handed over to Dr. Saint-Paul when he inaugurated a research project that he called "an inquiry into sexual inversion." Saint-Paul explained in his introduction that the subject, which was no longer taboo, would have an intrinsic interest for the readers of the *Archives d'anthropologie criminelle*, since "a detailed investigation of the normal or pathological functioning of one of the most powerful factors in human behavior—in fact, the essential reason for so many heroic or criminal acts—should fascinate not only those interested in sociological problems but indeed every thinking human being." To conduct this inquiry Saint-Paul issued an open call not only to medical doctors but also to "writers, professors, and lawyers" to send in "observations, notes, documents, or confessions that they had collected in their fields." He provided a lengthy set of questions that focused on the subject's own medical history and that of his family, that probed for evidence of criminal behavior in the subject or in his relatives, and that delved into the subject's sexual history. The questionnaire included a theoretical section asking the respondents to speculate on the origins of this phenomenon. Like other surveys launched in the *Archives d'anthropologie criminelle*, entries were solicited from "everyone regardless of profession," and responses began coming in soon thereafter.[7]

One respondent was Marc-André Raffalovich, a wealthy Russian émigré raised in France, but who was then living in England. Despite his lack of medical or other scientific training, he became a frequent contributor to the *Archives d'anthropologie criminelle*, submitting book reviews and theoretical articles about male same-sex sexuality and debating the topic with other writers. He agreed with many of the doctors who published their views that same-sex sexuality was an innate condition, but he disagreed with them when they labeled it a degenerative trait. Instead, he argued that many "unisexualists," as he termed them, had an innate predisposition for the spiritual or intellectual life, and he believed equally ardently that, in order to attain this life, they had to practice a form of chastity.[8]

Another respondent was, of course, Emile Zola, who sent Saint-Paul the letters that we have translated here. In his analysis of the case Saint-Paul claimed that the young man exemplified a specific type of homosexual—the invert—who possessed an inborn tendency to same-sex sexuality. In the next chapter of his book he contrasted this case with that of Oscar Wilde, who was at the time serving a term of hard labor in an English prison for "gross indecency." Wilde, Saint-Paul argued, had acquired his "perversion" through bad company and other corrupting influences; he was, therefore, a "pervert."[9] These two concepts—sexual inversion and sexual perversion—were much debated in French medical literature at the turn of the century. Inversion was considered an innate trait that sprang from a form of hereditary degeneration, whereas perversion was an acquired vice that developed in an immoral environment.

In an ironic twist the author of what Saint-Paul had called *The Novel of an Invert* found the doctor's treatise on display in a bookstore, bought a copy, and read his own words. Like Raffalovich, the "invert" agreed with Saint-Paul about some of his analyses, but he rejected many others. He wrote a letter of rebuttal directly to the doctor, in which he offered a different interpretation of his sexual history. He also gave additional information about his sexual history as it had developed over the previous seven years. However, unlike the respectful tone that he used in his earlier correspondence with Zola, the letter writer adopted a defiant tone with the doctor.

Some of our interest in these letters comes from the author's experimentation with literary genres. Each of the letters is somewhat different in its framing of the story that the writer is telling. The first letter resembles a conventional autobiography, moving from family antecedents to childhood memories to adolescent experiences. It culminates in the author's great romance with a petty officer during his military service. The second letter fills in a gap in the young man's experiences. It deals with his seduction by and his affair with one of his father's acquaintances while he was still an adolescent. Thus it functions as a commentary and a critique on the "truth value" of the first letter as it reveals, in stark detail, what the first letter elided. If the first letter reads like a romance in its narrative structure, the second letter more closely hews to tragedy. In the third letter the author offers a character sketch—one that was perhaps not too dissimilar to the kinds that Zola was known to have made before writing his novels. The fourth letter—written seven years later and addressed to Dr. Saint-Paul rather than Zola—lacks the literary pretensions of the first three letters. Instead, the "invert" confronts the doctor's analysis and offers a different interpretation of his own sexuality, explaining that he took pleasure in recounting his affair with the petty officer, but felt guilt about his relationship with his father's business associate. Nevertheless, by the time that he wrote to Saint-Paul, he seemed to have come to an acceptance of his sexual nature. The dramatic asides and appeals to heaven, nature, or fate that characterize the earlier writings are absent; a matter-of-fact frankness bordering on the cynical has replaced them.

The author of these letters insisted early and often on his story's authenticity, referring to his words as a "confession" that neither "priest nor psychologist" had heard before Zola had received it. In this way he acknowledged rather subtly another famously frank (and yet not entirely truthful) autobiographical model—Jean-Jacques Rousseau's *Confessions*. No doubt he wished to appeal to the secular instincts of the letters' intended audience—Emile Zola. Contemporary readers must have been wary of the writer's narrative strategies, as Saint-Paul's title suggests. The writer shaped and presented his account selectively, as all memoirists do, and although Saint-Paul assured his readers that certain information the man provided was verifiable, other parts of his life story remained undocumented. His first-person account is clearly not the pure raw material that he wanted Zola to accept and fictionalize; nor was it solely useful as documentation for Dr. Saint-Paul's medical theories; it was really something of his own invention. As an example of self-conscious life writing, it is an intriguing document for social history. According to Saint-Paul, even Zola was impressed with it, recalling that "when I received that very interesting document a few years ago, I was struck by its great social and psychological interest. It touched me, too, by its absolute sincerity, for I could feel the intensity, I might almost say, the eloquence, of the truth there. And you must take into account that the young man who is unburdening himself is not writing in his native language. Don't you think that he succeeds in conveying and expressing profoundly lived emotions in certain passages? This is a guileless, spontaneous, complete confession of a type that few men can hope to achieve."[10]

8. Caricature of Emile Zola by André Gill. Source: *L'Eclipse*, April 16, 1876. Courtesy: Bibliothèque nationale de France, Paris.

The Novel of an Invert

By Anonymous (1889, 1896)

FIRST LETTER (1889)

To Monsieur Emile Zola in Paris:

It is to you, Sir, who are the greatest novelist of our times, who, with the eye of a scientist and an artist, perceive and paint so powerfully all the oddities, all the infamies, and all the maladies that afflict mankind, that I send these *human documents* so sought after by the learned men of our times.

This confession, which no spiritual director has ever heard from my mouth, will reveal to you a frightful illness of the soul, a rare case—if not an unique case, unfortunately—that has been studied by psychological experts, but that, until now, no novelist has dared to dramatize in a literary work. Balzac wrote *La Fille aux yeux d'or*, but he only touched upon this horrible vice that was depicted in this story.[1] Sarrasine truly loved Zambinella, but he believed he was a woman and stopped loving him after he discovered the truth.[2] Therefore, it's not the same kind of horrible case that I want to talk to you about today.

You yourself, Sir, in your admirable *La Curée* have only touched upon one of the most frightful vices that dishonors mankind in the character of your Baptiste.[3] That man is ignoble because the debauchery in which he engaged has nothing to do with love and is only an absolutely material thing, a question of congenital malformation, which doctors have more than once observed and described. All of this is very common and very disgusting and has nothing to do with the confession that I'm sending you, and which could perhaps be useful to you.

I'm not French, even though I know the most important cities of France, and I've even lived for some time in Paris. I write you, therefore, no doubt in a very incorrect manner. It has been a long time since I've spoken or written in this language. Would you please excuse the improprieties and the mistakes that undoubtedly infest these pages?

I don't know if you know Italian. If I could write you in that language, I'd certainly express myself better. I'm not concerned with style here, but I'll simply say what could be of interest to you. In these poorly written lines you'll discover, with your eagle eye and your artistic heart, the plight of a soul who seems to be pursued by a horrible fatality, who's ashamed of himself, and who'll certainly find peace and happiness only when he sleeps in this earth that you've described so marvelously.[4]

I am twenty-three years old, Sir, and I was born into a family with a rather high and independent financial status. In this matter I've nothing to desire. My father is Catholic. He calls himself a deist, but his religion is more like a kind of pantheism, which he doesn't want to admit to. My mother is a converted Jew, but she's faithful to her religion, even though she observes only its principal practices. I'm the fourth son of this marriage. My father is one of the most handsome old men that you could imagine, with the head of a patriarch, who attracts attention even in the street. He was marvelously handsome in his youth and still is at such an advanced age.

Our family is originally from Spain but has been living in Italy for centuries. My father was married at nineteen; my mother was eighteen, and she was far richer than my father. They were very much in love and still love each other. My father has a very impressionable and nervous temperament, artistic right down to his fingertips. He has had a rather adventurous life with considerable highs and lows, but even at times when he was down on his luck, he didn't let himself get discouraged, and he always knew how to regain it. He has always earned a lot and spent a lot. Several years ago he made a great fortune on the stock market, but he lost it all once again. Without being rich, he's well-to-do now and can surround himself with the luxury that he has always liked. He has traveled to several European capitals, and his family has almost always followed him. He cares little for society and frequents it seldom, outside of business contacts.

He loves the arts with a passion and surrounds himself freely with beautiful things—pretty statuettes and handsome paintings. Even at those times when luck didn't much smile upon him, he did without the necessities of life in order to buy a beautiful book or a pretty engraving—something that considerably annoyed my mother, who was much more economical, due to the instincts of her race. He loves his family passionately and makes all possible sacrifices in order to see us happy and satisfied, but he has his days of ill humor, and then whoever approaches him had better watch out! He always makes extreme resolutions without much reflection and has thus gotten embroiled in many unpleasant business affairs. He has seen a lot, traveled a lot, earned a lot, and spent a lot. He has a passionate love of reading, and since we've settled down, he has collected a fine library. His intelligence is very well developed. His forehead is magnificent. He's only of medium height, but he seems very tall. Monsieur Desbarolles,[5] whom he consulted a number of years ago in Paris, told him that he was born under the influence of Jupiter and Venus and that he'd make a new fortune—something that has since come to pass.

He's fairly musical and plays the piano rather well. He succeeds in the interpretation of the *melody* but is in rebellion against the *harmony*. In his youth, he also took up oil and watercolor painting, but he no longer occupies himself with that because he says that, as soon as he touches pencils and paintbrushes, his business affairs go badly. He's very proud of his good looks and takes great care of his large beard and his beautiful silver hair. He remembers tenderly his own father, who, according to all who knew him, was one of the most handsome men of his times and was loved and respected by all who knew him. He died fairly young from a heart attack.

My mother was very pretty in her youth, even though she came from a very ugly and vulgar family. She's always had very little intelligence, and I've always reproached my father for allying himself with a family that was so ugly and had so little distinction. He tells me that he was very young then and didn't understand how important marriage was.

Looking at my mother, who at fifty-five still has a pleasing figure, even though her face is ravaged by age, I always think of your Angèle in *La Curée*.[6] She has the same softness, the same lack of energy, and an astonishing weakness of character; she can't read a small, sentimental anecdote without crying; she has a weak memory; and her only good point is her great kindness. In certain things, however, she's obstinate, and nobody can get out of her head what she has put there. I always think it's one of the qualities or one of the defects inherent in the race that she's descended from and that I feel no sympathy for. In fact, I feel a secret repulsion from it. Nevertheless, I love my mother, but in my imagination I'd like her to be otherwise—a sentiment that I regret a lot and that I always reproach myself for.

I was born ten years after my last brother, when the oldest son was fourteen. My birth was a disappointment to my mother, who had hoped, after three boys, to have a girl. I was, however, pretty and cute like a little girl, and I'm told constantly that those who saw me in the arms of my mother with my beautiful golden curls and my pretty blue eyes always said, "But it isn't possible that this is a boy!" Whenever she sees me, my wet nurse always reminds me that the women she knew nicknamed me the "Little Madonna," since I was such a cute and delicate child. I've a portrait of myself at the age of two, and I can swear to you that no one has ever seen a more beautiful child.

The entire family was very proud of me, my mother above all. My intelligence revealed itself very early on, and I was considered a little prodigy. I was then all alone at home, since my brothers were away at boarding school in a neighboring town. I was very proud of my charm, and, even as the small child that I was, I used to blush with pleasure at hearing my beauty praised. I still recall the thrill of joy and pleasure that ran through my tiny little body when I went out in my little dress of billowing, blue piqué with blue bows and a big Italian straw hat.

When I was four years old, my dresses were taken away, and I was dressed in trousers and a little jacket. When I was dressed as a boy, I experienced a real feeling of shame—I recall it as if it were yesterday—and I ran quickly to hide myself and to cry in the room of my maid, who, to console me, had to dress me again as a girl. People still laugh when they remember my cries of despair as I watched those little white dresses, which were my sole source of happiness, being taken away from me. It seemed to me that I was being denied something that I was always destined to wear. This was my first great unhappiness.

Childhood—First Deviations

At the age of five I was sent to school, but I only stayed there for a few weeks, since the school doctor noticed that I became pale and sickly if I remained seated too long on the school benches.

When I was seven years old, we moved and went to live in Florence. My father's business affairs went magnificently, and we had a splendid coach, footmen, and a beautiful house, where my father brought together everything beautiful and elegant it's possible to imagine. A governess was hired to care for me, and I quickly developed the most lively and exalted friendship for this lady, who was very distinguished and loved me a lot. I even preferred her to my mother, who was very jealous of her and tried as much as possible to detach me from her—something that she didn't succeed at. At seven I was as charming a boy as I had been a beautiful child, with an intelligence that surprised all those who approached me. I had the greatest admiration for all that was beautiful and grand, and I was taken with a real passion for all the beautiful ladies and queens in history whom I read about with my governess.

I had an intense admiration for the French Revolution, and one day, having found a summary of Lamartine's *History of the Girondins*, I devoured it in a few hours.[7] At night I dreamed about it, and I couldn't stop wanting to talk about this grand epoch in the history of France. Marie-Antoinette, Madame Elisabeth, and Princess de Lamballe[8] were my greatest passions. I didn't like the popular heroes and heroines as much, but I've always had a limitless admiration for the unhappy women—those heroines who were dressed in their velvet garments, dragging their ermine coats. I made rapid progress in my little studies, and I astonished my masters by the speed with which I learned and understood everything.

At that time I was completely innocent, and I didn't know anything about anything. I often visited the museums with my governess, where even at such a young age I took a lively interest in the arts, for which I still have a great fondness. The sight of a masterpiece moved me deeply, and the study of mythology, which I pursued along with that of these ancient masterpieces, filled me with so much passion that I dreamed only of heroes, gods, and goddesses. The Trojan War made the greatest impression on me, but the strange thing—and one that I paid attention to only later on—was that all of my thoughts, all of my enthusiasm, were for the heroes rather than the heroines. I admired Helen, Venus, and Andromache a great deal; however, my great love, my great admiration, was for Hector, Achilles, and Paris, but above all for Hector. I had a real passion for him, and I used to enjoy imagining myself as Andromache in order to be able to hold him in my arms. This hero, dressed in armor, with his handsome, athletic body, beautiful naked arms, and magnificent helmet, made me daydream for long hours at a time. I still recall the sweet emotions of those hours spent in the long corridors of the museums, where I saw so many handsome heroes and naked gods that my imagination became animated with them as they took on an imaginary life of their own. I spent long hours reflecting on the happiness of this whole world of marble, so perfect, so far above reality that I couldn't even explain to myself all that it meant.

I already loved solitude, and the games of the other boys almost frightened me. My brothers were too big to pay any attention to me, and besides they spent little time at home. I never had much affection for them. My oldest brother was very handsome, but the two others were less attractive, especially the third one, who, with his short legs and long arms, resembles my mother's family in every respect—a family that, thank God, lived far from us and that I didn't like at all. My brothers are all well established; they all have families and are very happy, especially the first two brothers. I stayed alone in the paternal home—something that I didn't regret at all.

Thus I continued my studies, but in a very irregular fashion. I learned several languages, and I devoured all the literature that made me enthusiastic for all that was beautiful and, above all, for all that was poetic. Poetry exercised a great influence on me. Its cadences gave me real thrills, and I learned long monologues and entire scenes from my favorite tragedies by heart.

Music also thrilled me. I was carried away by beautiful verses as much as by beautiful music. I truly lived in an ideal world, as perhaps only a ten-year-old child could do in his dreams. I was always fascinated with the beautiful heroines of history and poetry, and I loved them like friends, because women seemed to me to be exquisite and charming beings, so far from the earth that I almost made them into divine beings.

At that time I had the greatest fervor for the Virgin Mary, whom I considered the ideal type and model for all women. I was tempted to participate in the cult of her divine nature, and I spent several months in the most outrageous devotion, all the more extraordinary since in our house all religious practices had been abolished and nobody took any notice of them. My mother retained a hatred of churches and of all religious pomp from her former religion, but it was the pomp, above all else, that charmed me. I then changed my tastes, and instead of Helen and the goddesses and heroes of mythology, I took pleasure in the company of saints, virgins, and martyrs. The walls of my bedroom were covered with little images of saints and angels before whom I said my prayers at almost any time of the day or night. In the middle of my lessons I'd ask to leave for some reason, and I used to run to my bedroom to say my prayers to the charming Madonna, whom I considered a sister and a friend.

This devotion lasted a short time and disappeared all of a sudden. I don't know why. I always blame it on the little image of Saint Mary Magdalene of Pazzi,[9] which my mother's maid had, and which I found so horrible that I couldn't keep a straight face before this little monster. Since then my admiration for virgins and saints has ceased, and I've fallen back solidly upon mythology. I almost became an idol worshiper, and I even bought a statuette of Venus in order to burn incense to her and to bring her bouquets of flowers every morning.

For some time I was feeling a whole new life awakening

inside me. I could no longer stay in one place, and my imagination presented to me the most beautiful images, which kept me awake at nights. I read everything that fell into my hands and I devoured the illustrated novels that I found in my father's library. This stirred me up so much that I became so passionate, so nervous, that everyone was amazed by it. I always spoke out of turn, and in the ebullient outbursts of precocious youth I had the most audacious thoughts and the strongest susceptibility to sadness and dejection without any apparent cause. I often cried when I was alone, and in order to console myself, I'd take refuge in an imaginary world.

My passion for dresses with trains still stayed with me, and when I was alone, I placed myself before my mother's mirror and I walked up and down, trailing behind me bed covers and old shawls. Their long folds draped the length of my body and the rustling sound that they made on the carpets made me shiver with joy. I always felt a desire to cover myself with long veils, and this passion, which has never entirely left me since my childhood, obsessed me more and more.

One day a friend of my mother's jokingly told me that she was beginning to be able to see my moustache sprouting. I nearly strangled her, since this remark seemed to me to be so insolent, and the news made me very sad. I quickly ran to my mirror and was very happy to see my beautiful red lips entirely free of the horrible peach fuzz that would have frightened me so much.

I used to enjoy dressing up as a woman, and this was easy with my imagination and the beauty that I was endowed with. The adventures that I made up in my mind made me shiver with pleasure.

I was still very innocent at the age of thirteen, which I was at the time, and I had no idea about the union of the sexes nor of the differences that existed between them. This seems strange for a child so advanced for his age, but it's the simple truth.

I lived too much in my heart and in my imagination. I loved everything that was *ideal* far too much to be able to see things that were right in front of me.

A groom about fifteen years of age soon put an end to my innocence on this subject. It was during a stay in a resort town, and all our servants had come along with us. I often went to the stables to see our horses, and I enjoyed playing and speaking with a boy of my age that I was sometimes allowed to run with in the great garden. I was soon enlightened by this kid, who made me as knowledgeable as he himself was. When I learned how children were made, I was so indignant that I felt a profound disgust for my parents, who seemed to have no shame about having made me in such an awful manner. These conversations ended up upsetting me terribly, because, if I was very mature from the point of view of intelligence—too mature, alas!—I was far from being mature physically, and at thirteen I wasn't even a man yet. This young man masturbated in front of me several times, and although I was dying to imitate him and my hot blood was circulating in my veins, I couldn't succeed at it when I was alone.

Soon this boy was sent away, and if I didn't forget his lessons, I no longer thought of them much. However, what really astonished me was that he was always talking about sleeping with naked women and what he did to them, whereas I experienced no desire to do this at all and would have found it natural enough to sleep with a man. It seemed to me that I was too weak, too pretty, too delicate to sleep with a woman, whom I resembled so closely, and besides I'd never have had the courage.

Men seemed to me from that time onward to be much more handsome than women, because I admired in them a force, a vigorous form that I didn't have and that it seemed to me impossible ever to possess. I always imagined myself to be a woman, and from then on all of my desires were those of a woman.

At that time I had a few friends, and without being conscious of it, I had exaggerated feelings of friendship for them. I was jealous of them, and when they passed by with their arms around each other, I'd tremble all over. I envied them, and my greatest joy was to give them proof of my affection and to make small sacrifices for them. I was tormented by their indifference and their noisy games, which were so different from my own, but I still would've preferred it if they had associated with nobody but me.

However, mature men—men of thirty to forty years of age—attracted me the most. I admired their well-built shoulders, their deep voices, which contrasted in a striking manner with our own, still childlike voices. I didn't understand what I was feeling, but I'd have given the whole world to be held in their arms and to press my entire body against theirs. I spent whole nights dreaming of these things and trying to give them a semblance of reality. I didn't yet know the awful vice that I nourished inside me and that has since made me so unhappy, and I didn't even know to what depths it would lead me.

A servant, who was in our service for a short time and who had a striking face with a black moustache and sideburns, attracted all my attention. Through the petty ruses of a young boy, I tried to get him to speak to me about indecent things, and he gave in to it with all of his heart. I liked him a lot and always wanted to have him at my side whenever I went anywhere. In the evenings he came with me into my bedroom on the second floor, and he stayed near me until I was almost asleep. I made him tell me about his mistresses, about the bad places where he went, and I found so much pleasure in it that I stayed up for hours and hours, fully awake and filled with desires that I could barely understand. I'd have liked to have him sleep next to me, to feel his pale and sleek body. I'd have liked to kiss him and to have him next to me in order to take pleasure and to give him some in return. My desires didn't go any farther than that, and I didn't even conceive of any other kind of thing.

One night, after long conversations on our favorite theme, when I was questioning him about the most indecent things, I was seized suddenly with the desire to know him entirely and without any shame, and as a joke I asked him to show me his male member so that I could judge if it was as big and as beautiful as he said. At first he refused, but when I promised not to say anything, he opened his pants and showed it to me, stroking it into an erection, since he had been aroused by my words. He approached the couch on which I was lounging panting with desire and shame. Never had I seen the member of an adult male, and I was so overwhelmed that I couldn't utter a word. Pushed by an undefinable kind of force, by some innate desire, I seized it with my right hand and rubbed it in my face, saying, "It's so beautiful! It's so beautiful!" I was burning with the intense desire to do something with this member that filled my whole hand, and I wanted so eagerly to find in my body an orifice into which I could introduce it—this thing that I had such a violent desire for. Hearing some noise, the servant covered himself quickly and then went away, leaving me burning with desires that I had never had before and that I believed until then didn't exist. In the back of my mind there was already a sort of hopelessness, as if I knew that I could never enjoy what I had liked so much.

Every night I wanted to relive the events of that horrible evening, but the man apparently feared some indiscretion and no longer wanted to show me anything. I grew thinner with rage. One evening the servant was severely punished and was nearly chased out of the house by my father, who had discovered that he had been bringing one of his mistresses into our house almost every evening. Having heard about this—and learning that there was someone who enjoyed so much pleasure with him nearby—I cried with rage and cursed heaven that I wasn't born a woman. Soon this man left our house, but I was only a little saddened by that. I was then still very young, and my impressions, as strong as they were, didn't last very long.

Youth—First Acts

I developed a strong affection for a magnificent young man who had been working as a groom in our stable for some time. He was truly superb—young, with a little brown moustache. He was of medium height, robust, and very well built. In secret I used to bring him cigars that I took from my father's smoking room. I also brought him cakes and sweets, which I deprived myself of for him. He was a very honest boy who loved to talk freely but who didn't allow himself any liberties. One day, while joking with him, I asked him to show me his naked body. He scolded me and didn't want to indulge me in my desire. I liked him more than ever, and my desire to see him, to be near him, and to touch his face became truly an obsession.

As I could hope for nothing from him, I tried to make myself believe that I was a woman, and at night I placed my pillow next to me and kissed it and bit it as if it were a living person. I thought of the handsome young man who was so robust and so fresh, and by making some movements I tried to give myself the illusion of sleeping with him. And in doing so, I experienced my first ejaculation almost involuntarily.

I was so afraid of such a thing that despite the pleasure I felt I promised myself that I'd no longer commit such an error. I didn't keep my promise very well, and soon I fell into the most degrading vices that one could fall into. My lively imagination gave me the most pleasant of images, and I enjoyed this frightful pleasure by evoking the images of men who attracted me and whom I'd have liked to be with. However delicate I was in appearance, my constitution was very strong, and I wasn't harmed by something that might have undoubtedly killed another.

At that time my father's business affairs went very badly, and we had to leave Italy for France in order to start over. We lived for several months in Paris, which I had already visited many years before. A very simple life took the place of our luxurious lifestyle, and I can assure you that it was the saddest time of my life. My father's character became embittered. Even in Paris his business affairs went from bad to worse. My governess left us at this time, and I enrolled in one of the Parisian boarding schools as a day student.

I couldn't stand my school lessons, and in order to have more time to myself and not to follow the regular course of studies, I declared that I didn't have the ability to be an engineer, which is what my father wanted me to become. Instead, I wanted to study painting since I had enough natural talent for drawing. Through my charms and my persuasive abilities I succeeded in convincing my father that I needed to leave the boarding school in order to study with a painter. I went to his studio very rarely because I preferred strolling around Paris and visiting the galleries and museums. I used to go to the painter's studio in the morning, since he lived very far from my parents, and in the afternoon I used to occupy myself with reading and drawing.

That time was very pleasant for me, but the desire to be with a man still plagued me, and I became thoroughly unhappy to belong to a sex that my soul didn't belong to. I continued with my solitary vice, which soon had no more attraction for me, and which I therefore abandoned because it began to tire me, both in body and soul, and because it no longer offered me any pleasure.

After several months in Paris we returned to Italy, where business had once again called my father. I then entered an academy of fine art, but I no longer had any passion for it, and I only went there in order not to be forced to do anything else that would particularly repel me. I was especially prone to such a condition, given the psychological state that I found myself in. The boys who attended the school of fine art with me seemed to be horribly common and vile. They had frightful hands, while mine were the most beautiful and best-groomed hands that anyone could find. In addition, I was very proud of my birth, my travels, and my superior education, and I had no desire to mix with those little boys, most of whom were the sons of butchers and merchants. Nowadays several of them are gifted artists, while I haven't made any progress at all in the art that I had chosen—on a whim, it's true.

I was usually free during the day because I went only rarely to school, and I spent my time meditating and reading. It was during this time, accompanied by several of my friends and cousins who were my own age, that I visited a brothel for the first time. I left it feeling discouraged and distressed. The women didn't attract me at all, and I felt nothing but repugnance for them.

One of them kissed me, and I felt such a violent disgust for this frightful person that I disengaged myself from her as quickly as I could and ran away as fast as possible, to the great astonishment of those who had accompanied me there. I went back several times, hoping to overcome my repugnance and to do what all the others did, but I never succeeded. I remained absolutely frigid under the most passionate caresses, and I felt only the most horrible disgust.

One day one of my friends, a young libertine, wanted me to be with him at one of his love-making sessions with one of those women, but I couldn't get over my innate aversion, and the scene of debauchery left me cold. Nevertheless, those places of ill repute inspired a sort of mysterious attraction in me, and many times I envied not those who went there, but those who lived there.

I began to think of myself as an exceptional and fantastic being—a being in whose making nature had made a mistake—and as one who, while recognizing the horror of his existence, couldn't do anything to remedy it. I lost my taste for everything. My sad and gloomy soul abandoned itself to a profound feeling of discouragement, and I fell into a deep depression.

I spent my mornings and afternoons walking in the gardens and along the promenades all alone, afflicted by a great sadness, doubting everything from nature to God. I wondered why I was born into such a miserable condition and what crime I had committed before my birth to be punished in such a frightful manner.

No one around me noticed anything, and they attributed my silence and my sadness to a bad character and an unnatural strangeness. My father was too absorbed with his business affairs and with rebuilding his fortune, which preoccupied him a great deal, and my mother thought about the house and her visits and wasn't, in any case, of such a nature as to worry about the afflictions of the soul. My brothers were far away, so I lived all alone, prey to my sorrows and my sad thoughts. I saw before me an entire life destroyed by a horrible passion that blind nature had inspired in me. I felt treasures within me that nobody would ever want, that would stay forever enclosed within my soul, and that would end by slowly annihilating me.

I came to desire death and to call for it in the awful solitude that I found myself in. I could never describe all the horrible tortures that afflicted me then. Nevertheless, from these long, painful moments I sometimes emerged with the most magnificent energy, with joys that had no causes and hopes that would never be realized. I tried to change my nature though serious reading and through religious devotions. Everything was useless, and each new attempt left me more discouraged than ever.

I wanted to feel affection for women, for young girls, even for children, but I couldn't. To me women were lovely and sweet friends. They could have slept next to me in all security, because I wouldn't have experienced the slightest of desires for them.

Men struck me as charming and handsome because of their strength and vigor, and I felt attracted to them by an unknown force—an irresistible attraction. I used to like to see handsome young men passing by in the streets, and when someone pleased me, I'd retrace my steps to see him again. Thus I had spiritual lovers whom I loved and followed in silence, without any of them suspecting a thing. I visited nobody, out of fear of betraying my frightful secret, which made me tremble and feel ashamed. I won't tell you how I suffered then or the frightful thoughts that suddenly popped into my head. You can imagine them easily enough. Thus I reached my eighteenth birthday without any of these moral torments having noticeably affected my constitution or my health.

I was then what I am now with only slight differences. I'm of medium height (five feet four inches), well proportioned, with a slender, but not too thin, frame. My torso is superb. A sculptor wouldn't have found anything to criticize about it and wouldn't have found any great difference between it and that of Antinous.[10] I've very broad shoulders—perhaps too broad. My hips are well developed, and my pelvis is large, like that of a woman. My knees are slightly bent inward, and my feet are very small. My hands are superb, and my fingers are curved with shiny, pink, polished fingernails that are carefully manicured, like those of antique statues. My neck is long and rounded, and the nape of my neck is charming, covered with down. My head is pretty, and at eighteen it gave me a distinct advantage. Its oval shape is perfect, and everyone is struck by its childlike form. At twenty-three, people still take me for seventeen at the most. My complexion is white and pink and becomes crimson at the least sign of emotion. My forehead isn't handsome; it slightly recedes, with deep-set temples; happily it's half covered with curly, sandy blond hair, which is naturally frizzy. The shape of my head is perfect because of my frizzy hair, but from a distance it reveals an enormous protuberance at the back. My eyes are bluish gray, with long, dark eyelashes and thick, arched eyebrows. My gaze is liquid, but my eyes are almost always dark, with circles under them. They're also subject to swelling, which passes rapidly. My mouth is rather big, with large red lips; my lower lip hangs down a little. People say that I've an Austrian mouth. My teeth are dazzling, and even though I've three badly discolored teeth, luckily nobody ever sees them. My ears are small, with colored lobes. My chin is round, and even at eighteen it was smooth and velvety, like that of a woman's; at present a light beard, closely shaved, hides it a little. There are two black and velvety beauty spots on my left cheek, contrasting with my bluish gray eyes. My nose is thin and straight with soft nostrils, which are slightly, but imperceptibly, curved. My voice is sweet, and people always regret that I didn't learn to sing.

This is my portrait. Perhaps it could serve you in the reconstitution of the strange being that it pleased nature to make, to my great despair.

Military Service

At the age of twenty I had to become a soldier, having attained the age for military service. My father's fortune, having been rebuilt once again, made it possible for me to enter as a volunteer earlier than the deadline established by law. My father chose the cavalry for me, which cost much more and was consequently much more chic. Besides, he was told that the strains of military service were much more bearable in this branch of service. Therefore, before I turned nineteen, I joined a garrison regiment in a small town, far from the eyes of the general commander, whose officers, we were assured, were very well brought up and very polite. They treated their volunteers well.

I had always had a real horror of military life. Its physical toll, its constraints, its terrible discipline frightened me a great deal, and I'd have given I-don't-know-what in order to be delivered from the horrible boredom of spending a year in so disagreeable a fashion. The first few months seemed to me rather hard, but little by little I grew used to this life. Besides, distractions weren't lacking.

I had several companions, young gentlemen proud of their nobility and wealth, whom I quickly became quite friendly with. Everyone soon befriended me because my pretty, child-like face contrasted attractively with the hussar's uniform that I wore, giving me the charms of a transvestite.

The various duties, the riding lessons, and the open-air life all had a very positive effect on my health and my spirits. The parade days, the long rides on horseback, the suppers and the dinners, all ended up by reconciling me to the military life, while the indulgence of the officers made the rest of it bearable enough for us.

What pleased us above everything else was to play the great lord and master with the ordinary soldiers and to put ourselves in a superior position vis-à-vis those poor people.

We all slept together with our platoon in large upper rooms. We'd have liked to have a separate room, but this was impossible for us, and I haven't regretted it since.

The petty officer who slept with us was an old grump, very sullen and boring. We had very little influence over him, and he didn't want to accept anything from us for fear of compromising himself or of not being able to scold us at his leisure. The other petty officers were, on the other hand, very friendly to us and never refused what we offered them or the dinners we invited them to.

In this exciting and busy life my senses calmed down and the incessant hallucinations that had pursued me for such a long time quieted down and almost ceased. We were too tired to dream about anything else except our duty. The men who slept with us side by side didn't tempt me at all. They were too rough, too ugly, too stupid to inspire in me any desire for them. They were, in addition, very dirty, and they never tempted me in any way.

Six months passed and spring arrived. Part of the regiment changed its billet, and other platoons came to take the place of those who left. In our room there was a real revolution the day that the new troops arrived. I took advantage of the situation to change my place and put my cot in the most convenient and the most remote corner of the room. My bed was across from that of the sergeant who commanded the platoon that had just arrived.

This man was young (twenty-five or twenty-six years of age) and had a very handsome face. At first I didn't pay a great deal of attention to him; I didn't even think about him. He was very silent and modest, treating the soldiers sternly and not speaking much when off duty. He commanded the platoon with a lot of grace and energy, and later I came to admire the charming and chivalrous manner in which he handled his horse. On the parade ground he made him jump over ditches and other dangerous obstacles that I was terribly afraid of.

The first feeling I had for him was jealousy and envy. He seemed to me to be too tall compared to my small and slender size. He seemed too courageous and too skillful compared to the rest of us. He had a way of commanding that I envied and that I'd never achieve.

Ordinarily he went to bed very early, whereas my friends and I didn't. We went to the theater, or we stayed all evening long in the regimental canteen, playing music and dancing very gaily. One evening, taken by an inexplicable fantasy, I left the company of my friends and retired to our dormitory. Many soldiers were already asleep, and their sergeant was in the process of undressing.

I did the same and lay down to sleep, without missing a single movement of my neighbor. He was already stripped down to his shirt, and soon, seated on his bed, he took off his last piece of clothing and jumped into his bed with only his nightshirt on.

I was struck by the beauty and the perfection of his body. In the feeble light of the lamp that was suspended from the ceiling, it appeared to me to be of a marvelous beauty, surpassing the antique masterpieces that I had been so passionate about earlier in my life. But those were made of marble, and this lovely body was full of strength and youth. His legs impressed me especially; they were perfectly shaped—wiry, thin, and supple all at the same time. His entire handsome body suggested an extraordinary strength joined with the most graceful form. The next day I watched him with a great deal of attention, and I was struck by his handsome face, by the elegance of his manners, by his well-kept hands, and by his short nails. I felt overcome with friendship for this young man who did his duty so sadly, was so sober, and went out so little. However, I didn't have any desire for him. I admired him as if he were a handsome statue, and I didn't think that he'd ever be able to understand me. In the evenings I often sat next to him, and I enjoyed having him tell me about his country, his home town, or his family. He didn't have a mother, and his father had several children with another wife. This is why he stayed in the military. His father was a petty clerk and had given him some education. He wrote very well, and in his free time he read books translated from the French, especially those by Dumas the Elder.

I began to like his company more and more, and soon I developed the most tender friendship for him. Several times I invited him to come to the theater with us, and this didn't seem to disturb my friends, who were also friendly toward this young man. He also came to dinner with us a couple of times, but he was always very cold and reserved. He had a great many duties, and in the evenings he was often so tired that he preferred not to leave the barracks. I'd have offered him money, but I was afraid that he wouldn't accept it.

Soon I couldn't do without him, and I looked for every occasion to please him. I was content to take his hand and sometimes to stroke his fine, sleek, dark brown hair and his head, which was so charming and serious. I noticed and admired the beauty of his teeth and of his handsome mouth, which was adorned but not hidden by a little brown moustache. I saw in him my favorite heroes, and when he passed by in his handsome black and yellow uniform on his beautiful horse, I compared him to Hector or Achilles.[11]

I was jealous of him, but I enjoyed having him recount his military adventures and his passing love affairs. Even though he had a remarkable physique, he went out to find women only twice a month at the most, because they were too expensive and he had so little money.

Besides, he had been involved with women and love very little, since he had been in the military since the age of seventeen and had not had the leisure of becoming sophisticated. I fiercely envied all the women who took this young man in their arms and made him happy, even if only once, since I looked upon him as a god. I'd have given an entire lifetime of joy to be able to have that satisfaction at least once. I was definitely very unhappy! And I'd never have this immense pleasure next to which all else pales.

And nevertheless, I'd never have dared to say a word to him about all of this. I'd have died of shame before having finished this horrible confession. But what had to come to pass came to pass. One evening we all dined together, and our friend had joined our party. Everyone was drunk. Near our lodging several of us got terribly sick. The soldiers were no longer sleeping with us but in a neighboring room. Our eight or ten beds remained in the immense, somber room, lit by a very small lamp that went out in the middle of the night.

We were more or less excited, and our escapades were prolonged well into the night. The quartermaster, who slept in the little room next to ours, was dead drunk and snored horribly. My bed was in the most remote corner of the room just opposite that of the young petty officer, who was himself in very high spirits thanks to the generous amount of wine that he had drunk, which he wasn't accustomed to for all sorts of reasons.

My companions were asleep before too long, and we hadn't even undressed. Finally I decided to do so, and taking off my uniform, I curled up in my fine linen shirt and got into my little bed. I had my young friend sit on my bed, and in our excitement and in the intoxication caused by the wine and the noise that we had just made, I lavished upon him the sweetest caresses and the most flattering words as if in jest.

I was half lying down on the cushion that we were allowed to keep on our bed. He was half undressed, sitting on my cot when he leaned very close to me. I was speaking to him as if in rapture or in a semi-intoxicated state caused by sleepiness and the warmth of the bed. This was beginning to overwhelm me, when he stretched out on top of me. He took me in his arms and gave me a lengthy kiss on the cheek, all the while slipping his hands under the covers and grabbing handfuls of my flesh. I felt as if I had died of an immense joy that had seized me all of a sudden. We pressed against each other for several moments, one against the other, face to face, with burning red cheeks, my mouth pressed against his mouth as if against a sweet, warm pillow. I had never been so happy!

The lamp resting on the floor threw mysterious rays into the immense dormitory, where in the far distant beds my companions slept. It left that corner where we were thus in ecstasy in the deepest shadows. I was afraid, however, that someone would see us, and wanting to enjoy completely the abandonment of my friend's lack of restraint, I whispered in his ear, while kissing it, "Go and turn out the light, and then come back, but do it quickly." He got up, stumbling, and went to drink from the pitcher that was resting on the floor next to the lamp. The dormitory was no longer illuminated by anything but the lamp in the neighboring dormitory. As a result you could see only a little in the center of the room; everything else was in deep darkness. I saw him in the shadows coming back to his bed, which was in front of mine. I heard him undressing himself very quickly and coming toward me as he tried to stifle the sound of his breath.

This short period of time seemed to me to last a century, and when I felt him next to me under the covers, I seized him around the waist; I touched him; I kissed him passionately, nearly crying with joy and pleasure. He offered himself to my love with enthusiasm. In an instant we were naked, our bodies becoming one, so closely were we intertwined. Never would I have believed it possible to taste such pleasure. Our tongues joined each other in our mouths. We held each other so closely that we could barely breathe. My hands ran across, in all senses of the phrase, this beautiful body, so ardently desired, this sweet and virile head, which was so different from my own. At last our pleasure reached its climax, and what transported us most was that we achieved orgasm at the same time. We stayed intertwined for a long time, exchanging sweet words. "Never have I had such pleasure with a woman," he said. "Their lips and their caresses aren't so hot and so loving." These words filled me with joy and pride. I was holding him at last—this man whom I had desired so much. And what a charming man! All women would have envied me. Finally we separated, promising to love each other forever and to do whatever was possible to stay together.

The next morning, when we got up, we didn't dare look at each other, shame having momentarily succeeded our foolish passion, and in the fresh air of the morning we sobered up completely. All morning long we only spoke very few words to each other, but in the evening, as soon as we were in bed and alone in the profound darkness of our corner, my desire for him was rekindled, and so I got up, holding my breath, and went to find him. He was awake and waiting for me, or so he said.

We prolonged that night of pleasure for as long as possible, and I don't believe that there has ever been anyone more in love or more passionate than we were. We wrung from each other such lustful spasms as to drive each other nearly mad, and my charms exercised such an attraction on him that he took my foot and kissed it wildly.

During that night all our restraints left us, and from then on we spent nearly all the other nights together in bed, kissing and caressing each other. "What beautiful cheeks you have," he told me. "They're as soft as those of a woman, and your feet, they're like those of a child." These remarks filled me with joy. I no longer wanted to be a woman, because I found this terrible passion so much more delectable and enjoyable, superior to what ordinary love could offer, especially since it didn't attract me at all. I felt so much affection for this handsome young man that I ended up loving him more than anyone else in the whole world, and I thought of nothing but him. I wanted to see him handsome and well kept; I wanted to make him a new and elegant uniform to my liking; I wanted to see him beautiful, perfumed, and well groomed. Money meant nothing to me, and I spent it on him liberally without regret. At first he didn't want to accept anything from me, but soon I convinced him to take whatever I gave him. He never asked for anything, but I knew what he needed and what would satisfy his desires.

I wanted him to eat with us, but he didn't want to embarrass my companions or to let some know-it-all guess at our passionate friendship. I withdrew from my companions as much as possible, finding some forced pretense to excuse myself from taking part in their amusements. I isolated myself completely from them so that they went walking in town or to the theater by themselves. Instead, I went to a furnished room that I had rented in town, where my friend came to join me on Sundays and holidays. There we had debaucheries of fine dinners and sumptuous meals only for the two of us; and we always ended them in the same way. The thought of my friend was constantly with me, and it never left me. I'd have sacrificed everything for him. Nevertheless, we took our pleasure in the most innocent of ways, that's to say, in the least criminal of ways.

He wasn't used to the sweet perfumes or perfumed waters that I bathed myself in, and even though he took the greatest care of his own hygiene, he didn't know about these sorts of refinements, which charmed him nevertheless. According to the fashion of the time, I wore silk nightshirts with drawstrings, which felt good and were soft to the touch. The good food and the fine wines that I fed him acted powerfully on his nature. He wasn't used to such a refined and easy lifestyle, but he did feel all of its sensuality.

When he came to the apartment, I was almost always in bed. He'd kiss me, saying, "God, what a lovely spouse you'd make! But that's of little importance! You're no less than my little wife!" And in that small dark room there were endless whispers and caresses and burning kisses in the big bed covered with a fresh white quilt that I had brought from my father's house. That quilt had nothing in common with the gray, rough blankets of the army.

But where we experienced the greatest intoxication was in the bathhouses of this charming, agreeable city, where we bathed together on Sundays and holidays in the same cubicle. There were two bathtubs, and we'd douse ourselves with scented water from a flask. Often we would sit in the same bathtub, embracing each other in the hot water.

My friend grew so used to me that he couldn't do without me, no less than I could do without him. He had never been so loved, and he had never experienced as much pleasure as I offered him. We even took some excursions by carriage into the countryside surrounding the town. When he drove across the fields illuminated only by the moonlight, we experienced perfect happiness.

He also wanted to show his friendship for me and to demonstrate that he thought of me as much as he thought of himself. One day on one of our regimental marches, he jumped over an enormous ditch in order to get me a bunch of grapes that I had wanted. In the end, never were there truer lovers than we were, who were as happy as we were, who had greater passion in their hearts than we had in ours. The horrible and accursed passion that burned inside me since my childhood had at last found its way and had taken flight and had entangled with it a being that was innocent of its faults. Only an accursed passion could have ensnared and poisoned such an innocent soul. I've often reproached myself for having corrupted a young man through my influence. He had probably never suspected such abominable passions. However, at that time I didn't think of such things, and I didn't find anything reprehensible in my conduct. It was only later that remorse seized me and that I bitterly regretted my fault and his.

My year of military service was almost at an end, and I regarded my approaching departure with real terror—something that I'd have believed impossible a year before. The idea that I'd have to separate myself for a long time, if not forever, from my friend was unbearable to me. At night we'd often cry together. He still had several years to serve, and he saw with sadness that the time would come when he'd be left alone and isolated, now that he had a friend who was so passionately attached to him. I'll not tell you all that we suffered on those days before our final farewell. I neglected my comrades a lot in those last few weeks, and although they didn't suspect a thing, they noted with displeasure that I preferred to be with a young man whom they didn't consider their equal in rank.

Finally the terrible day arrived. Our good-byes were made in our little room, where so many happy hours had been spent, and I delayed my departure in order to enjoy the company of my dear and beloved friend one last time. I left him all that I possessed in terms of money, and I gave him several mementos, begging him to write to me as often as possible. He promised me to do so, and at last I left.

When I returned to my father's house, I felt a frightful void, and the habits of the family seemed unbearable to me. Everyone gave me the warmest of welcomes, and they pampered me in the most tender way. My nerves were so worn out, though, that an insurmountable melancholy took hold of me and kept me in its grip relentlessly. I had such intense nervous crises and fevers that I was advised to seek a change of climate and spend some time in the center of Italy. Everything was useless, however, and my only consolation was in the letters that I received from time to time.

Nevertheless, at the end of three months I had regained my health completely, and I began to take an interest once again in painting and literature, which had interested me so much in my youth. The image of my friend soon faded and lost all of its charm and vivacity. He still wrote me sometimes, but I only responded with colder and colder letters at longer and longer intervals. Soon he stopped writing to me, and I wasn't too upset about that.

Six months after my departure his regiment was placed in charge of a garrison, and he was killed by a pistol shot by one of his drunken companions, who had had a quarrel with him about their military service. He died immediately on a road lined by fir trees that went from the town to the fortress. His murderer was condemned to the galleys for life. I didn't regret his death, which I first learned about through the newspapers. Later a petty officer whom I had met afterward gave me the full details of his death. The passionate friendship that I had for him had burned itself out, and there remained nothing of it, not even ashes. I'd have had no pleasure in seeing him again, and I'd have been ashamed for him and for me. The earth would have kept this secret, and only these pages to you will have divulged it. I've told you only the pure and simple truth; you're free to believe it or not. Its *dénouement* may seem romantic to you, but it's nevertheless very real.

I now live alone as a virgin, having no taste for a life from which I get no pleasure at all. The desire for men pursues me still, but now having no longer any occasion for weakness, I'll surely not fall again into the horrible errors of my senses. I won't have a family; I'll never have children. Everyone is surprised to see me so sad and mournful, especially at my age with my face and in my position. If you knew me, Sir, would you share in this surprise? I don't believe so. Everyone tries to figure out what causes my sadness and my desolation. I've almost retired from the world, and I live in almost complete solitude, to the great astonishment of everyone. My health is much weakened, but this I say with pleasure, because I want to be dead already, especially since I don't fear death.

Forgive me, Sir, if these pages are so badly written, but I won't even reread them because, if I did, I wouldn't send them. Doesn't such a terrible illness of the soul deserve to be described? Or at least known by the greatest compiler of human documents in our time? I don't know whether you can do something with the terrible passion I've confessed to you. In any case, I'm content to have made it known to you. If, in the sublime descriptions of human miseries, this misery that afflicts me can find some place in your work, please, Sir, don't make me too odious. I live with death in my soul and no longer have any joy to wait for here below. I feel guilty and afflicted by a frightful destiny that I can't escape from. Have I not already been punished enough?

It has now been five hours since I began to write, and the pen is falling from my hand, due to fatigue. If I can help you with anything through these pages, then I don't regret the time I've spent in writing to you, especially since it wasn't a terrible motive that caused me to take the pen into my hand.

SECOND LETTER (1889)

New Confessions

This morning I reread the pages I finished last night. I only glanced at them, but I was tempted to throw them into the fire. I didn't do that, sure that I'd have regretted it later. These pages must have some interest for you. For this reason I'm going to fill in a gap that I voluntarily left out through a false sense of shame but that certainly didn't escape your clairvoyant eye. Since I've confessed so many horrors, I can't help confessing others and reveal myself completely. I'd have liked to spare myself this rather dirty recitation, but then you certainly wouldn't understand how a young man of nineteen, completely virginal, could have corrupted a man of twenty-five so easily—a man who had already known several women. That's something that was and still is absolutely unknown to me and something that I don't even want to know. However deeply corrupted my morals are, and even though I've dreamed from a very young age of the most exquisite depravation, I didn't lose what could be called my innocence until the age of sixteen. Until then I was content with imaginary debaucheries and solitary pleasures.

My first tutor was a friend of the family, who had been a friend of my father's since his youth. He was a former captain in the Piedmont cavalry, having served in all the Italian wars, where, as they say, he brutally cut down many Austrians. He was looked upon as a completely debauched person, and it was whispered that he had lived for a long time with a young man whom he had helped to squander three-fourths of his inheritance. This captain lived off his pension and the numerous horse deals he made. He had traveled a lot, and he had been in Hungary for a long time. Even though he was from the lower classes, he frequented the best houses. Ladies could barely tolerate him because of the poor esteem that he showed them both in his acts and in his speech. Men, on the other hand, especially sportsmen, received him with open arms.

He came to see us sometimes, but at first he paid no attention to me. However, I felt attracted to him, and I had a lot of warm feelings toward him. He was tanned, very tall, with a frame that seemed indestructible, from which bulged muscles as firm as steel, taking the place of seemingly nonexistent flesh. For me he was the archetype of the old baron in a suit of armor, and I never saw him without thinking about one of the characters in *Ivanhoe*.[12] His head was superb, brown like that of a mulatto, with a great hooked nose that slanted slightly to the left; his black, deep-set eyes shone forth with an extraordinary clarity; and his long black moustache showed only the contours of his mouth—a mouth that mocked everyone, with large, brown lips and strong, white teeth. His enormous head was almost entirely bald and covered with a down of short, black bristles only at the back and on the sides. His hands fit the rest of his body; his voice was harsh and deep; and his entire athletic body had a herculean force about it. He could bend horseshoes with his bare hands. He had a way of looking at people that made them lower their eyes, and he didn't spare anyone.

He took the greatest of liberties with me, tickling me under the chin, and when he met me in the corridor or when I walked him to the door, he pinched and caressed me for a long time, even in the presence of my father, who didn't see anything bad in it.

As I've already told you, I knew nothing at the time except through hearsay. I trembled with desire to know something through my own experience, and when this man touched me, my blood rushed through my whole body. One day, when he was talking to my father about the wounds he had received during the war, he wanted to show us a scar he had on his thigh. He had avenged himself for it by splitting the head of the German soldier who had given it to him. He unbuttoned his pants, and to my great joy, he showed us his enormous, gleaming, shiny, bronze thigh, covered with coarse, black hairs, crossed by a large, pink gash, which seemed to me quite handsome in the middle of the somber flesh and hair that gave it a brown border.

I held my breath in order to see what he was touching under his shirt, but I saw nothing except a dense, black bush that made me tremble violently. Despite this, I didn't have any affection for this man, but he did seem to me to be so masculine that I very much wanted to belong to him, even if only for a few moments. Ever since that day, whenever he looked at me, I was very moved. I blushed, and when he touched me, I trembled with desire. Even today, in writing these lines, I feel the emotion I would like to stifle welling up inside of me once again, and I feel that, if he were here now, I'd abandon myself to him completely. As a man accustomed to all sorts of adventures, he understood what he could get out of my pretty youth and my charms—the charms of a young girl disguised as a boy. He invited me to come and see the horses in his stables, which, I believe, he was soon sending away to I-don't-know-what country. I went there full of desire for an adventure where I could at last learn something and indulge my own tastes. These tastes had grown so overwhelming, since they had not yet been satisfied, that they didn't leave me any peace. After the visit to the horses, which I admired a great deal without understanding anything, he showed me his apartment. It

consisted of a living room off the landing, a bedroom, and a
toilet. For servants, he had a groom and an old porter.

When I entered this furnished room, which was engulfed in
smoke, smelling of cigars and the stables, and where everything was lying about, I was dumbfounded, and my desire gave
me such violent palpitations that I could barely breathe. I felt
my extremities freeze. Even now I still have this cruel and delicious feeling at times.

He sat me on his sofa, caressed me, laughed in a very forced
manner, and looked at me with such strange eyes that I was
afraid, while at the same time I was charmed. I didn't know
what to say; I was ashamed, and I was as red as a peony. He
took me by the hands, and placing me on his knees, he began to
kiss me on the ear, whispering things so quietly that I couldn't
hear him. At last he got up, saying, "Do you want to? . . . Do
you want to? . . ." with a husky voice that nearly frightened
me. I didn't respond—I was so terrified!

He got up abruptly, locked the doors, and closed almost
all the shutters of the window. Then he came toward me. I
was the one who was panting with desire, shame, and fear.
He undressed me in the blink of an eye, all the while running his hands over my body, removing everything, including
my stockings and shoes, throwing off my shirt, and carrying
me, like a little child, to his bed. Just as quickly he was completely naked and lying next to me while I was, as if in a dream,
unconscious of my acts and my thoughts.

He stretched out on top of me, panting and sighing strongly,
pressing me so violently in his arms that he cut off my breath,
and he began to writhe upon my body. He held my penis
so tightly that, when he moved on me, he aroused me most
delightfully. Meanwhile he licked my ears and slipped his
tongue in my mouth and caressed my whole body with his
hands. In a broken voice, he spoke to me most sweetly and
most wildly. When he ejaculated, he inundated me with it. Nor

did he stop moving, but he bellowed just like a bull. Meanwhile I had a copious orgasm, and for a long time we stuck fast to each other as though we were dead and truly cemented together. We had to struggle to disentangle ourselves.

At that moment I no longer had any shame, and he himself seemed completely happy. He let out a long sigh of pleasure and satisfaction. Afterward we got up and dressed with care, and I looked at myself in the mirror. I was struck by the strange and almost frightening beauty I had at that moment. My face was flushed; my lips were as red as blood; my eyes sparkled with all their most beautiful radiance. I was proud of myself—of the pleasure I had given and of the pleasure I had received. I felt grateful to the captain, and I felt as if I belonged exclusively to him. He made me promise to come and see him often—something that I did with all my heart. I never had such bright and happy days, and it seemed to me that I began to live from that day forward.

From that time on I went to him often. We used to take a late breakfast at a spa; then we lingered for many hours in a closed cubicle. Truly, that man was a satyr! I think he was some sort of Roman from the last days of the Republic—one of those who knew how to invent such skills in wantonness. He used to say that it was best to move all the limbs in pleasure and that he had done it all. He also used to dream up new positions and motions, alternating and repeating them again and again, leaping and twisting in an odd way. I can't begin to describe all that he showed me.

When I got to know all of his repertoire, he said to me, "Now you must belong to me completely, and I must possess you completely." I couldn't ask for anything better; my nature pushed me toward it, and I panted with desire to know new and secret things. I soon understood what he wanted; it seemed quite natural to me, and I didn't refuse. He didn't expect me to abandon myself so completely, and it made him burst with joy. He told me that I was his treasure, that he loved me a great deal, and that he'd give me the greatest pleasure that I'd ever know.

I watched his penis, full of fear, as it distended enormously and stood up fully erected while he anointed it with cold cream. I didn't think that it'd be possible to introduce this enormous thing into my soft and delicate body. He smeared me with the cream, and I went along with this, albeit with an angry spirit and as much uncertain expectation as desire. He arranged me on the bed as usual, with my legs placed on his shoulders so that he might touch my body with his penis. Just then he seized my shoulders, and he drove home the first stroke. I felt such sharp pain that I bucked wildly to oust him, and just as strongly he tried to hold me still. Finally I freed myself from him and leapt off the bed, refusing to start over.

He ground his teeth, he treated me roughly, he begged me, but I was unyielding. How can I confess it to you? It was the physical pain that made me withdraw from the violent act; it wasn't shame or any other feeling. I yielded to my nature, which only wanted what I really was.

He had to content himself with the liberties he had already taken with me, because I never wanted to satisfy him in the manner that I found so painful. I preferred more delicate pleasures that wouldn't leave any trace. I wanted to try this way of love with my friend, but that time too the pain was too strong, and I had to renounce it, even though I did so with regret.

Otherwise, I loved dearly that centurion, who indeed felt himself to be most manly when he saw me so delicately and so charmingly feminine. He often asked me, weeping, to fulfill his desire in every respect, but I never would. That man, however, took the greatest pleasure with me, and he often said he preferred me to the most beautiful virgins. When he took me in his arms, he used to kiss me, suckle me, bite my flesh. Each day, when he ejaculated, he'd bite my shoulder so violently that the marks would remain for days. Never did I delight him so sincerely as I did on those occasions.

I didn't think it was possible to create a man so robust. I often marveled at his naked body. He had, and still has to this day, a complexion the color of darkened copper. He bears the scars of three or four wounds. He had the vigor of Hercules despite being forty-two or forty-three years old, which he wouldn't admit, for he said he was forty-eight, which is false. His virility was at its height. He told me that when he was growing up, he'd have intercourse three or four times a day, but now he was able to have intercourse only once a day. When he ejaculated, you thought you were undone, since he showed so much pleasure at those times that he'd roar like a lion. It was never possible to be prepared for that man's love-making, but he always wanted me to be prepared. I was jealous of him, but no more so than of anyone else who might have been even more charming or even more graceful and youthful.

He was my instructor, and if I had gotten such instruction in other subjects, I wouldn't have complained at all. He was often away, and after a few months I felt new and sweet longings for him, but I'd soon see him again, and no matter how often he was away, I always hoped he'd see me again in the future.

I then had an adventure with a young Spaniard, who was for me what I had been for others. He followed me around every-where for a long time, waiting under my balcony for hours on end, and walking along the riverbank when I was there. When I met him, he showed me the most passionate friendship. I had him come to my place several times, but he had the same char-acter as I had. He was very shy, and I took an immediate aver-sion to him, being used to powerful men. I took leave of him in a way that wasn't quite honorable, and I haven't seen him since. I believe he returned to Spain with his family.

One day, while in town, a man followed me. My captain was traveling, my Spaniard bored me, and I was in need of distraction. We understood each other very well very quickly. I agreed to meet him in the captain's apartment, to which I had the key. I was disgusted with this man, who had the same vice as your Baptiste. He was cold and sticky, a bitter and disagreeable blond; I could do nothing with him because I was so disgusted with him. He went away as quickly as he came, and I never saw him again.

Here, Sir, is the confession I wanted to make to you. It's now finished. Maybe you'll pity me, which is the gift that great intellects have in knowing and understanding both the good and the bad. In the society where I live and where I pass through, isolated because of my own thoughts, I feel profoundly sad and profoundly disgusted. This torpor leaves me only in those instances when I can abandon myself to a foolish passion, and those instances are rare, because I don't want to let anyone know my sad secret. Ladies make a big fuss over me, and more than one of them has made gallant advances toward me—advances that I've always refused smilingly, but with genuine despair and great regret. I like women's company a lot. It truly does for me what women in *La Curée* do for your Maxime, whom I resemble a little.[13] But, being more unhappy than he, my nature won't allow me to love, and it leaves me only with cold debauchery, which ends up by making me hateful.

People often joke about my melancholy and my Werther pose,[14] but if they could read my heart, they'd pity me, or maybe they'd just laugh at me. As I've already told you, I don't have any hope here on earth, and everyone else's joy seems to me to be an insult to my existence. I'll remain always what I am—a pretty, cute, perfumed, irreproachably elegant, frivolous, and secretly debauched being. I say "secretly" because nobody knows what I am and what I do. When I say "nobody," this means that I do make exceptions for three or four people who truly do know me, but since they share my weaknesses and my shame, I don't blush before them, or at least we blush together.

And why should I feel shame for what I do? Wasn't it nature that made the mistake in the first place and condemned me to eternal sterility?

I could have been an adorable and adoring woman, an irreproachable mother and wife, but I am only an incomplete being, a monstrous being, desiring only those who are forbidden to me and desired by those who could only be regarded as my friends, not as my mistresses. Do you know of a more terrible torture? But our sins, aren't they forgivable?

I'm sure, Sir, that you'll keep this confession as one of those human documents that are the least examined and that you'll be grateful to me for having addressed you.

I'll tell you once more about those things that might interest you about my entourage and the environment that I live in. . . .[15]

. . . and if it weren't for the dowry of my mother and for some lucky speculations, we'd be very sad representatives of the nobility. The marriage of my father will explain to you the rest of our decline and the source of our wealth.

My brothers are all well established, and they all have beautiful families. I always pray to God that none of my nieces or nephews will resemble me either physically or morally.

I feel that, as I grow old, I'll become more and more devout, since it offers me the only possible consolation. But my most ardent desire is not to grow old at all but to die in the flower of my youth and beauty. If I was to grow old, I'd despise and hate myself too much.

I've nothing more to add to these pages, which are already too long. I'm afraid I've bored you terribly, if you've, indeed, reached this point. No matter. I've unburdened my soul a little, and I've written with a sort of retrospective pleasure about the abominable and intense scenes of which I've been the author.

It's useless to assure you that everything in this recitation is *true*; I've no reason to lie, and you yourself will perhaps recognize the truth of all that I've written to you. It seems to me that I've treated myself rather harshly, that I haven't flattered myself either physically or morally.

Please forgive my awful scribbling, but I've written to you with an open heart, as if I were confessing to a doctor or a friend, and I haven't paid attention to form or spelling.

Here, Sir, is what I've had to say.

One of your most passionate admirers.

POSTSCRIPT: Do you know, Sir, what caused me to write to you from where I am for the jubilee of the Holy Father? It's because of the intense desire and the raging feeling that I've experienced in seeing a young man who is the most perfect and noble beauty, for whom I've the most ideal passion, and whom I've never spoken to nor ever will. I love him so much that I hate him, and I wish him death so that he'll never belong to anyone else. Can you ever imagine such a martyrdom?

THIRD LETTER (1889)

Sir:

I hope you've received the package of badly written pages that I sent to you. I wrote them with pleasure, sure that in your profound studies of mankind, of its sicknesses and misfortunes, such a confession could only please you.

I wrote you during a very boring and sad day, so much so that the rain came down in torrents, and its melancholic traits spread out to all things. The last part of this confession was written yesterday morning when a frightful rain beat at the window of my banal and badly furnished room.

What I've written shows the effect of my disposition and the sadness and boredom that surround me. I've exaggerated all of my traits with the blackest of hues, and I've shown myself to be what I am—perhaps—but what I am not always—certainly. This is what I am, and I have this melancholy and this sadness, which have become the foundation of my character, but I do come out of it often, and I don't always feel so unhappy. I'm writing you this letter after a delicious dinner in the company of numerous friends where I received plenty of compliments and where the generous wine and the brilliance of a rich house enchanted my heart and my spirit. I want, therefore, to complete the study of my personality, which I often consider favored by nature, since it has made me a being that even the most audacious poets haven't learned how to create.

Personality

As a man charming in body, I possess the spirit, the charms, and all the tastes of the most delightful women. I can therefore profit sometimes from the combined gifts of the two sexes, even if I blame myself at times for being neither a man nor a woman. I like to compare myself to the ravishing heroes of mythology and to tell myself that Hyacinth, Ganymede, and so many other ravishing creatures didn't differ from me in any way at all and were adored by the most handsome and powerful of gods.[16]

I've a repugnance—the most absolute kind—for women, but I do consider women to be most like me, and I've the most lively friendship for many of them, who also have a tender friendship for me. Perhaps they're astonished—without knowing the cause—by my reserve and my innocence in regard to them.

I'm in regular correspondence with several charming women, who often confide their most intimate feelings to me and whom I've entertained through conversation that is more than a little licentious. Several of them pretend to believe that I'm courting them and have made me the clearest of advances. I've immediately felt repugnance for them and have kept them at a distance. I always pretend to be in love with another woman, and I give them details about these imaginary persons and tell them all sorts of things that I've learned in books or that I know about through my friends.

Once a married cousin stayed with us for several days. She slept in the room next to mine, and only a wall separated our two beds, which were placed in the corners of our respective bedrooms.

During the night she knocked on the wall of my room, laughing and joking, because she was very lighthearted and always played at being a spoiled child. (She has since died from meningitis.) I feared that she'd get the idea to call me, and so I pretended to fall asleep immediately. I believe I could have slept completely naked with her without the slightest desire ever touching me.

I could have the greatest sympathy for ladies—I say "ladies" because the others seem to me to be gross beasts—but I could only be their friend and never anything else. My feelings awake in a terrible and powerful fashion only when I'm by myself or when I see a man who pleases me—no matter what his social level is, it's true. Nevertheless, I prefer distinguished, well-placed men, especially military men.

Yesterday, when I went to the post office to send the long letter that I had addressed to you, I was struck by the good looks of one of the postal clerks. Romans are in truth very handsome! Today I've mailed several letters just so I could return and see him. I've had a very good time talking to him and looking at him. He's definitely a charming man!

I've a real passion for men, and if I were a woman, I feel I'd be terrible in my loves and in my jealousies! Don't believe that, when I use the word love, I only understand it to mean what

I wrote to you about yesterday. I think there's a much more beautiful and much more noble way to love. Alas! I can never experience it, because a truly noble and charming man like those whom I know would certainly not want to have anything to do with me, and I must be content with depraved men. It's true that they're more humorous and better placed than others, but that's my only consolation. I'd like, however, to be able to love somebody with a beautiful and noble passion. I understand all the sacrifices you can make when you love truly, and I shudder at not being able to know this feeling, especially at not being able to be loved with a heart-felt passion and with the spirit with which I feel I could love.

I'm afraid at the present time that the young military man's love for me was only a calculated thing—a way of enjoying my money—because I made him do certain things that he didn't know. Maybe my personality was also agreeable to him. I'm afraid that this may truly have been all there was to it and that he had no other feelings for me.

As for the captain, he's a debauched man whom I maintain contact with because I've nothing better right now, and to whom I belong through habit. Maybe I love him better than I think. When he leaves, it upsets me, and these long absences are very disagreeable to me, even though I don't truly love him. Until the present time I've only experienced true love once in my life, and maybe I won't experience it again with so intense an explosion of tender and delicate feelings and with such frightening jealousy.

I think the captain truly loves me; he says so at least. But I've noticed more than once that he changes after the thing is consummated and that the ardor and passion that he shows before changes after he has done what he wants. This wasn't so in the first months of our relationship, and I believe that he only considers his pleasure and the strangeness of my face and body and cares less about me personally or about my feelings or affections. Besides, he gets tired of me a lot.

Although he was strong, and perhaps because he was strong and robust, he worked himself up a long time before he achieved an orgasm. But I'd ejaculate soon, and while he worked toward his climax, I expected very little until my senses returned. I was therefore able to study this man, who was made powerless by his own lust. His face seemed to me then to be both wild and vile, and though he was grateful to me before, he was now so full of lust that he produced a feeling of loathing and almost terror in me. I wanted to flee, but it was only fair that he should be able to take his pleasure, since I had taken mine. This exhausted me greatly, and I lay there with a frozen expression and all rigid like a piece of wood. At those times I hated him, but when at last he'd ejaculate, I felt true joy. And on the days when I loved him madly, I surrendered my body and soul to him, and I made every effort to please him. It was a great sadness to me that I wasn't able to receive his semen into my body, which, it seemed to me, was his greatest desire. This desire of his tormented me enormously. At times I longed most sincerely to be a woman.

After my resistance the first time and after several attempts, he nearly gave up trying to possess me entirely, as he had wanted to do and as I had desired myself. Despite the atrocious pain that I felt at these attempts, he never succeeded at anything because of the extremely delicate nature of my body. In order to please him, I'd certainly be willing to suffer a little, but when I'm there—and we've tried it three or four times—I only feel the pain, and despite his efforts and his persistent prayers it's better for me to refuse.

Perhaps you'll be surprised that I speak to you with so much passion about a man who's no longer young, even though he's worth more than several young men put together. I haven't spoken to you so much about my other passion, which was just as strong. The reason is that the other one is no longer and that this one has lasted for four years. I always live in the present, and I still often enjoy this one. Besides, I'm relatively more reserved about the other one because I loved him more, and I never did, nor did I ever condescend to do, to him what the captain taught me and made me do, sometimes in a very brutal fashion. This charms me in secret and makes me docile in everything. I feel very small next to him.

In the confession I've written to you, that I've chosen you to hear—because of my admiration for you and in the hope that I could be useful to you in something—I didn't want to speak to you about the delicious debaucheries that I've indulged in with this man. I had decided to speak to you about the delicate ones that I had in the regiment, but in the middle of my excitement I couldn't resist evoking the delightful scenes I saw arising in my memory with an immense pleasure and desire, even though they've often left me sad and weary.

The only person who perhaps had a true love for me was the young Spaniard, with whom I enjoyed myself perhaps a dozen times, and who loved me to delirium, even though I was very cold toward him. I found him much too similar to myself. He was a virgin, like myself, even though he didn't want to admit it, but you could tell from his conversation, and the man advertised it blatantly. He was delicate but not handsome, and he had superb eyes with greenish brown irises, like precious marble. He told me one day that, when he was following me without knowing me—this lasted several months—and not having seen me for fifteen days (I was then in Palermo), he cried for a long time, believing me to be sick or dead. He also kept an oleander leaf that I had picked up, nibbled at, and thrown on the ground without taking any notice of it. He kept it as a relic and showed it to me placed in a frame under glass. I always laughed at him, and secretly he was very disagreeable to me, even though I wanted to appease him sometimes. I've since been afraid of inspiring the same sentiment, and this has placed me particularly on guard against myself and the facility I have in becoming impassioned at first sight.

I've also been very reserved in my conduct in society toward my lover, with whom I don't permit myself any pleasantries and whom I treat with complete indifference. I even act like that in our intimate conversations, and I abandon myself completely only in his closed apartment in the semiobscurity of his room. Before now I wasn't always so reserved, but the customs of the world have taught me how you must behave in these strange and exceptional situations.

When people speak of him, I'm silent or I say something bad about him. Often people have had to defend him from my attacks. What's worse is that I'm sincere in my criticism, and the bad things that I say about him are what I think of him. I treat him very badly with my words, and I'm not afraid to contradict him and everything that he says in the presence of others. However, as soon as we're alone and he shows himself to be the master, I feel my impertinence—which is artificial—recede, and I fall into his arms, happy enough to see him in his excitement and in his ardor for me. It's no doubt because of him that I don't seek other distractions, and besides, habit has made him my master, and only briefly do I want those others who attract me.

Yesterday, in the last pages that I wrote, I described the despair and rage evoked in me by the sight of the young man whose beauty has recently struck me. He's so handsome that I'm entirely carried away by him, but I consider him a work of art more than a man. I envy the woman who'll have him and who'll enjoy him, but I'd like to have him as a lover rather than a husband. He's too perfect and must in the end become monotonous. This doesn't prevent me from ever seeing him without emotion, and I'd like to be loved by him passionately, to hold him in my arms, so that he'd be in love with me.

Alas! This is impossible, and I must be content with what I have—which isn't little. Maybe everyone isn't as happy as I am. I've loved passionately, and maybe, had I been corrupted by a charming young man with elegant virility, I'd have known all the ardors of jealousy and of satisfied passion, if not completely, at least in a satisfying way. Instead I'm loved with a horrible and violent love by an old warrior in possession of all the power of his virility and next to whom a lot of other men seem weak and small. He showers me with his passionate tenderness, and if I weren't a little tired of him, I'd be absolutely happy in my satisfied desires.

I'm sorry about and will regret often the contrariness of nature and the inability of enjoying sex in body and soul, but in the end I'm young, pretty, charming, and rich. And if my soul is monstrous, I console myself in thinking that I'm the vicious but gracious product of a refined and delicate civilization.

In the rest of this letter I want to speak a little about my actual character—something that might also interest you and give you a complete idea of my strange personality. I love everything that is beautiful, and almost nothing—in all the genres—is beautiful enough in my eyes, so I love that which is exceptional, rich, and elegant. In my imagination I invent palaces more beautiful than all of those that already exist, filled with masterpieces chosen from among all of the masterpieces of the entire world. The sight of a work of art—artificial and yet real—holds me in ecstasy for hours, and I dream of it during the night. Beauty in my eyes takes the place of everything, and all vices, all crimes seem to me to be excused by it.

One of Balzac's characters who has charmed me the most is the handsome Lucien. I still imagine that I resemble him, and I've always thought that the love of the terrible Vautrin was of a nature more physical than what Balzac could have openly described.[17]

Flowers please me infinitely, especially flowers from greenhouses and rare, expensive, and unusual plants. Above all, roses and great exotic flowers charm me, even in paintings. I've a real aversion to lilies and all flowers of the fields, especially those that grow wild.

Among the human family I only like distinguished, well-born, and elegant people, who, I believe, are the only ones entitled to the dignity of the name "man." The others don't count for me. I make an exception for artists, who, thanks to the refinement of their souls and the beauty of their work, can be allowed a little laxness in their appearance. Other people don't count at all for me, and I've only aversion for them. I much prefer a magnificent dog—a King Charles spaniel, for example—to all of the workers and peasants of the world. The latter are odious to me. I make exceptions for some of the former, especially if they're handsome and muscular—something that happens from time to time. If I had been a beautiful lady, I believe I'd have liked to try out some of them, only to send them back afterward—that's understood, of course.

For me, the word "woman" conjures up ideas of luxury, emblazoned coaches, satin, velvet, white and perfumed skin, perfect hands, and the easiest of virtues. A woman who walks the street seems to me to be low and fallen, and for me these women are something horrible, even if they're beautiful from an artificial point of view.

It's not necessary to tell you that—however indifferent I am to everything political—I'm a royalist by instinct. To me kings and queens seem to be made differently from the rest of humanity.

I'm a Catholic without conviction, an unbeliever really. I like the pomp and circumstance of the Church, and I'm proud to belong to it. I like rich churches—those of the Jesuits above all else, with their gilded decorations and their polychrome marbles. And I like the religious and solemn ceremonies, which cause something unknown and mysterious to shiver inside me.

I despise the republic. It seems to me—you'll perhaps laugh—to be peopled by ragged, dirty beings.

I enjoy being only in very rich and magnificently furnished apartments—a taste that my father shares. He has spent a substantial fortune on art objects, especially on china and on superb and unusual objects from Japan. I love rooms lined up in a row, with velvet hangings and mirrors as far as the eye can see. I adore greenhouses and overheated rooms, where I like to daydream about everything by evoking mysterious and voluptuous images. I've always been vain, and a real shudder takes hold of me when I pass through the gates of our garden in our carriage, especially when people stop and stare before going on their way.

I love being admired and I'm proud of my beauty, which I try to heighten as much as I can. I've always found in myself a resemblance to the busts of Madame du Barry—a du Barry with short hair and dressed as a boy.[18] One evening, a number of years ago, I was thrilled by the sensation that I caused at the skating rink in Paris. Several ladies believed that I was cross-dressing and gave unmistakable signs of their surprise. I was charmed!

In paintings I prefer scenes of a style completely different from others, above all if they depict rich and modern interiors. Moreover, I've a real fanaticism for the great Makart, whose sensual and troubling works enchant me. My favorite painting by this artist is *The Death of Cleopatra*, a scene that I've always admired and envied.[19]

There's a deep vein of cruelty in my personality. I love the sufferings of others, especially if it's I who inflicts them. I deliberately tormented animals during my childhood. I carried it out with the utmost refinement, and I experienced an acute pain in the process, which pleased and excited me.

I've always been very arrogant, and at times when business was going badly I missed luxury terribly. It's a real necessity for me, and I can't live with less.

I hate everything that is ordinary, especially everyday things, and I adore the extraordinary and the impossible in all things.

Often, in the absence of my parents, I used to sleep all day long. I'd turn on all the lights in the apartment and stay up, drinking and eating all night long, in a Greek dressing gown, after having taken a hot bath scented with perfume.

I paint very beautifully, especially in watercolors, and I work on ladies' albums and fans.

I'm cunning and treacherous, but at times I've a silly ingenuousness. Everyone who meets me adores me and nobody resists my charms. I've always had my way with people by using my emotions, and I've always succeeded in making them do whatever I want, whereas others, imposing their will by force, don't get anywhere. I've often noticed that my friends and companions would be punished for the same kind of misdeeds and failings for which I'd escape all chastisement—thanks to the innocent and melancholic air that I have.

I've always tyrannized those who loved me. I immediately become more and more rude and authoritarian. Although I'm weak and effeminate myself, I hate the weak and love only the strong—those who do battle and win. I've always regretted not being able to console the great and the powerful after their fall from the heights. I think that, if I had been Marie Louise, I'd have followed Napoleon to Saint Helena. Maybe I wouldn't have done so if I had known and loved the handsome Neipperg, despite his glass eye.[20]

I admire enthusiastically, as I've already told you, all that's beautiful and delicate, but the strange thing is that ugliness, especially if is grandiose, primitive, and powerful, pleases me as much in a man as beauty does—maybe even more so.

I've a very lively and alert intelligence, despite my failings and my weaknesses. I understand all things, both the good and the bad, and I also admire the one as much as the other, provided that there isn't anything vulgar about it.

I never could learn arithmetic beyond the four rules[21] and never knew how to do the third rule, even though I had a master mathematician as a tutor for a long time. I also don't understand anything about financial affairs, even though I've heard them discussed in my family at length. Now, thanks to God, we no longer talk about them because we no longer need to.

I can learn a poem that pleases me in five minutes, no matter how long the text is, but I can't get two lines of unpleasant prose into my brain, even if I spend hours at it. I play the piano well enough, even though I don't have the patience to practice it for a long time. I prefer to play melancholic pieces, those of Schubert or Mozart above all. I also play operas, and while playing I like to evoke the scenes and passions of the characters from the librettos. My favorite composer is Verdi, whom I adore. In literature I prefer the descriptions of feelings and the long and inevitable evolution of passions to all the jumbles of adventures. I wanted to read the works of Ponson du Terrail, but I couldn't finish them; I found them too boring and impossible.[22]

Historical novels don't attract me in the least, except for *Ivanhoe*, because I like to believe that Rebecca could be one of my grandmothers.[23] The novels of Dumas the Elder have interested me for a long time, but I find consulting historical documents and memoirs of the times much more stimulating. I've countless volumes on Marie Antoinette, my favorite heroine, and on several other celebrated female personages. I like to collect their actual portraits, even the ugly ones, but I don't show them to anyone in order not to embarrass my beloved heroines. I keep them for myself. I've paid two hundred francs for some volumes that don't even interest me just to acquire a small engraving representing Queen Marie Antoinette on the scaffold. It's from a drawing made in 1793.

The history of France is the one that interests me the most, even though, if I could have chosen an epoch and a country in which to have come into the world, I'd have chosen Rome at the height of its decadence, under Hadrian, for example.

(The court of Henry III would have also pleased me.) I'd have
been ravishing in a Roman costume, and I've even worn one
at a masked ball, where I caused quite a furor showing off
my naked arms and legs, with lavish sandals that left my feet
exposed and my toenails shining like agates. The captain (I call
him that even though he's no longer a captain) was a gladiator,
and he was superb in his vest the color of coffee with cream
(it was actually darker than that), which showed off superbly
his whole robust body in its upright posture, with his legs and
chest clad in armor. That evening we abandoned ourselves to
mutual delight.

I've a real passion for animals, for sea birds and rare dogs
above all; I've some adorable Japanese pugs. At another time I
also adored children, but now I can no longer put up with them,
and I never hug them, not even those who are close to me.

Naples is my favorite city, and when I leave it, it's always
with difficulty, even if it's only for a few days. It's almost ori-
ental with its enormous palm trees and its blue harbor illuminated by strange lights that seem impossible when seen in
paintings. If Naples were inhabited by the French with their
refined civilization, it would be divine; there wouldn't be a
more beautiful city in the world. If it had belonged to the
English at the time of the Spanish conquests, it would have
been a beautiful paradise! As it is, it's nevertheless superb. I'd
like it to be better groomed and more refined; then it would be
the paradise of Mohammed.

I only like nature in its most savage solitude—in a forest,
for example—but since man has come into it, I prefer a perfect
civilization with all its refined delicacies and distractions. I like
English gardens, but the gardens at Versailles, and especially
those at Caserta,[24] have more charm for me.

It's pointless to tell you that I'm crazy about your works,
which I read with admiration, even though for me the subjects
of your latest books weren't very pleasant.[25]

The book that I like the most is *La Curée*, where I found characters with feelings similar to my own and a social sphere that I've almost always lived in, that I was born in, and that I still live in. *Madeleine Férat* made the strongest impression on me.[26]

I've written these pages this evening with the most intense pleasure. The room is very gay with its gaslight lit, its warm carpets, and the noise of the hotel swarming with people. I'm almost happy. How long will this state last? A long time, I hope. I no longer want to think about anything except enjoying what I have without searching for anything else. I've written this for myself, but what I've written I'm sending to you. Will I have been useful to you in anything? Or will I have wasted my time?

In any case, I don't regret these hours. I've relived all my life in its frightful sorrows and its guilty and delicious joys.

Further Thoughts

I thought I could sleep, but all the memories brought up in these pages have made sleeping impossible, and I've got to go back to my writing. It makes me relive many long years during a few short hours. Also, my abstinence during these last few weeks because of my friend's trip has made me particularly excitable. He hasn't yet told me when he'll return, and I feel an intensity of desire and passion that prevents me from taking a long rest. I'll thus pick up the thread of my conversation with you, but without a doubt this letter will be the last that I write to you, because if not, I'm afraid I'll never finish it, or I'd send you a real tome that would end up exhausting you. I think that I've finished, but then I always find something else to tell you. In addition I enjoy talking about my little self so much that I'll never stop revisiting myself in my imagination as if I were gazing at my image in a mirror. I don't think you can ever tire of talking about yourself and examining yourself down to the most minute details, especially if the being that nature has made us is as exceptional as I am. After all that I've written to you, I'm sure that you'll be able to guess at the rest of my character and my ideas and even of those around me, but since this is so enjoyable for me, I'll go on a bit longer—more for my benefit than for yours.

You've already deduced that I'm as much of a gourmand as Brillat-Savarin.[27] I don't eat a lot, but I love fine wines, even those that aren't really excellent except for their famous names and high prices. I've a passion for game, especially for pheasants, and all gamy meats enchant my palate. I love the rarest cheeses, particularly the strongest-smelling ones. All the accouterments of dining enchant me, and I can't enjoy a dinner unless the table is brilliantly set and the service is flawless. I adore Turkish coffee, and I drink a lot of it, but in small quantities and very hot. I like liqueurs, too, but in very small doses. I've always dreamed of Roman feasts, and one of the scenes that has enthralled me the most is the feast of Arbaces in *The Last Days of Pompeii*.[28] I adore that city, and I often stroll through it, reflecting on its dead charm and its life snuffed out by Vesuvius.

I've the most intense passion for equestrian shows, and the beauty of their athletes with their strength and perfect bodies has a very strong effect on me. On the other hand, tumblers and acrobats in the circus inspire only pity and disgust in me. I love beautiful horses, but I prefer driving in a carriage to riding on horseback, even though I do ride rather well. I almost never miss the wild animals at the circus, and I've always gone to watch the feeding and exercise of the lions and tigers with the secret desire of seeing a little blood flow. I prefer a handsome lion tamer to all the seedy poets of this world. When I see men—and in my passion for them I want to see splendor, courage, strength, and beauty in them—delicacy in them doesn't attract me at all, since I'm so delicate myself.

I love gambling passionately. The riskiest games please me the most. I'm fairly lucky at them, but money does slip through my fingers and never stays in my pockets. I've often repaid the gambling debts of my friends—as small as they are. I spend little money on myself, and that's almost always limited to books, curios, and my wardrobe, which is very important to me. I love the severe and proper style of the English, whose simple and unique style we've all adopted. I love the color black, which brings out my blond and pretty face. I love sparkling white linen and the finest, most stylish boots. I'm very elegant in appearance and never seem self-conscious. I don't like jewelry on men and only wear very simple tie pins. My watch is truly a marvel. On my left pinky I wear a simple iron ring with a big diamond, which my mother gave me. Canes are my great luxury. I've some by Verdier, which are marvelous, especially one with a head made of superb rock crystal.

I don't believe I've spoken to you about my hands, which are truly superb and perhaps the loveliest part of me, except for my hair and my complexion. I'm very proud of them, and they're so generally admired that people often tell me that it's a pleasure to be touched by them. A great sculptor, who unfortunately has just died and whom I knew well, wanted to make a cast of them, and I've a copy of this cast in my bedroom, displayed on a blue velvet pillow. The shape is perfect but strange, long and tapering without showing any joints or muscles. The fingers are long, broad at the base but tapering like a spindle at the tips. Even though my fingers are of an unheard-of delicacy and of an extreme fineness, they're square at the tips, and I've got to cut my fingernails so that they resemble precious stones, colored bright red, as if they were polished. My nails are all the shades of pink from the pale half-moons at their base to the bright red color at their very tips. Although they're square, their shape is flawless, and the expanse of flesh that surrounds them is as fine and white as an eggshell. I'm admiring them while I write to you, and they're truly marvelous. My thumb is ravishing, rounded with an oval nail. My hand is like white velvet, with shades of pale, almost imperceptible, blue produced by the veins. The last phalange of each finger is curved oddly upward and is a hearty pink color that contrasts with the whiteness of the rest. My palm, which was once examined by a German lady who does palm readings and table rapping, is crossed by deep, long, well-marked lines that don't break off anywhere. They're, however, crossed by one diagonal line that is chipped and broken and crisscrosses all the others. This lady explained these lines to me, but in a fantastical German way, I fear. I inherited my beautiful hands and my handsome face from a paternal ancestor who was stunning and whose arms and hands were so superb that even Canova complimented her on them one day.[29] She was, they say, the mistress of . . .[30]—if they only knew I dared to write this! But other than that she did nothing for the family, except perhaps that we owe to her the shape of our lips and our chins.

My grandfather was unhappy in his marriage and died very young from the distress caused by his wife. After all that, she only survived him by a little while and died before my birth. As I've already told you, my brothers are hearty and well built. The eldest is superb; he resembles my father, but he's perhaps a little less handsome. The other two aren't good-looking, especially the third one, who takes after my mother's family, who are repulsive to me. They're all much taller and stronger than I am, and they were born one right after the other. I came into the world ten years after the last one and only after my mother had suffered a terrible illness, which brought her very close to death. I think it was one of those deadly fevers. All my brothers' children are attractive, strong, and well made. There's one little girl who resembles me strikingly, people say. She died eighteen months after her birth in only a few hours, without any symptoms forewarning of a sudden death. I'd like to die in the same way.

Otherwise I'm perfectly made, with a great deal of nervous energy, spirit, and considerable vivacity. Sometimes I fall into a funk, but I recover from it with a great deal of joy and a healthy desire to laugh. Then I don't leave anyone alone, and I become everyone's favorite because of my talk, my flattery, and the chitchat that I shower on everyone around me.

All of a sudden, however, I become silent and sad, and everyone is astonished by these quick and seemingly inexplicable—to them at any rate—changes. My facial expression, especially where my upper lip is separated from the nose by a little indentation, changes as the colors of the sea do on a stormy day. My eyes are almost always melancholic, overshadowed by their long lashes. You can hardly see them, and their color is indefinable, sometimes blue, gray, or green; often they turn a shade of violet.

People say I seem arrogant—mocking and taunting. In reality I often assume that attitude to hide my shyness and my awkwardness in public. I keep society at a distance in this way. I believe there are few people in the world as egotistical as I am. I'd sacrifice anybody for one of my passing fancies, and only in the grip of one of my momentary desires do I understand a sacrifice made on the behalf of others. In my family, who have always spoiled me, everyone complains about my coldness, and they often treat me as an ingrate because of it. That has often caused my father great distress, because he has such a weak spot for me, and even when he was disinclined to do so, he never denied me any of my wishes or any of my extraordinary and useless whims. In truth, I don't care much for my family. I've said as much to them when I've been in an ugly mood—the cause of which no doubt you'll have guessed. I see them as the cause—innocent, to be sure—of my extraordinary and perverse nature, and I can't forgive them for having made me this way. I hold it very much against them, but now I'm trying to let go of this awful feeling and to force myself to show them some affection, which is sometimes genuine and which I do sincerely feel.

They've often hurt me cruelly by speaking to me about or by joking with me about my presumed love affairs, especially about the love some women have for me. At those times I hate them, and I respond in a very brutal manner. They only tolerate this behavior from me, and they'd protest against it if others showed them so little respect.

My father socializes very little. He's consumed by his house, and decorating and furnishing it takes all of his attention. He ignores the rest of us, except for his grandchildren, who adore him and whom he loves passionately. I'm jealous of them and can't stand them.

I pay a great deal of attention to my health, even though at the age of fifteen or sixteen — before meeting the captain, when I was alone and had made those awful discoveries about myself — I wanted to die, without really knowing what that meant, except that it would be a change in my intolerable situation. I quickly abandoned that feeling, fearing the horror of the void and of bodily putrefaction. At that time I spent hours at night on my balcony, practically nude, in very cold weather, trying to kill myself and thereby escape my passions, which no one was satisfying at that time. But I didn't even catch a cold, and I quickly stopped such foolishness. I've since understood that as long as you're alive, you can enjoy yourself, and I hope to live out the rest of my youth. Perhaps, when I've reached the end of my youth, I'll still want to live all the way to the age of one hundred! It's possible!

I always take showers and take care of myself as well as I possibly can in order to have all my strength ready to serve my passions and to satisfy my master, who is far away at this time and whose return I eagerly await. He writes to me frequently and tells me about Hungary, about his horses, and about the native women of that country. God only knows how badly he treats me, but as long as he doesn't cheat on me with other boys, I don't care! That's the only thing I want and desire. His name day passed just recently, and I sent him a superb whip with a beautifully carved handle. He also wrote me that despite the journey through barbaric and boring lands, he's in exceptionally good spirits. He always keeps a lovely photograph of me close at hand, and it never leaves him. He told me he only thinks about returning and he often dreams of me and of my favorite cologne. He rarely wears anything but the severely cut waistcoat and elegant collars that I insisted upon.

I forgot to tell you that I'd like you to give a few more details about the physique of your characters. Don't the physical attributes explain the moral aspects of nations and individuals?

I've just read *Mademoiselle de Maupin*,[31] and it charmed me completely. Oh! What a beautiful book! What lovely corruption, so sweet and delicate!

Please excuse the horrible handwriting and all the mistakes in French and in spelling, but my soul and my passions have carried me away. To write this, I haven't looked anywhere, except inside myself.

Postscript: In the hotel where I'm staying, I've made the acquaintance of a man of about thirty years of age. It was at the dinner table. He tried to seduce me openly, and soon he'd have gotten what he wanted. He's tall, has a rather kind face, and is very pale and elegant, with long thin arms. He's from Milan. If I had wished it, how quickly it could have been done. But should I embark again on such a similar adventure? My blood boils, and I'm afraid of not being able to resist the temptation. If he came right now, it would be done quickly, I'm afraid. If the captain knew about it, it would be a lovely affair! He'd be capable of strangling me. In any case, we'll see this evening. I'm getting dressed now and going down to dinner. It'll be a decisive evening. It seems to me that he doesn't have good teeth. He has a long moustache that covers up his mouth. It'll be there at the dinner table that I'll make up my mind—come what may! Besides, this man will soon be leaving again. Let's hope that he doesn't get attached to me!

It's pointless to tell you that I gave a false name and a false address at the post office where I sent my letters, and besides, in a couple of days, I'll no longer be here. You'll no longer know anything more about me. Farewell, Sir, and, perhaps, good-bye. The clock sounds and I must go into a real battle.

Seven o'clock in the evening.

POSTCARD (1889)

To Emile Zola, Man of Letters, Paris, France

Sir,

Not knowing your address, I've sent you by registered mail three letters that I addressed to your editors, Monsieur Charpentier and Company. I hope all of them will get to you and they'll not remain too long in transit. Since your person is so well known, I'm sending this one without an address. I hope that it will get to you as well. That which must come to pass has come to pass. I've the most delicious memory of it and was perfectly happy this morning, I can assure you. I'll shout it from the rooftops. There where everyone else had failed, he has succeeded!

While strolling through the streets of . . . , where I was staying for a time, and while stopping by chance at the display window of a bookstore, I was struck by the title of a book whose preface had been written by Monsieur Emile Zola. A strong emotion overwhelmed me because I suspected what it was about, and I guessed that I'd see my own story reproduced in it—the confession that I had sent Zola a number of years ago. I was hoping to see the strange emotions that had enslaved me since my earliest childhood years reproduced by the pen of this master. In each new novel by Zola I hoped to find a character who was modeled after me, but my wait was always in vain, and I ended up by being convinced that this writer lacked the courage to put such a terrible passion into a novel and that he had retreated before the enormous difficulties that an unhappy heart and spirit like mine had presented to him. Nevertheless, why ask our modern writers to do what Balzac himself didn't dare to do?

It was therefore with a rapidly beating heart and with my blood surging through my body that I entered the bookstore and bought the volume written by you, Monsieur Laupts. The title of one of its chapters, and especially the name of Monsieur Zola, had already caused me to guess its contents.

You're a very knowledgeable man, Sir, and from what I can gather from your writing style, an open-minded and tolerant fellow. I want you to understand, therefore, that I read your book thoroughly. Like all sick persons who see in their doctor a friend, even if he knows that the illness is incurable, I feel as if I've been overwhelmed by friendship and gratitude for those who take care of the perfidious affliction that persists in me. And, like a friend to those who are dear to him, I try to help them by showing them what it is that they are searching for so tirelessly and that I, on the other hand, know so well through an innate science.

The feeling I experienced at last was that of pleasure at seeing myself published just as I am—something that I'd have much preferred to have relived in the pages of a novel and not in a treatise of medical science. Having been next to Hyacinthus, the sweet friend of Apollo, or of Alexis, the handsome lover of Virgil,[32] and then finding myself finally in the pages of a treatise on anthropology in company with a Parker or a Taylor[33]—that was a bit hard to take, believe me, Sir! I'm not complaining; I'm simply stating the fact, that's all.

What I can tell you, however, is that I'm more egotistical than ever, that my heart is very tranquil, and that I consider it a degenerate organ that only feels something under the influence of an intense emotion. It gives me terrible sensations, but spasmodically, and except at those times I'm very calm. And I could even say very happy.

My mind is the same. I know, however, what I am and what I want. I've chosen my role in this life, and I look for all the happiness that I can find without troubling myself about the rest. The memories of my past trouble me a little, and those who have crossed my path in associating themselves with my pleasures, be they living or dead, now interest me but little. I live in the present, not dreaming at all about the past and not thinking very much about the future. When the memory of my past reemerges in my soul as in a mirror and these same joys are seen as bad and the pleasures as cruel, then this painful feeling lasts only a short while. It quickly leaves my thoughts. Perhaps my brain itself has atrophied and no longer conjures up images with lively, crude clarity!

What should I tell you about my passion? About this passion that fills all my waking hours, all the moments of my life, never giving me any respite? It's still there, but despite being extremely intense at certain times, it no longer has the terrible power that it did before, and it can no longer be compared with the delights of earlier times, even though the sight or even the thought of an undressed man causes me to burn with all the flames of hell.

Being rich and independent, I've been able to arrange my life in my own fashion—a fashion that is a little strange, like everything I do. All of the tastes I confessed to Monsieur Zola earlier remain with me still. They've even become stronger. I still love luxury, and the apartment where I live is a real museum that would charm the most demanding artist. Statues, paintings, family mementos, handsome books, magnificent furniture, Persian rugs, and so on—all of these things are amassed in my apartment. I live there in the midst of a small circle of intimate friends, and I don't of course lack a favorite, who has a lovely beard.

Literature still interests me a great deal. I've journals in many languages everywhere. I devour a large quantity of books. Paintings, especially those by others, please me in an extraordinary way. But the art that thrills me most is music. I spend long hours listening to my favorite scores on the piano and following in my fantasies the episodes of the diverse dramas that play out in my imagination. Music evokes them with an intensity that borders on hallucination. This lasts a long time, until weariness takes hold of me and makes me fall into a half sleep that I emerge from aching all over, but with a feeling of laziness and calmness of the most delicious kind.

Some charming women friends come to play music with me, to look at my engravings and art objects, to sing and to chat with me. I've inspired some foolish passions in these women, who are distressed by my coldness and who would throw themselves into the fire—as useless as that may be—in order to bring it to an end. I've never ceased being a virgin—oh! what a strange word for my pen!—and I'll remain one always. Monsieur Raffalovich would have nothing to fear on that score! Women are for me what they've always been: delightful companions, good friends, whom I shun only when they show me some vague, amorous desires and make me understand that they want a less platonic friendship on my part. I only entertain married women, which allows me to disguise my extreme coldness as the result of my friendship with their husbands and the honor that I don't want to betray. What a comedy! Several of these women are seen as quite compromised in the eyes of society because of me, and one of them, a very petite, beautiful woman, full of spirit and passion for literature and music, was mistaken for my mistress for a long time. I laughed a great deal at the allusions that people made about us, because our entire relationship was based on the music that we made together and on our frequent conversations.

The only thing that you could suspect me of doing is the one that would make me feel odious . . . My nature is perverse, as it has always been, but it has acquired more moderation, more calmness, and more sophistication. I spend months in the most complete abstinence, in the most absolute chastity. It seems as if I've water in my veins instead of the lava that's there at other times, but when the occasion presents itself, a simple glance, an ambiguous handshake, a word in the ear suffices to awake the demon of lust in me—a demon of the most frightening kind—and I burn as if I had burning sulfur in my body.

I know Venus and her formidable fires
Of the blood that she inflicts with such inevitable torments![34]

When I wrote to Monsieur Zola, I was about twenty-three years old; I am now thirty. Many things have happened. My parents are dead; they died less than a year apart from each other. Many changes have occurred around me. I myself haven't changed. I remain the same. *Semper idem* . . .[35]

Oh, Sir! To feel different from the way that everyone else feels is sometimes a great pleasure, but what hours of anguish sometimes punish a few moments of pride and infernal pleasure!

Do you want another atrocious example? I was at the deathbed of a person who was related to me through blood and affection when I received a letter that gave me a welcome surprise and filled me with emotion. It was from a young friend of mine whom I had previously treated badly and who, after many years, while passing through the town where I lived, remembered me and asked me if I had, as he did, the same desire to see him again. All of a sudden my head was on fire and my blood began to boil more than that of Saint Januarius![36] I forgot about everything, especially the sickbed, which turned into a deathbed on the following day. I even forgot about my affection and my duty and everything else. I only lived for the next day—the day of our meeting.

My young friend arrived, greatly changed in appearance, with a handsome moustache and a small beard like that of Henry III, dressed in the most perfect elegance, with a self-assurance and an audacious air that I had never noticed before. He's in the diplomatic corps and, it seems, has not lost any time. We talked about unimportant things, but he looked at me with a vague, drunken look that I recognized, and since I complimented him on his handsome appearance, he said to me, "It's you who are still handsome, more handsome than ever!" I got up to show him an album because I felt a certain discomfort being next to him, as I had on other occasions. But when I was near him, he grabbed both my hands and kissed them ardently, and from time to time he murmured sweet nothings into my ear. I was very moved myself (not however as much as I was with the other ones), and I caressed him as well. I found him very fine and delicate, and this displeased me about him, even though my senses were already aroused. And for lack of anything better to do, I was content with this adventure. Since there were some other people near us, I had to take leave of him, and we separated, promising to see each other again two days later.

It was the day of the funeral when I saw him again. On the previous evening in the room where the young creature was laid out—a chamber illuminated and filled with beautiful flowers—I felt as if I were at a festival, and I trembled with pleasure to think that I was alive and that sensuous pleasures were waiting for me on the next evening. And nevertheless, I had cared very much for the being who had passed into eternal slumber after such horrible suffering. I had almost watched him being born, and I had always cherished and celebrated him—but isn't lust stronger than anything else? The more criminal it is, the more it eats away at your heart, and the more it kills all other emotions.

I surprised everyone with my gay air, which contrasted with the sadness of the others. I had to leave in order to hide my exaltation and the foolish joy that I felt at having seen again the one who was now so charming, who had loved me to distraction, and whom I had almost driven away with scorn. At that moment I desired him passionately, and I don't know what I'd have done if he had not come. He arrived at last, but as always I felt cold toward him, and even if he covered others with ardent caresses and passionate kisses and even if he received their caresses with delight, still he gave in to me on other points only with extreme resistance, showing me a very strange and truly incomplete nature. He was a being definitely lacking in something, but maybe there was something in our natures—something too much the same—that made us unable to make each other truly happy.

He told me about an adventure that he had had in the capital of his country with an engineer, whom he had met at the opera and whom, he told me, he had loved passionately. He showed me his portrait. He was a very handsome man with brown hair and a very masculine air about him, who had, as my friend told me, taught him a great many things. They wrote to each other constantly, and this man burned with desire to see the other again. This anecdote left me feeling extremely cold, and we said good-bye after exchanging a few friendly kisses and nothing more. We felt as if we were of the same sex, and this thought, which had caused our first rupture, separated us forever. So the young diplomat went away without any warning, without even sending me a few lines. I've since learned that he was sent to a country that's very far from our own—across the ocean. May he enjoy himself! That's what I wish for him with all my heart!

As for me, I've known true passion only once with its delights and its torments, with its jealousies and its transports. When we are two, we become one only with the person we love. By my art and my seductions I caused a certain feeling to arise in a young and simple man, but one that was so chivalrous and so handsome that he himself perhaps didn't understand it. It was a feeling made up of admiration and gratitude, of sensual love and true friendship. I shared this feeling with him passionately, and by unsettling the brain and the senses of my friend, I threw him into the most burning and the most unrelenting pleasures. This seemed completely natural to him, I can assure you, and he showed no surprise at it, since the thing was accomplished without premeditation and virtually against his will—and maybe even against my own will. I truly loved him then with my head, my heart, my senses, with everything. It was like a nightmare, a dream, and when I woke up far from him, my passion had burned itself out, and there only remained ashes in my heart—but not in my blood, which burned and burns still. What would I not give in order to experience once again one minute of this happiness, which is the equivalent of centuries of beatitude? For an instant of these joys I'd renounce an eternity of happiness in the company of all the saints in heaven! Alas! I feel old in my heart and in my soul; and vice, instead of passion, still attracts me.

The captain, as I always called him, died not long ago from

a horrible illness that required a cruel operation. He was given chloroform, but he never woke up, and he died of a hemorrhage that nothing could stop. His debts and other financial difficulties had made him live far away from me, but I went to visit him sometimes because I missed him, and I always saw him again with pleasure. He was a real demon, but I liked him because of the grandeur of his vices and because of the energy and force that never abandoned him. He'd be old at the present time—it's best that he's dead! He'll keep good company with Satan and he'll teach even him a thing or two! . . .

The adventure at the hotel was only fleeting. The liaison was short, but decisive. In opening up new horizons, it allowed me to become what I am and what I've never stopped being. The man was still young, enterprising, and audacious. He didn't stop looking at me throughout dinner. He noticed my discomfort and the glances that I gave him from time to time. At the end of the meal he approached me under some pretext, and then he began to engage me in small talk. I could hardly answer because I was so nervous, and I replied to his conversation in almost unintelligible monosyllables. But, without saying anything explicit to each other, we understood each other. I sensed it. I spent the rest of the evening strolling through the streets, and even though it was fairly cold, I burned like a lit fuse. Toward eleven o'clock I found myself back at the hotel, and I can assure you that I could take no more of it. My heart beat in my chest; my head was on fire; my whole being was in a state of overstimulation that's impossible to describe. I entered the lobby without glancing at anyone, and I pretended to look at the illustrated newspapers that were on the table. Out of the corner of my eye I had already noticed him sitting on a sofa, and he was looking at me over his newspaper. I felt a shock to my stomach. Without even thinking about it, I gave him a long glance and left slowly. He left the lobby almost as soon as I did, and he followed me at a distance, watching me climb the stairs with an indifferent air. I did this very slowly, turning around only once to look at him as I let go of the handrails and entered the long corridor where by chance—by a happy chance, I should say—the two of us were lodged. I entered my room nonchalantly enough, without turning the bolt.

I did everything for him that I know, and that was not a little. (Remember the mentor and the care in which I was always maintained?) But he wasn't satisfied with that. Because of his pleas, his ruses, and his art he succeeded in his attempts, which were, after all, made a little easier by previous attempts on other occasions, but which had never before succeeded. Perhaps his physique corresponded better to my own, perhaps he was more patient, or perhaps I was more willing. In any case, I responded to his desire with a violent desire of my own.[37]

He left at dawn, and I fell into a deep sleep, not awakening until eleven o'clock the next morning.

My body was sore and my spirits were exhausted, and in order to revive myself I had to take a hot bath. That did marvels for me, and every trace of fatigue and pain disappeared immediately. After splashing my entire body with a bottle of eau de Cologne, I felt full of life and joy. I had never been happier and only reproached myself for having taken so long to learn this new pleasure. At lunch the man didn't show up, which didn't bother me too much, especially since I'd have been a little ashamed to have seen him at midday. In the evening he did return, and we hardly looked at each other. But as soon as I was in bed, he entered my room. I accepted with patience, almost with joy, the pain that I experienced again, but my entire being was so aroused and so distracted that the pain passed almost imperceptibly and the pleasure was immense . . . What delighted me most of all was the joy he seemed to experience, the ardor and the passion he seemed to feel. He was supposed to leave the following day, but he couldn't make himself do it, and he stayed with me another three weeks, despite the pleas from his family and those who needed him. What we did together seemed very natural to us, and we talked and laughed before and after as if nothing had happened. Oh! Such delicious nights!

Finally he did have to leave, and he showed some regrets, which I only partly reciprocated. He wrote to me from time to time, got married, and had a child, all of which didn't prevent him from taking me to a hotel once, where we spent a night of supreme passion after we met each other by chance.

When I pass by the hotel where we had our first encounter, I always look up at the window of the two adjoining rooms where for the first time I accomplished my life's goal: to take and to give a sterile pleasure—but a pleasure superior to all the others. And furthermore, may I make a confession to you? I really didn't like this man at all. He was very good-looking, still young (thirty-six years old), with muscles of iron; he was a work of art, an unbelievable feat of craftsmanship. He acquainted me with pleasures I thought I had already given up. Still, I had no feelings for him, and if during the night another man, equally strong and equally handsome as he was, had come along to take his place, I'd have accepted him without any regrets.

Despite the passion that burns inside me, the ones who have had the privilege of my company have been few in number and carefully chosen. I've made exceptions during my foreign travels. One day I met a young and handsome train operator in Belgium, and I pestered him and spurred him on so much that finally I went with him to a small hotel where he lived and where I went to join him. This was a real amusement for me.

The others were the captain, my handsome hero, the man at the hotel—Sardanapalus, as I called him[38]—and two others—one who *was* and the other who *is*—these are the relationships that have charmed me the most. I don't count the young E——, who was an impossible being, and two or three—let's make it four—passing affairs of no consequence. Except the little diplomat and the young sergeant, all the other men have possessed me completely, including the former captain after the adventure in the hotel.

It would be pointless to talk to you about the adventure that occupies me at the present time. I bring to it a wild passion and an extraordinary taste, but my whole body is not taken by it as it was before, and I don't bring the same cruel and bitter intensity to it with which I had adored the only one whom I truly loved. Still, I'm happy that he's dead! He'll live forever handsome and young in my memory, and, after all, what could life have offered him in the future? He was not in a brilliant situation; his future had nothing in it that could promise him more than a few happy hours; and after having known me and after having lived a very strange, fantastic, and exceptional life for several months, wasn't dying the best that he could do? Destiny had taken charge of him, but don't you believe that, instead of the hand of another, his own hand should have been the one to fire the pistol that shortened his life? As for me, I'm sure that I don't believe that he could have ever reentered normal life. I had distracted him too much for that, and his soul had been altered and molded by me too much for him to be able to be content with a life of ordinary pleasures. May he rest in peace! He was a decent fellow! I had written him a number of passionate letters that could have greatly compromised me. He returned them to me at my request. I was a monstrous ingrate toward him.

As for me, since I had youth, vigor, and beauty, I was happy to be alive, even with a corrupted and sick heart and mind. That's what I am in a moral sense at the present time!

Physically I've changed very little. People think that I'm no more than twenty-four years old, and as I've already told you, I have a very youthful and charming air about me. My physical attributes have kept all their fine features and their perfect regularity; my eyes are full of life and expression; my complexion is always rosy and delicate; my hands are more handsome than ever. I feel more and more like a sexless idol, but nevertheless an idol, who only asks to enjoy life and to be adored. That's what I am at this moment, because all of those around me, even my servants, whom I tyrannize, have a certain amount of idolatry for me. But as for myself, I no longer adore anyone. Let me love—that's all that I can do from now on.

Before finishing the description of my psychology, I must tell you, Sir, that you're wrong when you insinuate that I must like to dress in women's clothing and thus to disguise myself as one of those whom you like to call my accomplices. I can assure you that you're very grossly mistaken, because I abhor men disguised as women, and I naturally apply this feeling to myself. I like the most serious, the most correct, the most masculine kind of elegance—the *chic anglais*, in fact. Everything that seems out of place in a man disgusts me, and I reject all feminine outfits and all useless ornaments with contempt. I dress like a gentleman, not like a man-girl. I've never worn bracelets, and only one diamond and one superb emerald that I inherited not long ago shine on my fingers. I like this last piece as much as Dorian Gray liked his, and in reading that beautiful book, I was struck by his taste for emeralds—a taste that I share.[39]

What I say about my clothing I can also say about my face. No one, in seeing me, could guess the feelings that I harbor in my breast, and my face, as charming as it is, is still, especially for the last few years, that of a young and handsome *man*. If those of my sex turn around to look at me and to follow me, it's because of the bold and persistent looks that I give them when an internal fire burns in me. My appearance is not at all effeminate. Rather I've the look of a handsome cavalryman or an elegant page more than of anyone else. I'm of medium height, I've a long torso, and my svelte and polished body has nothing ambiguous about it, even though I do have radiant satin skin, above all else. Most people don't even see it, and only a few privileged souls have been able to touch and admire it. As I've already said, I inspire love—a very lively love—in women, and from this alone you should understand that I don't look like a girl. I look like an ephebe, not a malformed person.[40]

And now, Sir, after this work, let's review a little how it all came about. You've heard that the studies on the mixing of the races are very interesting. I can tell you something about it, and I want to review for you certain ancestral types about whom I've elsewhere made only brief sketches in a very summary fashion. This will certainly help you to understand certain things and explain how nature proceeded in making those kinds of beings. In recognizing the strangeness of those who have preceded us in the stream of generations, you begin to understand the strangeness of those who have followed them and have been created by them. In all that follows I beg of you to use the utmost DISCRETION.[41]

I must tire you by repeating the same thing, but I still want to tell you that I love still and I love often, but only with my senses. My heart and soul are no longer susceptible. Is it true that you love only once in your life? My being has become more and more passive and lets itself be taken rather than search for prey, as it did earlier. As soon as a man, in whom I immediately detect this vice and this passion, looks at me, and as soon as our eyes meet in a certain way, I experience a shock to my stomach, my blood rises to my face and head, my ears begin to tingle, my extremities freeze, and I'd be able to follow this stranger through thousands of dangers, over mountains and valleys, across deserts and forests of the wildest kind; I'd follow him into the flames of hell! But when I've satisfied my passions, I become extremely cold toward him and toward others. Men repel me until lust traps me again and throws me into their arms without my even realizing it. Often a great sadness overtakes me in thinking about my solitude . . .

A completely nude man doesn't attract me much; it's a seminude man that makes me dreamy and makes me want to explore, to feel, and to caress. I'd give myself to him body and soul. Everything disappears from my brain, and only one idea, or rather only one sensation, remains—that of a desire that nothing can stop and that wants to be satisfied. Unhappiness no longer exists at that moment. For a long time now my body has become habituated to what used to frighten it at other times. It's a temple destined for lust, and it inspires in me the respect that is owed to sacred things. I live an artificial and monstrous life, but isn't my existence a privileged one? I'm at times perfectly happy and tranquil, but at other times I'm hardly happy at all, and I'd like something new, but I don't know where to find it. Ah! Why didn't nature give me at least ten senses? Five are too few . . .

My friends have all been or are men of the world, of the best society, people with taste, whether perverted or refined, but virile in all their manliness. I've felt delicate and weak near them and less manly. They've submitted themselves to all of my caprices, and I've tyrannized them in a completely incredible manner. My friends have been few in number and rarely more than one at a time. There have been some genuine affairs with all of the preliminary trappings, and then there have been some ordinary relationships. Jealousy, remorse, scenes, break-ups, letters, messages, nothing has been lacking in these liaisons—and all of this without anyone around me suspecting a thing. I've feigned devotion in order to blind others more thoroughly, and I've succeeded in this completely. At the present time I no longer need to account for my conduct to anyone, and I'm free to do whatever I want without constraint. May the gods be good to me!

In my relationships I want a young man, but always a few years older than myself. I want him to be independent and rich enough not to need to suspect the motive that drives him. I want a passionate lover in whom I could enjoy exciting vice, seeing desire grow in response to extreme, violent advances, and even satisfying him. All of this thrills me, but the man must attract me. If not, he's quickly dismissed in a most cavalier manner. I'm very arrogant with those who are *too* passionate toward me. If he seems to be neglecting me, I experience the most awful jealousies and hatreds; I contemplate committing a crime. If we lived in the old days, I surely wouldn't hesitate having it done or doing it myself. Then I'd dream only of daggers or poison, especially the latter. But this passes quickly, and it's I who is the first one to go from feelings to carnal pleasures.

Isn't pleasure everything here below? And doesn't it justify everything? What do we demand of life if not pleasure? And when we have it, what do we want more of? Ah! How foolish I was to have despaired! But now, how I've made up for lost time!

My thoughts often turn to the East and the strange people[42] who hold such a place in the history of the world and whose blood I often feel burning in my body, which is too fine and delicate for them. In my brain surge all the debaucheries of Tyre and of Sidon in which the Jews have so often participated, fornicating with the gods whom the prophets railed at.[43] How many times have I not thought about the feasts of Astarte and of Moloch while I was contemplating the small bronze idols that are now sitting on the fireplace in my living room and that have turned green after centuries?[44] I turn my reverie toward the time when they celebrated their bloody rituals; and the priests of Baal smile in my imagination more than those of Christ![45] I'm a convinced materialist. Didn't I already say that I believe in atavism in an absolute way?

The memory of these two different civilizations haunts my brain, and these two enemy people launch themselves into battle in my veins. What do I make of those heroic and religious memories of relatively recent times when I feel this ancient ferocity, this strangest and most passionate perversion bubbling up in me? Nature has created a being where diverse elements have corrupted each other. But isn't it rather the shock of the two civilizations that I was born in? There are plenty of poisons everywhere, and ardor, spirit, and rage, which have devoured me and which continue to devour me, come from far away and are traced back to the world's earliest ages. Do they come only from there? The gracious and classical vices of Greece, the hypocritical debauchery of England, the fiery spirit and crimes of Italy—have they not also contributed to making me what I am? What's certain is that I live a sterile life, and except for pleasure, you'd get nothing good from me. When I love, I corrupt, and my entire being is like a beautiful flower whose perfume kills.

I've nothing more to tell you, Doctor, and my task is finished. I'll have nothing new to confess about my life. I'll still have loves, adventures, maybe even passions, but have I not searched my entire being and described it? And what could I still reveal that you don't already know? I've told you the causes and the effects; it's for you to study them and to make them beneficial to science and humanity. It's a beautiful thing to make the world better or at least to have the desire to do so. As for me, such as I was born, I will live, and as such I will die.

Secret Confessions of a Parisian by Arthur W——, "The Countess," was first published as Arthur W——, "Confidences et aveux d'un parisien: La Comtesse (Paris, 1850–1861)," in Henri Legludic, *Notes et observations de médecine légale: Attentats aux moeurs* (Paris: Masson, 1896).

"Loves" by Anonymous was first published as "Ma confession" in Ambroise Tardieu, *Etude médico-légale sur les attentats aux moeurs*, 5th ed. (Paris: Baillière, 1867).

"Observation 1" by Anonymous was first published in Jean-Martin Charcot and Valentin Magnan, "Inversions du sens génital," *Archives de neurologie* 3 (1882): 54–56.

"Autobiographical Notes" by Gustave L—— was first published as "Notes autobiographiques" in Paul Garnier, *La Folie à Paris: Etude statistique, clinique et médico-légale* (Paris: Baillière, 1890), 385–91; reprinted in Paul Garnier, *Les Fétichistes: Pervertis et invertis sexuels: Observations médico-légales* (Paris: Baillière, 1896), 98–113.

"Autobiographical Notes" by Louis X—— was first published as "Notes autobiographiques," in Garnier, *Fétichistes*, 113–48.

"Letter to My Parents" and "My Autobiography" by Antonio was first published in André Antheaume and Léon Parrot, "Un cas d'inversion sexuelle," *Annales médico-psychologiques*, 9th ser., 1 (1905): 459–72.

"Mental Hermophrodite and Other Autobiographical Writings" by Charles Double consists of three original manuscripts containing *Etat psychologique et mental d'un inverti parricide*, *Impressions d'un condamné*, and *Hermaphrodite mental*, all of which are located in *Fonds Lacassagne*, MS 5366, Bibliothèque municipale de Lyon.

The Novel of an Invert was first published as "Le Roman d'un inverti" and presented by Dr. Laupts [Georges Saint-Paul] in *Archives d'anthropologie criminelle* (1894): 212–15, 367–73, 729–37; (1895) 131–38, 228–41, 320–25 (first three letters to Emile Zola); reprinted as "Le Roman d'un inverti-né" in Dr. Laupts, *Tares et poisons: Perversion et perversité sexuelles* (Paris: Carré, 1896), 47–95 (first three letters); Dr. Laupts, *L'Homosexualité et les types homosexuels* (Paris: Vigot, 1910), 47–95 (first three letters); Dr. Laupts, *Invertis et homosexuels: Thèmes psychologiques* (Paris: Vigot, 1930), 69–128 (all letters).

INTRODUCTION

1. Jean-Jacques Rousseau, *The Confessions*, translated and with an introduction by J. M. Cohen (New York: Penguin Books, 1953). First published in Paris in 1781.

2. Mark Traugott, ed., *The French Worker: Autobiographies from the Early Industrial Era* (Berkeley: University of California Press, 1993); Alfred Kelly, ed., *The German Worker: Working-Class Autobiographies from the Age of Industrialization* (Berkeley: University of California Press, 1987); John Burnett, ed., *Useful Toil: Autobiographies of Working People from the 1820s to the 1920s* (New York: Penguin, 1984); John Burnett, ed., *Destiny Obscure: Autobiographies of Childhood, Education, and Family from the 1820s to the 1920s* (New York: Penguin, 1984); Victoria E. Bonnell, ed., *The Russian Worker: Life and Labor under the Tsarist Regime* (Berkeley: University of California Press, 1983).

3. Patricia Ann Meyer Spacks, *Imagining a Self: Autobiography and the Novel in Eighteenth-Century England* (Cambridge: Harvard University Press, 1976); Estelle C. Jelinek, *Women's Autobiography: Essays in Criticism* (Bloomington: Indiana University Press, 1980); Estelle C. Jelinek, *The Tradition of Women's Autobiography from Antiquity to the Present* (Boston: Twayne Publishers, 1986); Sidonie Smith and Julia Watson, eds., *Women, Autobiography, Theory: A Reader* (Madison: University of Wisconsin Press, 1998). See also the special issue devoted to "French Issue: Autobiography and the Problem of the Subject," in *Modern Language Notes* 93, no. 4 (1978): 573–749.

4. Denis Bertholet, *Les Français par eux-mêmes, 1815–1885* (Paris: Olivier Orban, 1991).

5. Philippe Lejeune, "Autobiographie et histoire sociale au XIXe siècle," *Revue de l'Institut de Sociologie* 1–2 (1982): 209–34; Philippe Lejeune,

"Les Instituteurs du XIXe siècle racontent leur vie," *Histoire de l'education* 25 (1985): 53–104; Philippe Lejeune, "Crime et testament: Les autobiographies de criminels au XIXe siècle," *Cahiers de sémiotique textuelle* 8–9 (1986): 73–98; Philippe Lejeune, "Autobiographie et homosexualité en France au XIXe siècle," *Romantisme* 56 (1987): 79–100. See also Philippe Lejeune, *On Autobiography*, edited and with a foreword by Paul John Eakin, trans. Katherine Leary (Minneapolis: University of Minnesota Press, 1989).

6. The best example of how prosecutors used autobiographies to construct their cases is *Moi, Pierre Rivière, ayant égorgé ma mère, ma soeur et mon frère . . . : Un cas de parricide au XIXe siècle*, presented by Michel Foucault (Paris: Gallimard/Julliard, 1973), translated by Frank Jellinek as *I, Pierre Rivière, Having Slaughtered My Mother, My Sister, and My Brother . . . : A Case of Parricide in the Nineteenth Century* (Lincoln: University of Nebraska Press, 1975).

7. On the use of writing as a diagnostic and investigative tool in nineteenth-century penology, criminal justice, and social science, see Philippe Artières, *Clinique de l'écriture: Une histoire du regard médical sur l'écriture* (Le Plessis-Robinson, France: Synthélabo, 1998); Philippe Artières, *Le Livre des vies coupables: Autobiographies des criminels (1896–1909)* (Paris: Albin Michel, 2000). On the influence of criminologists and psychiatrists on the professionalization of medicine in the nineteenth century, see Robert A. Nye, *Crime, Madness, and Politics in Modern France: The Medical Concept of National Decline* (Princeton: Princeton University Press, 1984); Robert A. Nye, *Masculinity and Male Codes of Honor in Modern France* (New York: Oxford University Press, 1993); Ruth Harris, *Murders and Madness: Medicine, Law, and Society in the Fin de Siècle* (Oxford: Clarendon Press, 1989); Vernon A. Rosario, *The Erotic Imagination: French Histories of Perversity* (New York: Oxford University Press, 1997).

8. Michel Foucault, *La Volonté de savoir* (Paris: Gallimard, 1976), translated by Robert Hurley as *The History of Sexuality: An Introduction* (New York: Vintage Books, 1978), 69.

9. Foucault, *La Volonté de savoir*, 63.

10. Foucault, *La Volonté de savoir*, 65.

11. Foucault, *La Volonté de savoir*, 64.

12. Foucault, *La Volonté de savoir*, 64.

13. Arthur W—— [Arthur Belorget], "Confidences et aveux d'un parisien: La Comtesse (Paris, 1850–1861)," in Henri Legludic, *Notes et observations de médecine légale: Attentats aux moeurs* (Paris: Masson, 1896), 235–349. Selections reprinted in Pierre Hahn, *Nos ancêtres les pervers: La vie des homosexuels sous le Second Empire* (Paris: Olivier Orban, 1979), 269–332. Reprinted again as *Arthur X——: Mémoires d'un travesti, prostitué, homosexuel ("La Comtesse," 1850–1861)*, presented by Jacques Chazaud (Paris: L'Harmattan, 2000). The date, 1861, in the original title is obviously a mistake, since Belorget ended his account with his release from prison on July 22, 1871.

14. Legludic, *Notes et observations*, 220–22.

15. Ambroise Tardieu, *Etude médico-légale sur les attentats aux moeurs* (Paris: Baillière, 1857, 1858, 1859, 1862, 1867, 1873, 1878).

16. "Ma confession," in Tardieu, *Etude médico-légale*, 5th ed. (1867), 187–89; 6th ed. (1873), 215–17; 7th ed. (1878), 210–12.

17. "Observation 1," in Jean-Martin Charcot and Valentin Magnan, "Inversions du sens génital," *Archives de neurologie* 3 (1882): 54–56; reprinted in Jean-Martin Charcot and Valentin Magnan, *Inversions du sens génital et autres perversions sexuelles*, presented by Gérard Bonnet (Paris: Frénésie, 1987).

18. Gustave L——, "Notes autobiographiques," in Paul Garnier, *La Folie à Paris: Etude statistique, clinique et médico-légale* (Paris: Baillière, 1890), 385–91; reprinted in Paul Garnier, *Les Fétichistes: Pervertis et invertis sexuels: Observations médico-légales* (Paris: Baillière, 1896), 98–113. Louis X——, "Notes autobiographiques," in Paul Garnier, "Notes autobiographiques de Louis X——," *Annales d'hygiène publique et de médecine légale*, 3d ser., 23 (1895): 393–405; reprinted in Garnier, *Fétichistes*, 113–48; reprinted in Hahn, *Nos ancêtres les pervers*, 215–28.

19. Antonio, "Lettre aux parents" and "Autobiographie," in André Autheaume and Léon Parrot, "Un cas d'inversion sexuelle," *Annales médico-psychologiques*, 9th ser., 1 (1905): 459–72; reprinted in Autheaume and Parrot, "Lettre d'un suicide," *Masques* 3 (1979–80): 88–93.

20. Charles Double, *Etat psychologique et mental d'un inverti parricide, 1905, suivi de Impressions d'un condamné et Hermaphrodite mental*, presented by Philippe Artières (Lille: Gai Kitsch Camp, 1995). Reprinted

in Artières, *Livre des vies coupables*, 283–313. The original manuscript is located in the *Fonds Lacassagne*, MS 5366, at the Bibliothèque municipale de Lyon.

21. "Le Roman d'un inverti," presented by Dr. Laupts [Georges Saint-Paul] in *Archives d'anthropologie criminelle, de médecine légale et de psychologie* (1894): 212–15, 367–73, 729–37; (1895): 131–38, 228–41, 320–25. Reprinted as "Le Roman d'un inverti-né," in Dr. Laupts, *Tares et poisons: Perversion et perversité sexuelles* (Paris: Carré, 1896), 47–95; Dr. Laupts, *L'Homosexualité et les types homosexuels* (Paris: Vigot, 1910), 47–95; and Dr. Laupts, *Invertis et homosexuels: Thèmes psychologiques* (Paris: Vigot, 1930), 69–128. Selections reprinted in Hahn, *Nos ancêtres les pervers*, 232–66. Reprinted most recently as *Le Roman d'un inverti-né* (Lyon: A Rebours, 2005). On how Saint-Paul acquired the letters, see Dr. Laupts, "A la mémoire d'Emile Zola," *Archives d'anthropologie criminelle, de médecine légale et de psychologie* (1907): 825–41. On secondary sources, see Vernon A. Rosario, "Inversion's Histories/History's Inversions: Novelizing Fin-de-Siècle Homosexuality," in *Science and Homosexualities*, ed. Vernon A. Rosario (New York: Routledge, 1997), 89–107; Nicholas Dobelbower, "Des cas curieux: Narration et inversion en France au XIXe siècle," in *Règles du genre et inventions du génie*, ed. Alain Goldschläger, Yzabelle Martineau, and Clive Thomson (London, Canada: Mestengo Press, 1999), 277–91.

22. Foucault, *The History of Sexuality*.

23. Harry Oosterhuis, *Stepchildren of Nature: Krafft-Ebing and the Making of Sexual Identity* (Chicago: University of Chicago Press, 2000).

24. Sandra Frieden, *Autobiography: Self into Form: German-Language Autobiographical Writings of the 1970s* (New York: Peter Lang, 1983), 17–41.

25. Philippe Lejeune, "The Autobiographical Pact," in Lejeune, *On Autobiography*, 3–30.

PART ONE. THE DRAMATIZATION OF THE SELF

1. First published as "Confidences et aveux d'un parisien: La Comtesse (1850–1861)," by Arthur W——, in Henri Legludic, *Notes et obser-*

vations (Paris: Masson, 1896). Selections reprinted in Pierre Hahn, *Nos ancêtres les pervers*, 269–332. Reprinted again as *Arthur X——: Mémoires d'un travesti, prostitué, homosexuel.*

2. Lejeune, *On Autobiography*; Bertholet, *Les Français.*

3. Concetta Condemi, *Les cafés-concerts: Histoire d'un divertissement* (Paris: Edima, 1992), 86–87. See also Lionel Richard, *Cabaret, cabarets: Origines et décadence* (Paris: Plon, 1991); W. Scott Haine, *The World of the Paris Café: Sociability among the French Working Class, 1789–1914* (Baltimore: Johns Hopkins University Press, 1996); William A. Peniston, *Pederasts and Others: Urban Culture and Sexual Identity in Nineteenth-Century Paris* (New York: Harrington Park Press, 2004), 138–40. On popular entertainment in the period, see also F. W. J. Hemmings, *The Theatre Industry in Nineteenth-Century France* (Cambridge: Cambridge University Press, 1993); Vanessa Schwartz, *Spectacular Realities: Early Mass Culture in Fin-de-Siècle Paris* (Berkeley: University of California Press, 1998). On female impersonators, see Laurence Senelick, *The Changing Room: Sex, Drag, and Theatre* (New York: Routledge, 2000).

4. Condemi, *Cafés-concerts*, 86–87.

5. On female prostitution, see Alain Corbin, *Les Filles de noce: Misère sexuelle et prostitution aux 19e et 20e siècle* (Paris: Aubier Montaigne, 1978), translated by Alan Sheridan as *Women for Hire: Prostitution and Sexuality in France after 1850*, (Cambridge: Harvard University Press, 1990); Jill Harsin, *Policing Prostitution in Nineteenth-Century Paris* (Princeton: Princeton University Press, 1985). On male prostitution, see William A. Peniston, "Pederasts, Prostitutes, and Pickpockets in Paris of the 1870s," in *Homosexuality in French History and Culture*, ed. Jeffrey Merrick and Michael Sibalis (New York: Harrington Park Press, 2001), 169–87.

6. Peniston, *Pederasts and Others*, 67–147.

7. On Balzac, see Gerald H. Storzer, "The Homosexual Paradigm in Balzac, Gide, and Genet," in *Homosexualities and French Literature: Cultural Contexts/Critical Texts*, ed. George Stambolian and Elaine Marks (Ithaca: Cornell University Press, 1979). On homosexuality in French prisons, see Nicholas Dobelbower, *"Les Chevaliers de la guirlande*: Cellmates in Restoration France," in Merrick and Sibalis, *Homosexuality in French History*, 131–47.

8. On various slang terms, see Claude Courouve, *Vocabulaire de l'homosexualité masculine* (Paris: Payot, 1985).
9. Louis Canler, *Mémoires de Canler, ancien chef du Service de Sûreté* (Brussels: A. La Croix, 1862; reprinted, Paris: Mercure de France, 1968); selections translated as *Autobiography of a French Detective from 1818 to 1858 comprising the most curious revelations of the French detective police system* (London: Ward and Lock, 1862; reprinted, New York: Arno Press, 1976.) Céleste Mogador, *Adieux au monde: Mémoires de Céleste Mogador* (Paris: Locard-Davi and de Vresse, 1854); translated by Monique Fleury Nagem as *Céleste Mogador: Memoirs of a Courtesan in Nineteenth-Century Paris* (Lincoln: University of Nebraska Press, 2001). Pierre-François Lacenaire, *Mémoires, révélations et poésies de Lacenaire écrits par lui-même à la Conciergerie* (Paris: Marchands de Nouveautés, 1836); reprinted as *Mémoires et autres écrits*, presented by Jacques Simonelli (Paris: Librairie José Corti, 1991).
10. Ambroise Tardieu, *Etude médico-légale*.
11. Legludic, *Notes et observations*.
12. Legludic, *Notes et observations*, 243.
13. Tardieu, *Etude médico-légale*.
14. Legludic, *Notes et observations*, 243–45.

AUTOBIOGRAPHY ONE: "SECRET CONFESSIONS OF A PARISIAN"

1. *Cocotte* was a term used for a woman of easy virtue, kept woman, or courtesan.
2. Lake Saint-Fargeau might have been a small body of water on the estate of that name, which was located on the outskirts of Paris. It is now in the twentieth arrondissement near the present place Saint-Fargeau.
3. The Restaurant de Madrid was located in the Bois de Boulogne. Originally known as a gathering place for lovers and duelists, it became an extremely popular spot for the nobility during the Second Empire.
4. The Maison d'Or was a fashionable restaurant on the Boulevard des Italiens during the Second Empire. It was also the subject of a paint-

ing by Thomas Couture (1815–1879) that was exhibited at the Paris Exposition of 1855. Entitled *Supper at the Maison d'Or* and known as *Parisian Banquet*, it depicted four drunken, disheveled, costumed revelers and the remains of a festive meal.

5. Philippe Lejeune discovered in 1987 that the real name of the author was Arthur-Louis Belorget (or Belorger). He was born in Paris in 1837, condemned to ten years of imprisonment for desertion in 1861, transferred from Poissy to Fontevrault in 1866, and released in 1871. He was arrested another time in Angers for a public offence against decency in 1874 and sentenced to eighteen months in prison. Nothing more, other than these memoirs, is known about his life.

6. According to Lejeune, he was really born in Paris on April 13, 1837, not 1839, as he himself stated.

7. Charles Perrault (1628–1703) was the author of *Histoires et contes du temps passé* (1697), which included a number of popular fairy tales that have since become even more famous.

8. Panurge is the companion of Pantagruel in François Rabelais's (1494–1553) work *Pantagruel* (1532–1552). In the fourth book, Panurge bargains while at sea for a sheep from a dealer who had insulted him. When he had concluded the deal, he threw the sheep into the sea, and the rest of the sheep followed the leader, taking with them the dealer and his shepherds, who tried to save them.

9. The Théâtre de Montmartre was a "theater of curiosities," founded in 1822 on the place Dancourt. It remained open until 1914.

10. Dr. Legludic made the following comment at this point: "There he was exposed to examples of the most unwholesome behavior. The older students engaged in obscene acts, such as exhibitionism, fondling, and masturbation, and it was a young boy, a neighbor on the rue de Rumford, who initiated him into the practice of masturbation."

11. *Mignon* means "cute" and has long had a queer connotation. It originally designated King Henry III's young male favorites, who were known for their ostentatious makeup and provocative clothing. See Courouve, *Vocabulaire*, 158–61.

12. The term *complaisant* is attributed to an obliging person who is eager to please others. It has long had a sexual connotation. According to Courouve, in a medical text published at the beginning of the nineteenth century it denoted the "passive partner" in male homosexual relations. See Courouve, *Vocabulaire*, 80–81.

13. *Tante* literally means "aunt," but in nineteenth-century prison argot it meant an inmate who serviced other men. Gradually it became more generally used for an effeminate man. See Courouve, *Vocabulaire*, 207–9. *Tapette*, when applied to a woman, means "chatterbox," but when applied to a man, it is a derogatory term for a flamboyant homosexual. Courouve, 210–12. *Petit* literally means "little," but in the street slang of the nineteenth century, it was used to identify young (usually adolescent) male prostitutes. Courouve, 147–49. *Fille*, which literally means "girl," frequently referred to a female prostitute, but here Belorget is using it to refer to male prostitutes.

14. "Pederasty" or "pederast," originally derived from the ancient Greek term for "the love of boys" or "boy lover," was the most commonly used term for "homosexuality" or "homosexual" in nineteenth-century France. Unlike its English or American counterpart, it did not have the connotation of child abuser as it does in contemporary society. See Courouve, *Vocabulaire*, 169–78.

15. The Mazas prison in Paris was constructed in the 1830s on the new cellular model; it became the main prison for Parisian criminals.

16. The Bois de Boulogne is a very large park on the western edge of the city, originally donated to the city by Emperor Napoleon III in 1852. Its tree-shaded roads and trails attracted riders in coaches and on horseback, and it became a fashionable place for social display.

17. A comment by Dr. Legludic appears here: "Paula helped him with his wardrobe and gave him his first lesson in makeup and comportment."

18. The term *amateur* designated a pleasure-seeking gentleman who preferred younger men and was willing to pay for them. See Courouve, *Vocabulaire*, 43–44.

19. The term *tribade*, apparently coined from the Greek verb "to rub," was used in the eighteenth and nineteenth centuries to name women who engaged in same-sex sexual activity. For a discussion on its changing meanings, see Susan Lanser, "*Au sein de vos pareilles*: Sapphic Separatism in Late Eighteenth-Century France," in Merrick and Sibalis, *Homosexuality in French History*, 105–16.

20. Satory is a plain south of the city of Versailles; originally it was the location of a military camp, but in the nineteenth century it was the site of a horse-racing course.

21. Dr. Legludic inserted an explanatory note here, which may indicate an elision in the original manuscript: "When he returned home,
he found a letter from the marquis, informing him of his departure
for India. He enclosed a five-thousand-franc note with his good-bye
note, having paid off all his creditors and having prepaid his horse and
carriage for the next year."

22. These nicknames are all feminine. Roughly translated they mean
"The English Beauty," "Miss Charles," and "The Belgian Girl."

23. Dr. Legludic wrote here: "One night there was raid on the café-concert on the Champs-Elysées where he worked, and the Countess was
arrested. He spent three months in the Mazas prison."

24. *Garçon* literally means "boy."

25. The Poissy prison was opened in 1819 in a small town on the outskirts of Paris; it had originally served as a poorhouse. As a prison, it
housed approximately fifteen hundred men convicted of theft, fraud,
and other offenses against property and contained both cellblocks and
workshops.

26. La Roquette (also known as La Petite Roquette) was established in
Paris in 1836 as a prison for adult and juvenile offenders. During the
July Monarchy, it was known for its experimental regimen of solitary
confinement, which proved, however, to be unsuccessful.

27. The Fontevrault prison occupied the site of the twelfth-century
Fontevrault Abbey, which had contained five churches, the larg-
est of which—and the only one still standing in the nineteenth century—became a prison holding male inmates from eleven French
departments.

28. These institutions were juvenile detention centers. Mettray was an
agricultural penal colony established in 1840 and noted for a regimen
intended to discipline and rehabilitate young male inmates by incor-
porating them into "family" units, requiring set hours of schooling
and labor, and providing a healthy diet. Separating youths from the
older prison population into special institutions was an innovation of
the mid-nineteenth-century criminal justice system.

29. *Tantum ergo sacramentum* is Latin for "Come adore the Sacrament."
This phrase is the opening words of a hymn sung during the Catholic
Mass for the Eucharist. The text is attributed to Saint Thomas Aquinas
(1225–1274).

1. Rosario, "Inversion's Histories," 91.

2. For example, Tardieu asserted that the active sodomite's penis was long and thin like a dog's and that the passive sodomite's anus was funnel-shaped. For Tardieu, these two anatomical parts of these two different individuals complemented each other in an unhealthy relationship. See Tardieu, *Etude médico-légale*; reprinted as *La Pédérastie*, ed. Dominique Fernande (Paris: Le Sycamore, 1981), 9–83.

3. Tardieu, *La Pédérastie*, 64.

4. Vernon A. Rosario, "Pointy Penises, Fashion Crimes, and Hysterical Mollies: The Pederasts' Inversions," in *Homosexuality in Modern France*, ed. Jeffrey Merrick and Bryant T. Ragan Jr. (New York: Oxford University Press, 1996), 157.

5. Tardieu, *La Pédérastie*, 15–24.

6. "Ma Confession," in Tardieu, *Etude médico-légale*, 5th ed., 187–89; 6th ed., 215–17; 7th ed., 210–12.

7. Johann Ludwig Casper, *Handbuch der gerichtlichen Medizin* (Berlin: Hirschwald, 1856–1858); Karl Westphal, "Die konträre Sexualempfindung: Symptom eines neuropathologischen (psychopathischen) Zustandes," *Archiv für Psychiatrie und Nervenkrankheiten* 2 (1869): 73–108; Jean-Martin Charcot and Valentin Magnan, "Inversion du sens génital et autres perversions génitales," *Archives de Neurologie* 7 (1882): 55–60, and 12 (1882): 296–322; Arrigo Tamassia, "Sull'inversione dell'istinto sessuale," *Revista sperimentale di freniatria e di medicina legale* 4 (1878): 97–117, 285–91; Havelock Ellis, *Sexual Inversion* (London: Wilson and Macmillan, 1897).

8. Vern L. Bullough, *Sexual Variance in Society and History* (Chicago: University of Chicago Press, 1976), 638.

9. Robert A. Nye, "The History of Sexuality in Context: National Sexological Traditions," *Science in Context* 4 (1991): 387.

10. Paul Brouardel, "Etude critique sur la valeur des signes attribués à la pédérastie," *Annales d'hygiène publique et de médecine légale*, 3d ser., 4 (1880): 182–89.

11. Charcot and Magnan, "Inversion du sens génital"; reprinted as *Inversion du sens génital*.

12. Charcot and Magnan, *Inversion du sens génital*, 322.

13. Charcot and Magnan, *Inversion du sens génital*, 322.

14. Alfred Binet, "Le Fétichisme dans l'amour," *Revue philosophique* 24 (1887): 143–67, 252–74.
15. Charcot and Magnan, *Inversion du sens génital*, 322.
16. Garnier, *La Folie à Paris*, 385–91.
17. Garnier, *Fétichistes*, 113–48.
18. Antonio, "Lettre aux parents" and "Autobiographie" in Autheaume and Parrot, "Un cas d'inversion sexuelle," *Annales médico-psychologiques*, 9th ser., 1 (1905): 459–72. Reprinted in Antonio, "Lettre d'un suicide," *Masques* 3 (1979–1980): 88–93.
19. Laurent Mucchielli, ed., *Histoire de la criminologie française* (Paris: L'Harmattan, 1994); Gordon Wright, *Between the Guillotine and Liberty: Two Centuries of the Crime Problem in France* (New York: Oxford University Press, 1983).
20. On Lombroso, see Mary Gibson, *Born to Crime: Cesare Lombroso and the Origins of Biological Criminology* (Westport, CT: Praeger, 2002).
21. Mucchielli, *Histoire de la criminologie française*.
22. Philippe Artières has compiled many of the autobiographies of prisoners collected by Lacassagne and has published them with his analysis of the historical background in *Le Livre des vies coupables*. The original manuscripts are located in the *Fonds Lacassagne* at the Bibliothèque municipale de Lyon. Double's autobiography appears as "Etat mental et psychologique d'un inverti parricide," "Impressions d'un condamné," and "Hermaphrodite mental!" in the *Fonds Lacassagne*, MS 5366. It was first published as *Etat psychologique et mental d'un inverti parricide*. It is also included in Artières's *Le Livre des vies coupables*, 283–313.
23. Harry Oosterhuis, "Richard von Krafft-Ebing's 'Step-Children of Nature': Psychiatry and the Making of Homosexual Identity," in *Science and Homosexualities*, 67–88; and Oosterhuis, *Stepchildren of Nature*.

AUTOBIOGRAPHY THREE: "OBSERVATION I"

1. *Apollo Belvedere* is the Roman copy of a Greek statue; the original is in the Vatican, but plaster casts of the statue were found in many museums and art galleries throughout the nineteenth century. It was considered the most perfect example of classical beauty.

2. Hypospadia is a medical term referring to a malformation of the ureter. It was frequently diagnosed as a form of hermaphrodism in the nineteenth century. See Alice Domurat Dreger, *Hermaphrodites and the Medical Invention of Sex* (Cambridge: Harvard University Press, 1998).
3. Maria Felicia Malibran (1808–1836) was a very well known contralto of French and Spanish descent, known for her passionate interpretation of operatic roles.
4. Potassium bromide is a strong sedative.

AUTOBIOGRAPHY FOUR: "AUTOBIOGRAPHICAL NOTES"

1. *Homosexuel* is the term used in the original. It is a translation of the German word *homosexual*, which was coined by the Hungarian writer Karl Maria Kertbeny (1847–1882), who published under the pseudonym Benkert. German psychiatrists, notably Richard von Krafft-Ebing (1840–1902), popularized it in the later half of the nineteenth century. Garnier's usage of the term here in 1890 might be the very first usage in French. See Courouve, *Vocabulaire*, 129–37.

AUTOBIOGRAPHY FIVE: "AUTOBIOGRAPHICAL NOTES"

1. On February 24, 1848, the Parisian insurrectionists converged on the Tuileries Palace and forced King Louis Philippe to abdicate. Immediately after his departure, they burst into the palace and looted it.
2. The asylum at Ville-Evrard was a psychiatric hospital in the French public health system located in Neuilly-sur-Marne. It is now the Hôpital Ville-Evrard.
3. Martial (40–104 CE), the Roman epigrammatic poet, referred to sexual matters, including pederasty, in his writings. Petronius (d. 66 CE), the Roman satirist, is best known for his work *Satyricon* about the misadventures of two male lovers. Aristophanes (448–388 BCE), the Greek playwright, frequently included sexual references and situations in his comedies.
4. Bois de Vincennes, a large municipal park on the outskirts of Paris, was a well-known cruising area for the male homosexual subculture of Paris in the nineteenth century.

5. Bois de Meudon is another forested park on the outskirts of Paris.

6. At the time, sodomy was not against the law; however, the police and prosecutors often used the law regarding public indecency to prosecute men soliciting other men in public. See Peniston, *Pederasts and Others*, 13–22.

1. *Dédé* (1901) was an early novel by Achille Essebac, the pseudonym for Achille Bécasse (b. 1868); it featured a doomed love affair between two teenage boys.

2. Plato (429–347 BCE), the great Greek philosopher of the classical era, was known for his frank discussion of the ancient Greek tradition of pederasty. Many nineteenth-century men used his philosophy as a defense for homosexuality. Anacreon (570–485 BCE) was a Greek poet whose verse often celebrated the love of older men for younger boys.

3. The terms *"uranism," "uranist,"* and *"uranian"* were invented by Karl Heinrich Ulrichs in 1862 to denote same-sex sexuality and the men who had sex with other men. Other late nineteenth-century writers, including Raffalovich, adopted the terms, but they were never widely used. See Courouve, *Vocabulaire*, 221–25.

1. The words *femme monstre* used in the text translate literally as "woman monster." In contemporary medical and scientific terminology the word "monstre" also denoted a congenitally deformed person, a "freak of nature."

2. Tantalus, the mythical king of Lydia and Phrygia, was punished because of a crime variously described as revealing the secrets of Olympia to mortals, stealing nectar and ambrosia, or cooking his son Pelops and serving him to the gods. His punishment in Hades also varies in different versions of the myth: he is either under a boulder on the verge of crushing him, or up to his neck immersed in water that recedes

every time he tries to drink, or just out of reach of a branch of a tree laden with fruit that moves away each time he tries to pick a fruit.

3. Dejanire was a legendary princess of Calydon, who married Heracles (also known as Hercules) and bore him five children, but because of her jealousy over his love for the captive Iole, she sent him a tunic dipped in the poisonous blood of the centaur Nessos, which she had kept as a talisman of marital fidelity. When he put it on, he died violently.

4. The Crédit Lyonnais, founded in 1863, was one of the major banks for small investors in the second half of the nineteenth century.

5. Marie-Caroline Miolan-Carvalho (1827–1895), the wife of the director of the Opéra Comique, Léon Carvalho, was a well-known operatic soprano.

6. Bourg-en-Bresse is the departmental capital of Ain, the department where the murder had taken place.

7. Anatole Deibler (1863–1939), the son and grandson of executioners, began working as an assistant to his father in 1882. He was officially appointed to the post of executioner in 1899 and carried out close to 350 capital punishments.

8. We have been unable to find any information about this criminal.

9. Jacques Vacher was a notorious serial killer, who was convicted of murdering four boys, six girls, and one old woman in 1897. All of his killings involved rape, mutilation, and throat slashing in a ritualistic manner. He claimed to be insane, but Dr. Lacassagne declared him "responsible for his actions." Dr. Lacassagne also wrote a book about the case, entitled *Vacher: L'Eventreur et les crimes sadiques* (Lyon: Storck, 1899).

10. Claude Carron was convicted of killing his mother during a robbery in Lyon in 1903. While waiting to be executed, he filled twenty-six notebooks for Dr. Lacassagne. Philippe Artières published extracts from them in *Le Livre des vies coupables*, 219–82.

PART THREE. LITERATURE, MEDICINE, AND SELF-EXPRESSION

1. Anonymous, "Le Roman d'un Inverti" presented by Dr. Laupts [pseudonym of Dr. Georges Saint-Paul] in *Archives d'anthropologie*

criminelle (1894); 212–15, 367–73, 729–37; (1895) 131–38, 228–41, 320–25.

2. "Le Roman d'un Inverti-né," in Dr. Laupts, *Tares et poisons*, 47–95; reprinted in Dr. Laupts, *Homosexualité et les types homosexuels*, 47–95. Selections from the first letter to Zola were reprinted in Pierre Hahn, *Nos ancêtres les pervers*, 232–66.

3. The last letter to Dr. Saint-Paul appears in the third edition of his book *Invertis et homosexuels*, 69–128. A new edition, which includes the complete collection of letters, has recently been republished. See *Roman d'un inverti-né*.

4. Claude Bernard, *Introduction à l'étude de la médecine expérimentale* (Paris: Baillière, 1865).

5. Bénédict-Augustin Morel, *Traité des dégénérescences physiques, intellectuelles et morales de l'espèce humaine* (Paris: Baillière, 1857).

6. Rosario, "Inversion's Histories," 89–107; Dobelbower, "Des cas curieux, 277–91.

7. Dr. Laupts, "Enquête sur l'inversion sexuelle," *Archives d'anthropologie criminelle* (1894): 105.

8. Marc-André Raffalovich, *Uranisme et unisexualité* (Paris: Masson, 1896). See also Brocard Sewell, *Footnotes to the Nineties: A Memoir of John Gray and André Raffalovich* (London: Cecil and Amelia Woolf, 1968); Rosario, *Erotic Imagination*, 97–109; Frederick S. Roden, *Same-Sex Desire in Victorian Religious Culture* (New York: Palgrave Macmillan, 2002), 157–89.

9. Wilde's well-publicized trials and imprisonment prompted fierce debates among French writers. See Nancy Erber, "The French Trials of Oscar Wilde," *Journal of the History of Sexuality* 6 (1996): 549–88.

10. Dr. Laupts, "A la mémoire d'Emile Zola," 833.

AUTOBIOGRAPHY EIGHT: *THE NOVEL OF AN INVERT*

1. Balzac wrote this short story in the years 1834–1835 about the rivalry between a young man, Henri de Marsay, and his half sister, Mme. de San-Réal, over a young woman with beautiful eyes, Paquita Valdès.

2. Balzac wrote this short story in 1830 about an eighteenth-century sculptor, Ernest-Jean Sarrasine, who fell in love with a Roman castrato, Zambinella, not realizing that "she" was a man.

3. *La Curée* (1872) is the second novel in Zola's series, *Les Rougon-Macquart*. In it, Baptiste, the servant, a minor character, is dismissed for sexual improprieties toward another man.

4. *The Earth* (1887), the fifteenth novel in Zola's *Rougon-Macquart* series, is about peasant life in France.

5. Adrien-Adolphe Desbarolles (1801–1886) was a painter and student of the occult, who lived and practiced in Paris. He published a number of books on his methods of divination, such as *The Secrets of the Hand* (1859) on palm reading and *The Secrets of Handwriting* (1872) on graphology. He became known as the "father of modern palmistry."

6. Angèle is the first wife of the main character, Aristide Saccard, in the novel *La Curée* and was depicted as a submissive wife.

7. Alphonse-Marie-Louis de Prat de Lamartine (1790–1869), one of the leading romantic poets of the era, also wrote a sensational polemic about the French Revolution, in which he detailed the excesses of the Reign of Terror.

8. Known as Madame Elisabeth, Elisabeth-Philippine-Marie-Hélène of France (1764–1794), the sister of Louis XVI, was executed during the Terror. Marie-Thérèse-Louise de Savoy-Carignano, Princess de Lamballe (1749–1792), a friend and confidante of Marie Antoinette, was killed by the mob during the September Massacres.

9. Saint Mary Magdalene of Pazzi (1566–1607), a member of the prominent Pazzi family in Florence, was a Carmelite nun known for her austerity and her ecstatic visions during which she exhibited the stigmata. Canonized by Pope Clement IX in 1699, she is honored as one of the patron saints of Florence.

10. Antinous was the youthful lover of Emperor Hadrian (76–138), who deified him upon his death in 130. His cult was quite popular in the latter part of the Roman Empire. Sculptures of Antinous depicted him as a muscular, handsome, often nude youth. Recognized as classical examples of male beauty, many of these sculptures were on display in European museums, including the Louvre, the Vatican, and the gardens of Versailles.

11. In Homer's *Iliad*, Hector was the son of the Trojan king and the military leader of his people. Achilles was the military leader of the Greeks and killed Hector in revenge for the death of his lover, Patroclus.

12. *Ivanhoe*, written by Sir Walter Scott in 1819, was set in the time of King Richard I of England (Richard the Lion-Hearted).

13. Maxime was the son of the main character, Aristide Saccard, in the novel *La Curée* (1872). He was depicted as an indolent character—rather effeminate at times.

14. Werther was the hero of Johann Wolfgang von Goethe's novel *The Sorrows of Young Werther* (1774). Werther committed suicide because of his unrequited love for a married woman.

15. At this point Dr. Saint-Paul inserted the following comment: "I skip certain details that are so personal that they might permit the indiscreet to discover the identity of the author of this confession. Suffice it for me to say, however, that, having verified the information that he gave me concerning his family, this family is, on the father's side, from the best and highest nobility."

16. Hyacinth was a Spartan boy loved by Apollo in Ovid's *Metamorphoses*. Ganymede was a beautiful boy, whom Zeus loved and carried off to Olympus in order to make him his cupbearer.

17. Vautrin was the master criminal who appeared in many of Balzac's novels. His relationship with Lucien de Rubempré, another character in Balzac's *Human Comedy*, was ambiguous—sometimes fatherly, sometimes lustful.

18. Marie-Jeanne Bécu, Countess du Barry (1746–1793), was the mistress of Louis XV.

19. Hans Makart (1840–1884) was an Austrian painter known for his large-scale interpretations of mythological and historical themes.

20. Marie Louise (1791–1847) was the second wife of Napoleon I; she refused to share his exile; instead, she lived openly with Adam-Adalbert, Count von Neipperg, an Austrian officer and diplomat, in Parma, Italy.

21. The four mathematical rules are addition, subtraction, multiplication, and division.

22. Pierre-Alexis, Viscount de Ponson du Terrail (1829–1871) was a popular novelist, known for his adventure series *The Exploits of Rocambole*.

23. Rebecca was one of the main characters in Sir Walter Scott's novel *Ivanhoe*. She was a Jewess, captured by a rival of Ivanhoe, who was defeated by Ivanhoe in mortal combat in order to gain her release.

24. Caserta is a city in south central Italy known for its royal palace and magnificent gardens, built in the eighteenth century.

25. Writing in 1889, he was probably referring to some of the following: *The Dream* (1888), *The Earth* (1887), *The Masterwork* (1886), or *Germinal* (1885).

26. *Madeleine Férat* (1868) was one of Zola's earliest novels.

27. Jean-Anthelme Brillat-Savarin (1755–1826) was the most famous gastronome of the nineteenth century, known for his work *The Physiology of Taste* (1826).

28. *The Last Days of Pompeii*, a very popular painting by the Russian artist Karl Pavlovich Bruloff (1799–1852), inspired Edward Bulwer Lytton (1803–1871), the English novelist and playwright, to write his work of the same title in 1834. Arbaces, "the Egyptian," is one of the main characters.

29. Antonio Canova (1757–1822) was an Italian sculptor known for his neoclassical style.

30. At this point Dr. Saint-Paul deleted the name of a king.

31. *Mademoiselle de Maupin* (1835) was written by Théophile Gautier (1811–1872); its main character is an adventurous, cross-dressing young woman who loves both men and women.

32. Hyanthus was the Spartan boy in Ovid's *Metamorphoses*, whose accidental death upset Apollo so much. Alexis was the shepherd boy in Virgil's second *Eclogue* with whom Corydon, another shepherd, fell in love.

33. Charles Parker was one of the young men that Oscar Wilde was accused of soliciting; his testimony at the trials led to Wilde's conviction. Alfred Taylor was Wilde's codefendant, accused of introducing male prostitutes to him; he was also convicted.

34. The verses "Je reconnais Vénus et ses feux redoutables / D'un sang qu'elle poursuit tourments inévitables" are a reference to the play *Phèdre* (1677) by Jean Racine (1639–1699). In his notes on the novel *La Curée*, Zola indicated that he intended it to have echoes of this play.

35. Latin for "always the same."

36. Saint Januarius was an early Christian martyr executed during the reign of Diocletian (circa 305). His relics are preserved in a church in Naples. The reference is to the miraculous liquefaction of the saint's dried blood, which is supposed to bubble up during the annual celebration of his feast day.

37. Dr. Saint-Paul made the following note here: "The document relates at great length details that I will not reproduce. It is with acute precision that the author describes the preliminary acts, the first attempt that almost succeeded, the second attempt that succeeded completely, and the following nights, etc. . . ."

38. A legendary figure, Sardanapalus was a king known for his debauchery who organized a collective suicide of his court, including his concubines and his eunuchs, when the Babylonians threatened to capture him. His story is the subject of a painting by Eugène Delacroix entitled *Assyrie* (1826).

39. Dorian Gray was the decadent hero of Wilde's novel *The Picture of Dorian Gray* (1890).

40. Saint-Paul added the following note here: "The author of this document gives certain details about his anatomy and sexual physiology that indicate that they are entirely normal."

41. Saint-Paul again noted the following: "I could not, even in summarizing it, reproduce the text. It is the history of a family, and despite the attractive, picturesque, and seemingly sincere description of the revealed psychologies, it is not suitable to publish these recognizable particularities without the family's knowledge just because it gave birth to an invert. I note, however, the following: 'I see my own family little, and I don't love them at all. Months pass without our even knowing whether we are alive or dead. I must, however, admit that they behave better toward me than I toward them. I've always shown them more than just coldness—a sort of aversion—and especially toward . . . , whom I can't stand. Those whom I love the most are dead—or rather it seems to me that I love them because they no longer exist.'"

42. Here Saint-Paul explained that the invert had included the following biographical notes on certain individuals whom he had known: "She was taken with a passion for silver, and she collected an enormous quantity of silver and ruby objects of an exquisite workmanship. She wore superb precious stones, furs, and admirable laces. I found in one of the jewelry boxes that belonged to her a stash of pretty things, among which was a superb phallus of admirable workmanship made of coral. It was mounted in gold, and it had on its upper part a ring,

which indicated that it was meant to be suspended on a chain and worn around the neck. It was perhaps an amulet."

And again: "All the same, she remained what she was since her birth—a deist par excellence. And she always had a limitless admiration for the "people of God," as she called them. The triumph of Israel filled her with joy, and she didn't hide it, but she was passionate about the people more so than about the religion. When the book by Monsieur Drumont appeared, she said: 'Here is the most beautiful elegy that you could make for the Jews. Even their enemies are forced to acknowledge their superiority over other races! Is it not to recognize this superiority and to bow down before it to declare, as this individual has done, that they have subjected and reduced to servitude various peoples amongst whom they themselves have come to live? And besides,' she added, 'if you wanted a God, it was necessary for you to come looking for him among *us*!' All of this caused considerable laughter."

43. Sidon was an ancient Phoenician city whose destruction by numerous other city-states throughout the centuries was usually attributed to its decadence. Tyre was another ancient Phoenician city that was besieged and conquered numerous times throughout the centuries.

44. Astarte, also called Ishtar or Ashtart, was the goddess of fertility and war in the ancient religions of Mesopotamia. Her cult was strongly condemned by the prophets of the Old Testament. Moloch was a local Canaanite deity denounced by Jeremiah and other Old Testament prophets.

45. Baal was a name given to many local deities in Canaanite, Phoenician, and Aramaic religions. Generally, he was an agrarian god of fertility or storms or a protector of a city or a state. His worship was carried out on mountain tops or in woodlands. The prophets of the Old Testament continued to denounce him throughout the history of ancient Israel.

www.ingramcontent.com/pod-product-compliance
Ingram Content Group UK Ltd.
Pitfield, Milton Keynes, MK11 3LW, UK
UKHW020000310125
454458UK00010B/563